Ngaio Marsh

Twayne's English Authors Series

Kinley E. Roby, Editor

Northeastern University

TEAS 481

NGAIO MARSH
Photograph by Pamela Chandler and courtesy of Douglas G. Greene

Ngaio Marsh

Kathryne Slate McDorman

Texas Christian University

Twayne Publishers
A Division of G. K. Hall & Co. • Boston

Ngaio Marsh
Kathryne Slate McDorman

Copyright 1991 by G. K. Hall & Co.
All rights reserved.
Published by Twayne Publishers
A division of G. K. Hall & Co.
70 Lincoln Street
Boston, Massachusetts 02111

Copyediting supervised by Barbara Sutton.
Book production by Gabrielle B. McDonald.
Typeset in Garamond
by Compositors Corporation of Cedar Rapids, Iowa.

10 9 8 7 6 5 4 3 2 1

Library of Congress Cataloging-in-Publication Data

McDorman, Kathryne Slate.
    Ngaio Marsh / Kathryne Slate McDorman.
        p.   cm. — (Twayne's English authors series ; TEAS 481)
    Includes bibliographical references and index.
    ISBN 0-8057-6999-4 (alk. paper)
    1. Marsh, Ngaio, 1899–   —Criticism and interpretation.
    2. Detective and mystery stories, New Zealand—History and
    criticism.   I. Title.   II. Series.
    PR9639.3.M27Z79   1991
    823—dc20   90-46276
                                                                CIP

7885 99/0

For K. the G., with love

Contents

Preface   ix
Acknowledgments   xii
Chronology   xiii

Chapter One
New Zealand Roots and British Branches:
Ngaio Marsh's Hybrid Nature   1

Chapter Two
Images of Commonwealth   20

Chapter Three
Country as Place and Character   46

Chapter Four
Characters: The Dress Circle   74

Chapter Five
Characters: Supporting Roles   94

Chapter Six
Theater: Murder on the Marquee   113

Chapter Seven
Marsh and the Golden Age of Detective Fiction:
Her Legacy   133

Notes and References   147
Selected Bibliography   151
Index   159

Preface

As a breed, mystery writers appear to have a penchant for explaining their basic precepts to others, like honest magicians eager to reveal how they make the rabbit disappear. S. S. Van Dine prescribed twenty rules, and Dorothy Sayers added some rather impressive injunctions of her own.[1] This inclination suggests authors who are eager to strip away the art to reveal the craft by which they function, a show-and-tell syndrome.

Other mystery writers choose not to write instructive essays but to make their statements through their characters. Agatha Christie's frequent heroine Mrs. Ariadne Oliver is a detective novelist who reflects on her actual adventures as she would narrate them in her books. Ngaio Marsh's detective, Roderick Alleyn, often comments about how dull the average murder case is compared with the accounts of detective novelists who conveniently neglect tedious routine. Perhaps such an artistic temperament is necessary for those who write about righting wrongs. It may be that only writers who could solemnly swear to write of "detectives who well and truly detect the crimes presented to them," without reliance on "Divine Revelation, Feminine Intuition, Mumbo-Jumbo, Jiggery-Pokery, Coincidence or the Act of God,"[2] could concern themselves with such artistic introspection.

Such authors are assisted in their search for truth by a relatively recent group of critics who review the literature for characteristics that distinguish them from authors of the "merely popular" romance, thriller, Gothic, psychological, analytical, and police procedural novels. Ironically, although these critics claim that the detective or suspense novel can be traced back to the Bible and has definitive roots in the nineteenth-century works of Edgar Allan Poe, Wilkie Collins, and even the venerable Charles Dickens, the critical heritage is almost exclusively twentieth century. Much as they might disagree about the genre's antecedents, however, most analysts appear convinced that the 1920s and 1930s in England and America represent the golden age of detective fiction. Then, they argue, the form was at last made manifest through the works of several major mystery writers. For reasons that are as yet unexplained, detective stories in the golden age were frequently by women writing about men solving crimes. Though the crime is always the most brutal one of murder, the setting is refined: "A bullet creasing a well-tailored dinner jacket, tea gently laced with arsenic in the Spode teapot, were the stuff of the English school of crime writing, served up with relish and wry."[3]

This English school was dominated by a formidable quartet of female talent: Dorothy L. Sayers, Agatha Christie, Margery Allingham, and New Zealand–born Ngaio Marsh. Of the four, Marsh enjoyed the second-longest writing career and wrote the second-greatest number of detective novels. She has been recognized for creating in her hero, Roderick Alleyn, a new "type" of detective for the genre: intelligent, well read, well bred, and a professional policeman. Despite several charming eccentricities, Alleyn is significantly different from Sayers's excessively mannered hero, Lord Peter Wimsey, Christie's Hercule Poirot, and Allingham's Mr. Campion. Alleyn, the aristocrat, falls in love, marries, and procreates, which was "not quate nayce,"[4] according to the strict conventions of detective fiction, in which romance, conjugal felicity, and the joys of parenthood were deemed digressions from the detection and therefore inappropriate. By challenging these classical limitations of the form (which had become rigidified into formula), Marsh transcended the conventions and contributed thereby to the survival of the detective story beyond the limitations of the puzzle or "locked door" mysteries.

This study analyzes Marsh's detective stories as they exemplify the model of the golden age. One can certainly ascertain the skeleton beneath the flesh of her mystery stories, which is almost identical to the framework employed by her contemporaries Sayers, Christie, and Allingham. A careful comparison of all four novelists reveals basic similarities in character and tone. An even closer reading of the detective stories of the "Big Four," however, reveals ways in which Marsh began deviating from her peers.[5] By the 1940s, Marsh's skeletal Alleyn had begun to rattle his chains and demand his freedom from the constrictions of the formulaic closet. By allowing him to go forth, Marsh expanded the classical detective story into the novel of manners and social commentary. It will be seen that her detective stories represent a synthesis of the three traditions: classic golden-age conventions, adaptations of those conventions to include a richer mix of environment and characters, and insights into the manners of her day. To analyze each of these aspects in proper depth, Marsh's work should be approached thematically rather than chronologically. This technique discloses which characteristics of English life she was most wont to portray in her novels and how she ranked their significance. In this endeavor, she was assisted by her unique viewpoint as an insider's outsider. She was New Zealand born and reared, and therefore classified as a colonial; at the same time, she was mightily attached to the London artistic community through her dedication to Shakespearean drama and her admiration for England's cultural heritage. She utilized her hybrid perspective to strip away with a sympathetic hand the mask of English social conventions and the illusions cultivated by the studied innocence of the upper-middle class. She employed the device of a theatrical setting in seven of her thirty-two novels to underscore the theme of illusion challenged by reality. She sent Alleyn abroad in seven novels (four times to New Zealand) to provide a contrast of cultures, setting in high relief Alleyn's very Englishness of manner.

As a social commentator, Ngaio Marsh earns our esteem by her sensitivity to the gradations of class in English society. She represented these gradations as dependent not on the overt repression of any group but on a rather generous, if discriminatory, set of assumptions, shared by many well into the twentieth century, about the deference owed to those who were by nature defined as gentlefolk. The very civility of these assumptions was attested to by the lack of social revolution in England. Alleyn and his police cohorts symbolize a new hierarchy based on profession but colored by traditional ideas of the social order predicated upon birth. Many of Marsh's novels repeatedly, if subtly, contrast numerous elements of English tradition with the modern milieu, most especially in social manners, style of theatrical productions, and the transformation of Great Britain from an imperial power to a partner in commonwealth.

Marsh's style supported these themes of contrast. She adopted the traditional detective formula when it suited her purposes and altered that formula for the same reason. Earl F. Bargainnier has written of her, "She has accepted the formulas and conventions of the Golden Age, but, while remaining within their boundaries, has adapted them in her own way through five decades into the 1980s, and that is no mean achievement."[6] This study takes Bargainnier's contention a step further; Marsh's adaptations and her originality have earned her a place as an author who did not merely embellish detective story traditions but who became a unique voice in English and New Zealand letters.

Acknowledgments

No scholar's work is ever completely her own. Without a compatible environment in which creativity is rewarded, ideas may wither and die. I am grateful to my colleagues at Texas Christian University for their encouragement and assistance in bringing life to this effort. I am especially indebted to Dr. Don Worcester in the History Department, who has encouraged so many of us to love scholarship and to pursue it by our individual and sometimes unorthodox paths. Like Professor Worcester, Dr. Fred Erisman has lent his considerable editing skills to this manuscript. Far beyond that Herculean chore, he has constantly challenged me to refine my ideas and has inspired me to press on in the inevitable times of discouragement.

I appreciate the professional skill and personal support of Dr. Christina Murphy, who interested me in the Twayne series and was always patient with my inquiries. Professor Douglas G. Greene, who edited *The Collected Short Fiction of Ngaio Marsh,* was most generous in providing the cover photograph. Walter Berry deserves special mention here; his wit and gracious generosity were delightful morale boosters. Susan Olson and Robyn Hydrick provided invaluable help in the preparation of the manuscript and in guiding me through the foreign territory of word processing. Twayne editor Barbara Sutton made many improvements to the manuscript. My thanks also to Vicki Muller, whose careful editing saved me from choppy sentences and numerous solecisms. Any remaining errors are strictly my own.

I also wish to acknowledge a group of friends without whom this book would not be—especially Rilda Bess and Gregg Franzwa, for their innumerable kindnesses and their unwavering friendship. Others who shared their strength and their belief in me throughout this project deserve mention as well. For the generosity of Barbara, Betty, Carol, Erinn, Sharon, and, of course, Jean Tant, I am also indebted in very special ways. Thank you for what each of you has contributed to my life. Your loving and steadfast encouragement was indeed the wind beneath my wings.

Chronology

1895?   Edith Ngaio Marsh born 23 April in Christchurch, New Zealand. (The archivist in New Zealand believes she was born in 1895, but the birth was not registered until 1899.)

1910–14   Receives her secondary education at St. Margaret's College.

1915–20   Studies painting at Canterbury University College School of Art, Christchurch.

1920–23   First theatrical tour with the Allan Wilkie Shakespeare Company.

1928   First visit to London.

1934   First detective novel, *A Man Lay Dead,* published; introduction of her detective hero, Roderick Alleyn.

1935   *Enter a Murderer* and *The Nursing-Home Murder* published.

1936   *Death in Ecstasy* published.

1937   *Vintage Murder* published (first New Zealand novel).

1938   *Artists in Crime* published; Agatha Troy introduced. *Death in a White Tie* published; Troy and Alleyn become engaged (thereby breaking Van Dine's prohibition on the detective having a serious love interest).

1939   *Overture to Death* published.

1940   *Death at the Bar* and *Death of a Peer* published.

1941   *Death and the Dancing Footman* published.

1942   Directs first Shakespearean production (*Hamlet*) at Canterbury University.

1943   *Colour Scheme* published.

1939–45   Serves in Red Cross transport unit during World War II.

1944–52   Directs ten Shakespearean productions and many modern plays. Is director of the first all–New Zealand Shakespearean company. Produces plays for D. D. O'Connor Theater management, including the British Commonwealth Company.

1945   *Died in the Wool* published.

1947   *Final Curtain* published; Alleyn returns from the war to
       Troy, who is now his wife.

1948   Awarded the title Fellow of the Royal Society of Arts O.B.E.
       (Officer of the Order of the British Empire).

1949   Marsh's British publisher, Collins, gives a "Marsh Million"
       party to celebrate growing sales of her detective novels. *A
       Wreath for Rivera* published.

1951   *Night at the Vulcan* published.

1953   *Spinsters in Jeopardy* published.

1955   *Scales of Justice* published.

1956   *Death of a Fool* published.

1958   *Singing in the Shrouds* published.

1959   *False Scent* published.

1962   Ngaio Marsh Theater opens at Canterbury University. *Hand
       in Glove* published.

1963   Awarded the doctor of literature degree from Canterbury
       University. *Dead Water* published.

1965   *Black Beech and Honeydew*, the first edition of her autobiog-
       raphy, published.

1966   Awarded the honor Dame Commander of the Order of the
       British Empire (D.B.E.). *Killer Dolphin* published.

1968   *A Clutch of Constables* published.

1970   *When in Rome* published.

1972   Directs last Shakespearean production, *Henry V. Tied up in
       Tinsel* published.

1974   *Black as He's Painted* published.

1977   *Last Ditch* published. Receives Grand Master Award, Mys-
       tery Writers of America. *Grave Mistake* published.

1980   *Photo Finish* published.

1981   Second edition of *Black Beech and Honeydew* published.

1982   Last detective story, *Light Thickens,* published. Dies 18
       February.

Chapter One
New Zealand Roots and British Branches: Ngaio Marsh's Hybrid Nature

Despite her protestations that detective fiction did not represent her truest vocation, Dame Ngaio Marsh will be remembered best for her thirty-two works of that genre. This self-professed squeamish and fastidious woman created exceptionally bizarre methods for dispatching her victims to the hereafter; each crime was subsequently solved by her thoroughly cool-eyed policeman, Roderick Alleyn, CID. These mysteries rank among the best of the golden age of English detective fiction, along with the work of Agatha Christie, Dorothy Sayers, and Margery Allingham. Although she had much in common with these three writers, Marsh introduced the unique elements of her New Zealand heritage and her theatrical career into her novels, thus broadening their scope beyond the "drawing room" milieu. As an outsider looking in at English customs and mores, she added a dimension of objective commentary on social conventions that, quite arguably, took her fiction beyond the detective formula and into the realm of the novel of manners. Though she referred to her fiction deprecatingly as "entertainments," it is clear that she crafted each novel with care and that her characters achieve dimensions beyond mere clichés.

For all her achievements in detective fiction, Marsh's reputation in New Zealand, and to some extent in England, rests on a different standard. She was a producer of ten Shakespeare plays, a founder of a New Zealand company devoted to their production, and a coach of numerous "student-actors," as she called them. For these latter accomplishments she was honored in her homeland and granted the Order of the British Empire in 1966. Peter Harrot, a theater historian, remarks in his *A Dramatic Appearance* that "her contribution . . . has not been as a writer but as a producer and an inspiration to young people. She has been responsible for a series of exceptionally fine Shakespearean productions with student casts. Her reputation lies in the philosophy she was able to expound, in the development of talent, and in the lessons of her own dedication."[1]

Marsh herself would have agreed with this assessment; she confessed that her work in the theater would always be regarded as her most valuable contribution. Yet discomfited as she might have been by judgments to the contrary, Marsh was certainly aware of the transitory nature of theatrical performances—even superb ones recalled with pleasure—when contrasted with the longevity of the pleasure of a novel. It was the mixture of these commitments, each of which enhanced the others, that shaped her contributions as an artist and her enduring reputation as writer, Bardophile, and teacher.

The life of Ngaio Marsh contributed significantly to the art of her fiction. She translated her experiences narratively and symbolically into her characters, her settings, and her major themes. Underlying all her detective fiction was the Victorian/Edwardian fastidiousness in which she was steeped as a child. Such propriety, however, did not prevent her from indulging in its paradoxical partner—a love of sensationalism and melodrama, nowhere so evident as in the Victorians' fascination with death.

In the Victorian age, death and mourning were raised to an art form, and at times it appeared that the Victorians' sense of propriety was exceeded only by their thrilling morbidity. With the "Widow of Windsor" as the most public practitioner, a virtual industry of funerals and death souvenirs developed. From elaborate coffins transported by mourning coaches bedecked with dark ostrich feathers to plaster casts of arms or hands of the departed littered about as a part of the decor, this industry thrived. Social class could be immediately determined by the nature of the funeral accoutrement; consequently, an etiquette of death requiring substantial financial investment had to be observed by the middling classes and those who aspired to social acceptance. Even the wealthy could incur sizable debts from funerals, and many of the less wealthy formed burial clubs to save for the inevitable expense. Given this emphasis on death, it is not surprising that the murder mystery as a discrete form of fiction was created by the Victorians and reached its apogee under a few women, including Marsh, reared just at the end of the era.

Marsh's family exemplified these elements of the age: a flair for drama and theatricals combined with her mother's prim suspicion of the easy emotionalism and "bohemian" habits of theater people. Indeed, it was the theater in Marsh's background that affected her so deeply—not only as a professional producer but also as a writer. Her style clearly reflected a well-honed ear for dialect and dialogue: extended conversations form the bulk of a number of her yarns. She portrayed verbal quirks that are often significant clues to character and class. A remarkable number of her novels take place in theaters, and those that do not nevertheless contain such a distinct placing of the action that one can almost sense a backstage rehearsal. Murders that occur in front of an audience fascinated Marsh. Not for her the "locked door" murder; her sense of drama demanded an audience and a stage for the action and rarely found scope in a surreptitious murder.

Marsh's earliest aspirations, however, were not theatrical but artistic. Her training as a painter affected her writing, endowing it with a visual clarity, a richness of detail and color seldom found in detective fiction and nowhere as consistently as in Marsh's novels. She created a painter as a major character in more than half her works and described with obvious relish the artist's eye, temperament, and talent. Marsh's novels are so filled with painterly detail and theatrical effects that solving the murder becomes almost a secondary business to discovering not the sleight of hand but the trompe l'oeil.

Marsh differed from the other "Big Four" mystery writers in that she was reared and lived out much of her life in a country other than England. Although the environment of Christchurch, New Zealand, was as close to that of England as its inhabitants could contrive, it was still a city in a very separate nation with a distinct, wilder, frontier feel to it. Marsh placed five of her novels in New Zealand, and in numerous others she featured characters from New Zealand or Australia. Marsh did not visit England until she was a young adult; she fell in love with it immediately yet never forsook her roots. Throughout her life she divided her time between the two countries. Her perspective from both inside and outside British society enriched her social observations of *both* England and New Zealand. Although firmly rooted in her native land, Marsh became a hybrid personality—capable of skillful commentary on both countries' values, honors, and gaucheries.

Even without venturing into the realm of psychoanalysis, it is apparent that Marsh's life had an inordinately large influence on her art and its major themes. Her theatrical avocation and her artistic bent inspired much of the color in her novels of suspense. Her peculiar social standing gave her a unique perspective on her characters and on class consciousness. Her heritage, born of a passing Victorian era, richly endowed her books with a sense of happening on the cusp of time—England was still Victorian in its sensibilities until at least 1921 and became "modern" only in the late twenties and thirties. These elements of Marsh's personal history, nurtured by family, friends, and two small island nations, are mixed and spun into thirty-two fine yarns that endure and even transcend their milieu.

Appropriately, Edith Ngaio Marsh's life began with a mystery. Though she was born on 23 April 1895, according to the New Zealand archives, her father registered her birth as 1899, thereby generating confusion that the author herself remained vague about in her autobiography. Throughout her life Marsh described her father, Henry Edmond Marsh, as an amiable eccentric, an indifferent businessman but a dedicated sportsman, an honest and lovable man. After her mother's death, she remained in Christchurch to care for him until his demise at well past the age of eighty. Marsh's mother and the relationship between mother and daughter was more complicated—a mixture of companionship and abrasion, as intimate ties tend to be. Her mother was the gifted actress of the family, high-spirited yet stable, an excellent anchor for her father's more fey qualities. Rose Seager Marsh appears to have performed the same function for her daughter—cautioning her against her more impulsive urges and inculcating a sense of propriety and responsibility. In her autobiography, Marsh was so reluctant to discuss any personal aspects of her life—her dreams or sentiments—that it is tempting to attribute her reticence to an upbringing in which such frankness was "not quate nayce."[2] Her mother's emphasis on discipline and forbearance may have been the legacy of her New Zealand pioneer background and, tempered by her personal flair for drama, must have produced a woman of formidable strength who could delight and powerfully influence others—qualities that her daughter inherited.

A combination of pioneer hardiness and artistry also appeared in Marsh's maternal grandfather Seager. Traveling by bullock wagon, he and his bride immigrated to Canterbury in the middle of the nineteenth century when the Church of England was giving land grants to all faithful Anglicans who wished to help settle the new township. As their family matured, the young schoolmaster turned his talents to organizing a police force, with dashing new uniforms, running the first jail of the province, and ultimately superintending the first mental asylum, Sunnyside. Lacking any medical training, Marsh's grandfather entertained his patients as his only method for improving their state. He produced plays, performed magic tricks, and, in the best psychiatric methodology of the day, practiced mesmerism. His patients and his children adored him, and his daughter, Marsh's mother, passed along to her only child his love of drama, his lively sense of humor, and his genuine compassion.

Marsh's initial contacts with theatrical production were not altogether felicitous. Some of her earliest terrors arose from listening to her parents rehearse their lines for an amateur theatrical production of *The Fools' Paradise*. Her childhood anxieties centered on an exaggerated fear of poison that would affect her throughout her life. Though Ngaio Marsh thought of many bizarre murder weapons, she almost never used poisons—a very common method for Agatha Christie. In her autobiography, Marsh described her gradual transformation from a fearful child to one who madly adored and anticipated the traveling productions of dramas, comedies, and children's plays that made a circuit through Christchurch. Her imagination, vivid and colorful, was raised to new heights by her ecstatic responses to those early plays.

Marsh's parents encouraged not only a love of theater but also a love of reading. Her mother admired Hardy, Galsworthy, and Conrad and read *Almayer's Folly* many times. Mrs. Marsh taught her daughter to read selectively, with an eye toward style as well as a good yarn. Her father gave her the collected works of Henry Fielding when she was twelve—even insisting that she read *Tom Jones,* of which more prudish families would doubtless have disapproved. She read Smollett, too, but enjoyed each of these writers far less than her father's ultimate favorite: Charles Dickens. Of all Dickens's works, *David Copperfield* appears to have won Marsh's prepubescent loyalty most thoroughly, although *Pickwick Papers* also enraptured her. R. H. Barham's *The Ingoldsby Legends* had a dramatic effect on her as a child. Marsh recalled how she used to shudder at the grim illustrations. She recollected later that she would sneak into the room where the book was kept and, for the sheer compulsive horror of it, torture herself with the ghostly eyes of the Dead Drummer. She returned to that book and that image several times in her own detective stories; in *Death and the Dancing Footman* (1941) Jonathan Royal remarks that he was frightened as a boy by these illustrations.

Marsh's father may have been the first to introduce his daughter to the cheaply published, sensational type of murder mystery known as a "shilling shocker." She remembered him devouring these books on occasion. He would become excited and jiggle his pipe in his teeth, exclaiming as he approached the climax. " 'Frightful rot!' he would say. 'Good Lord! Regular Guy Boothby stuff,' and greedily press on with it."[3] In her own writing, Marsh gave strong testimony to the literary influences on her. By marrying the traditions of character and place of the Victorian and Georgian novelists to the economy of plot and the puzzle of detective fiction, Marsh provided a link between Charles Dickens and Agatha Christie.

Although her parents were not wealthy—indeed, Marsh quoted Rose Macaulay in describing hers as a "have-not" family—they provided their only child with a fine education. After attending a "select dames" school known among the students as Tibs, Marsh studied with a private tutor–governess and then went to St. Margaret's College. St. Margaret's was founded and run by an Anglo-Catholic order of nuns, and it followed a rather demanding classical curriculum. Several important events in Marsh's life occurred at St. Margaret's, one of which was an adolescent fling with strict religious observance; she even denied herself the opportunity to see Henry Irving's son portray Hamlet because the play was performed during Lent. Though this behavior puzzled her nonbelieving father, Marsh would later explain it as a reasonably harmless outlet for the tenuous emotions of a teenager. Fortunately, that particular enthusiasm waned and Marsh wrote her first play while a student at St. Margaret's. She later recalled with amusement that the work contained long passages of very "torrid blank verse" and artificial conversations (*BBH,* 90). The play was performed at her school, with her mother playing the role of the witch with such frightening intensity that young Ngaio came to appreciate the magic that a fine actor could bring to an average or amateur piece. At St. Margaret's Marsh also found a family of friends, the Burtons, who, in what would be true Marsh fashion, became friends for life. She was learning, as an only child, to create extended families and siblings as a way of mitigating her aloneness. It was a talent she developed throughout her life, so much so that after her death many would comment on her remarkable capacity for friendship.

St. Margaret's made yet another contribution of inestimable importance to Marsh's character, her career, and her life. Her English literature teacher, Miss Hughes, was, as Marsh put it, "a dragon," but she was an inspiring teacher who set high standards of scholarship and encouraged her students to excel (*BBH,* 82). Most appealing to Marsh, the teacher gave her a passion for the plays and sonnets of Shakespeare, which dominated Marsh's life and her choice of careers. She not only directed the plays but also quoted widely from both them and the sonnets throughout her detective fiction. Making Shakespeare's plays a living experience for New Zealanders was certainly Marsh's fondest recollection of her life.

Upon graduating from St. Margaret's and leaving her extreme Anglo-Catholic enthusiasm behind her, Ngaio Marsh entered the Canterbury University College School of Art, which took a strict academic approach to art that both challenged and frustrated her. Marsh found that those who espoused the extremely conventional shibboleths about what constituted a "good" piece were too limiting, but the more creative instructors were too inarticulate. That she maintained her scholarship for five years testifies to her talent. In the revised edition of her autobiography, Marsh explained her failure to become a serious painter as a problem of personal resolution. The chief drawback to academic training in any of the arts is that technical virtuosity (which can be taught) practiced without an artist's sense of self and individual style (which many argue cannot be taught) does not yield great art. Yet Marsh benefited from art school in ways she did not yet appreciate. She acknowledged that she trained herself to become so attuned to visual detail that she saw everything in the context of lines and color. Her visual acuity and dramatic palette found their way into her novels in ways that set them apart from those of the other grandes dames of detective fiction. Many agree that had Marsh developed only her talent for description, she would have become a successful "straight" novelist. As it happened, Marsh was content to let Troy Alleyn paint landscapes and portraits, occasionally commenting about Troy's perceptions and the colors she observes. What Marsh felt she herself lacked the talent to become, she created in her fiction and enjoyed vicariously. In her early twenties, however, theater, like a seducer, drew her away from the early romance with painting and held her with a mesmeric power worthy of Grandfather Seager's best efforts.

Ngaio Marsh had already overcome many of her childhood fears about the strange world of theatrical pretense. In her days as an art student, she had been delighted by traveling productions of Shakespeare performed by the Allan Wilkie Shakespeare Company of New Zealand. She reminisced about her utter enchantment with the company's performance of *Hamlet* and her childlike wonder as she watched the opening scene. For the first time, the words she had read and the interpretations she had studied became breathing, pulsating theater. Ironically enough, she became involved even with theater through writing. Allan Wilkie himself reviewed a play she had written, and though nothing ever came of that endeavor, he was impressed with the young playwright and offered her a small role in the New Zealand/Australian branch of the company's next tour. Though Marsh's mother had refused a theatrical career for herself, she consented, with assurances of proper supervision from the Wilkies, to allow her daughter to go. Marsh later speculated that her mother was anxious to break the unsuitable attachments that her naive daughter had formed with two ardent young men. Whatever the source of her mother's consent, it changed Marsh's life. Her lifetime enthusiasm for theatrical production endured through innumerable hours of rehearsals, preparations, distractions, travel on several continents, and, later, the writing of detective novels.

Marsh spent that winter receiving the most intense education of her life. She learned stagecraft, acting technique, timing, assessing an audience, and the rudiments of managing a company. All these lessons would be valuable to her in later years when she managed her own company. She continued to paint, taking her gear with her to even the remote areas where the Wilkie company sometimes performed. The most important lesson Ngaio Marsh learned, however, was one in discipline, adaptability, and dealing with the vagaries of artistic temperament. She remembered these months as a time when she had unwittingly stocked a "little cellar of experiences" that she would eventually savor as "table wines of detective cookery" (*BBH*, 182). She discovered how conducive a theater was to mystery—even well lighted with a play in progress, it retained an air of things hidden in its cavernous depths. No one but a veteran of the theater could have conveyed as success-fully as she did in her books the same sense of heightened emotions on both sides of the curtain: audience and actors become witnesses, murderers, and victims. Besides being an adventure yarn, the detective story relies on the murderer's ability to deceive, to feign, to act convincingly. The detective as director must sort through the mannerisms of the murderer/actor and de-termine which ones betray the mask behind which he or she is hiding. Marsh typically underrated her skill at detective "cookery," but theater had trained her as a master chef, one who chose only the finest ingredients for her entrées.

Marsh's travels with Allan Wilkie's company helped establish what was always her fragile independence from her parents. Though she returned to the family home at the end of the tour, she began to show distinct signs of mild rebellion. When offered another tour with a New Zealand company performing light comedy, she accepted it over her mother's objections. Here Marsh found herself in much less respectable circumstances than the Wilkies had offered, but once again she learned a great deal about theater and about being flexible and creative when the show had to go on. These lessons proved enormously valuable in her subsequent theatrical endeavors. When the small company folded, Marsh returned to writing plays and ar-ranging for their performance in New Zealand. She continued to produce plays for several amateur theatrical societies, which expanded her group of friends and made her thirst for adventure. When a wonderfully zany family—known to the readers of her detective fiction as the Lampreys—"adopted" her, adventure was imminent. Not only did the high-spirited clan join in the theatrical life of Christchurch, but their own lives ranged between farce and melodrama, according to Marsh's recollections. She loved them fiercely and they reciprocated. When they returned to England, it was not long before they were writing to Ngaio to join them. Though leaving her mother may have been the single most difficult and wrenching emotional experience in Ngaio Marsh's life, leave her she did. Entering another period of change and new challenges, she was ready, as she put it, for *life*.

The sea voyage to England was memorable and is described in some de-tail in Marsh's autobiography, as are other voyages that followed. There are readily identifiable parallels with her travel experiences in her fiction: im-pressions, characters, and an acute sensitivity to atmosphere. Marsh certainly became more aware of herself, both personally and as a New Zealander. Heretofore she had seen only Australia and had noted the marked differences between the continental Australian and the insular New Zealander. Now on a much wider stage she observed herself reacting to distinct national customs, even though all were contained within the British Commonwealth of Nations.

At the first major port of call—Durban, South Africa—Marsh encountered the famous color bar, apartheid. As she would do so often in her fiction, Marsh demonstrated its implications on a small scale—in the ordinary event that brought so much into focus for an observant traveler. It was a rickshaw ride. She recalled her reactions to the Zulus, men magnificently garbed in native costume, standing by their rickshaws and competing for customers; she hesitated, musing that for her "it would be beyond the limit of anyone's imagination to envisage a member of one race running between shafts like a horse for the convenience of a member of the other" (*BBH,* 218). She felt the practice was a breach of humane standards.

Like all good travelers who wish to avoid a trip to the local jail or expulsion, Marsh "swallowed" her scruples and hired a rickshaw. Later, however, she questioned her decision: "Should I have given him a compensatory sum and a self-righteous commentary? An odious solution which he would no doubt have rightly interpreted as an insult to himself and his rickshaw" (*BBH,* 220). Finally she concluded that whatever her ethical and moral dilemma, the Zulu probably gave it no thought at all.

In 1928 Marsh found the Dutch Afrikaaners repulsive. She described them as "arrogant, small-eyed, muddily white." Yes, they were masters, but their mastery made them revolting. As the ship prepared to leave Durban, the passengers threw coins to the African children on the wharf. Marsh recalled that when one child began to prance too proudly, "an enormous Afrikaaner turned on him as if he were vermin and hit at him and the child cringed and fell back. It was the ugliest of sights" (*BBH,* 224). Still, she cautioned herself to make no "snapshot judgments" about all Afrikaaners. Did Marsh alter her opinion as a result of the events in South Africa in the last years of her life? There is no public record of her thoughts on this point. Certainly her fictional treatment of her own country's indigenous population, the Maori, suggests that she maintained an evenhanded approach. Though she was aware of inequities and injustice, Marsh was not a social reformer. She rejected any kind of social pronouncement or revolutionary creed. Her Victorian/Edwardian upbringing, which emphasized graciousness and good manners, would have rendered such an approach improbable. Her instinctive conservatism was readily apparent in her remarks about experimentation in the theater and, one suspects, in other areas as well.

Having visited some of her father's family in Cape Town, Marsh finally arrived in England. It was, as her father had predicted, a "homecoming." Neither she nor her parents knew that five years would pass before she returned to New Zealand. Throughout these years her daily regimen included visits, business enterprises, and London socializing with the Lamprey family. Many of these experiences and travels found their way into her detective fiction. Except for *Vintage Murder* (1937), all of her earliest work was set in an English locale. Many of the impressions and wonders of a naive young colonial were spilled breathlessly into her English works, which predominate the whole canon. She echoed her first impressions of "home" and the emotional link that she felt through her father's blood: "An ignorant and passionate sense of historical continuity rose up in me." She felt an extraordinary buoyancy and a finely tuned anticipation of "being carried high on the full tide of London" (*BBH,* 243).

Marsh's initial delight never quite faded as she began to explore the city and discover theaters and more theaters. From the more experimental playhouses rather incongruously stashed in working-class neighborhoods to the West End and the Old Vic, Marsh thrilled to Pirandello, J. B. Priestly, and, of course, Shakespeare. She visited all the appropriate tourist spots and discovered the nightclubs and fashionable restaurants. In the midst of these enjoyments a distressingly predictable Lamprey financial crisis forced more practical concerns into the minds of the revelers. With cash in short supply, Marsh and Charlot Lamprey opened a small gift shop in Brompton Road that turned a rather surprising profit in the Christmas season, allowing them to move the shop to Beauchamp Place, where they expanded from gifts and small items into specialty furniture and interior decoration. This Marsh-Lamprey enterprise endured a surprising two and a half years during which Marsh's mother came to London for an extended visit. The two women took a flat in Pimlico and lived together quite amicably. Mrs. Marsh shared Ngaio's devotion to theater, so the two made the rounds to all the plays. They renewed friendships with those colonials who, like themselves, had come back to England, some to retire, others just to visit.

Though her daughter was doing well and the pleasure of their reunion and mutual discoveries delighted her, Marsh's mother continued to encourage her to develop her creative writing. Marsh had already earned a name for herself in New Zealand with travel articles she had penned for a syndicated series in local newspapers. As Marsh herself put it, she had begun to develop some appreciation for the rhythm and balance of words. Secretly, she had begun an epic novel of New Zealand but had laid it aside in London because she felt so removed from her subject. What were to become her greatest writing accomplishments began inauspiciously on a rainy Sunday afternoon when, alone in her flat, she read a detective novel and decided to try her hand at one. In later years she would contradict herself on whether the inspiration had been Agatha Christie or Dorothy Sayers, but by that time it would not matter because her own name had drawn comparable attention. She began, as she sardonically remarked, in "a blaze of inspiration," imagining a weekend at a country house where the "murder game" is played, only with a real corpse. Her first book, *A Man Lay Dead* (1934), grew from a few penny exercise books into piles of them. Her mother soon discovered the manuscripts and, though perhaps disappointed at her daughter's choice of genre, remarked that she could not put the book down. This admission was remarkable, considering Marsh's lifelong protestation that neither she nor her mother were widely read in detective fiction. Even though she reported that the book poured forth from her with ease, she still regarded it as an undistinguished effort. Nevertheless, it was a turning point in her life, setting her on a path of creative success. This first success, however, was muted by family tragedy.

Shortly before the book was finished and typed, Marsh's mother returned home to New Zealand. Marsh, visited by a foreboding of death, felt overwhelming grief at her mother's departure. Within the next few months Mrs. Marsh wrote that she was ill, and shortly thereafter her father informed Marsh that her mother was dying. Marsh left the manuscript in the hands of an agent and returned to New Zealand to nurse her mother in her last days. After Mrs. Marsh died, she remained in her family home to care for her father and to write.

In the next year Marsh completed her second book, *Enter a Murderer* (1935). Here she moved into her familiar world of backstage theater with a cast of eccentrics whose Machiavellian plottings, nursings of ancient wounds, blackmail, and violence suggest the author was no dewy-eyed idealist about her dramatic craft or those who practiced it. Subsequently, Marsh's illness and surgery gave her material for the plot of *The Nursing-Home Murder* (1935), written in conjunction with her surgeon, Henry Jellett. When she felt well enough to resume a normal schedule, she decided to travel, returning to England in 1937. Shortly after her arrival in England, she departed for a three-month tour of the Continent, primarily Germany, Austria, and northern Italy. Her recorded impressions of Germany chronicled the uneasiness of the Jews living among the stern-faced Nazis. She felt that the latter were cheered on by the adolescent yearnings of the German people to swagger as though they were invincible adults in the community of nations.

Save for the one trip in 1937, Marsh remained in Christchurch from 1932 to 1949 and lived with her aging father. Theirs was a companionable home, and Marsh's mysteries pleased her "shilling shocker"–loving father. During World War II her father did his bit for the war effort by assisting on the home front in his own inimitable and eccentric way, while his daughter served as a Red Cross transport driver. After the fall of Singapore, New Zealanders feared an immediate invasion of their homeland; the resulting tensions almost inevitably affected Marsh's fiction. In two of her detective novels of New Zealand—*Colour Scheme* (1943) and *Died in the Wool* (1945)—Nazi spies commit murder to hide their mission of espionage. In both cases Alleyn, who has been summoned to the islands to assist the Foreign Office, solves the crimes and unearths the treason. In neither case is there a covey of spies—just lone Nazis gathering information to sabotage the Allied war effort. Though New Zealanders feared invasion from Japan, Marsh always portrayed spies as German sympathizers or fanatics.

At war's end Marsh suffered another personal blow when her father died. The years in which she was homebound, however, hummed with activity. Not only did she do her own war work, nurse her father, and produce fourteen detective novels, but she also rediscovered her theatrical roots. Over the war years she had worked intermittently with small New Zealand repertory societies that performed standard popular plays and occasionally attempted more experimental pieces. None were willing, however, to risk mounting a full-scale production of Shakespeare, certainly not one of the tragedies; Allan Wilkie had done his work almost too well—others were intimidated by his success. But in 1941–42 two young undergraduates of Canterbury University approached Ngaio Marsh about producing a play for them, and the venture proved so successful that the following year she and the students together produced *Hamlet*. The experience of directing *Hamlet* with a turbulent, unpredictable, but extremely enthusiastic group of student players offered yet another life transformation for Marsh. She later reported that she found the experience as utterly enjoyable as the day in her exuberant youth when in a celebratory mood she embraced a honeyed tree. And this pleasure would continue for the next thirty years as Marsh worked with successive groups of students.

Her *Hamlet* opened in the Little Theater of Canterbury College—which was not well suited to Shakespearean production—with a lame actor playing the prince of Denmark to a full house. The response was overwhelming and launched Marsh on an association that she called a "love affair." Following a similarly successful production of *Othello,* she and her student players embarked on a tour during their vacation period. After twenty years, she was again a traveling player, this time with her own company. All the lessons and experiences of the Wilkie company, the light-comedy tour, and her amateur repertory days now bore fruit. Marsh managed quality productions despite the vicissitudes of weather, improper theaters, poor costumes, and players whose loyalties were divided between theater and schooling. She was enormously successful. She brought the works of Shakespeare, Pirandello, and other fine dramatists to the remote areas of New Zealand and Australia. From this accomplishment came the offer from theatrical promoter Dan O'Connor to organize a company to perform in Australia and New Zealand, its members to be drawn from the best actors throughout the Commonwealth. Marsh accepted and returned to London to assemble her cast. The tour was only moderately successful, however, and after its six-month contract ended the venture was allowed to die and the cast was released. Most returned to England, but Ngaio Marsh headed to her home in Christchurch to recover her physical strength and refresh her sagging spirit.

Upon her return she joyfully renewed contacts with friends and cousins from the North Island, made new friendships among the members of a Stratford-upon-Avon traveling company, and celebrated her continued success in publishing detective novels. In 1949 she was the guest of honor at a party dubbed the "Marsh Million" by the hosts, publishers William Collins and Penguin. The two presses had good reason to honor Marsh, having published a million copies of her titles. By 1949 she had written only half of the thirty-two works she would eventually publish with them. In these years Marsh also renewed her work with the Canterbury University Drama Society, which was recovering from a disastrous fire that had destroyed its theater, costumes, sets, and equipment. Making do with the Christchurch Civic Theater, Marsh thereafter directed a Shakespearean play each year she was in New Zealand. By the time she ceased her active association with the university, she had overseen the building of a new campus theater, which was opened in 1962 and named for her. Ten years later she directed her last Shakespearean play in New Zealand. She had obviously preferred the tragedies in her long directing career, but she opened the Ngaio Marsh Theater with *Twelfth Night* and concluded her directing career with *Henry V.* Like a fondly remembered affair of the heart, the relationship between Marsh and her student players was sincere and faithful until its end.

In her reminiscences as in her fiction, Marsh displayed a lifelong love of travel. In her youth she and her parents camped in the forests, and as an art student she journeyed to the wild west coast to paint. As a youthful actress she toured towns and cities up and down the New Zealand islands and in Australia. Her trips back and forth to England by sea and some jaunts to Paris and Monte Carlo with the Lampreys stimulated her interests and whetted her appetite for more and wider vistas. With her increasing financial security in the 1950s and 1960s, she was able to satisfy these appetites for as long as her health and energy permitted. Her preferred method of transportation was by sea or train, but she traveled by many means, sometimes alone and sometimes in the company of devoted friends and student secretaries. Her sea voyages were most memorable, especially her first youthful departure from New Zealand, her first sight of England, and the stops in South Africa in between. Her experiences led Marsh to speculate on the meaning of the British Commonwealth, relations between the races, and the vulgarities of class distinction based on mere wealth. Her travels were essential to her developing maturity as a person and as an artist.

On a later sea voyage, a brief visit to Odessa in the Soviet Union was possible; although Marsh had secured all the necessary visas, she and the other passengers were denied permission to land there. Based on what she observed from the ship's deck, she thought Odessa the strangest and most exotic of all the cities she had visited. In the days of the cold war, Soviet officialdom intimidated even the bravest traveler; Marsh found the customs experience unpleasant but noted that the people she watched onshore did not appear to be unhappy. Like the wise traveler she was by then, Marsh suffered the confinement and inconvenience with good humor. Other travels found her in the Far East, the United States, the West Indies, and the great capitals of Europe. Like Somerset Maugham, Marsh had a consuming passion for colorful places and exotic customs and peoples. Also like Maugham, she used a few of her trips as settings for novels, though she still confined herself primarily to English and New Zealand locales. Unlike Maugham, Marsh faced the problem of how to transport her central character, Alleyn, out of England on a policeman's salary, which she solved in several inventive ways.

The years between 1965 and 1981 were extraordinarily fruitful for Marsh. Besides her travels she wrote eleven Alleyn novels and produced five Shakespeare plays for her student players. Her dual career as director and writer reached fullest fruition and earned her a number of prestigious awards. In 1963 she received the honorary doctor of literature degree from Canterbury University, just after the Ngaio Marsh Theater opened. Though not the highest award she would receive, the honorary degree may have meant the most to her because it came from home. Marsh also drew notice from the English dramatic establishment, which named her a Fellow of the

Royal Society of Arts and, from the king's list of 1948, an Officer of the Order of the British Empire (O.B.E.). In 1966, in further recognition of her contribution to Shakespearean production in the antipodes, she was honored as Dame Commander of the Order of the British Empire (D.B.E.) (her "damery," as she referred to it). The awards for her detective fiction were a bit slower in coming, but she finally received the Grand Master Award from the Mystery Writers of America in 1977 and became a member of the famous Detection Club of England, whose initiation ceremony she so humorously described in her autobiography. She was even more wry about the American award and described receiving it with her typical wit. Informed that because she could not attend the awards dinner in Los Angeles the honorary bust of Edgar Allan Poe would be mailed to her, Marsh remarked, "to coin a phrase, Poe was posted. I look up at this moment and there, to my pride, he stands: *stylese,* corpse-like, sheet-white, with closed eyes and black moustache, and there, fused into his pediment is my name and the date, 1977. An uninformed person might well make the silly mistake of supposing him, thus labelled, to be me" (*BBH* rev.ed., 308). Her gentle wit was tempered with graciousness, and Marsh concluded by saying that she was touched by the compliment.

Marsh's graciousness and her reticence about personal affairs were consistent with a humility that bordered on self-deprecation about her novels. Although she acknowledged that detective fiction was usually read by professional men and women, she continually denied not only her own talent but also the skill and imagination necessary to produce consistently good novels in any genre. In the first edition of *Black Beech and Honeydew* she expressed amazement that in England detective fiction was discussed as a serious art form; she maintained that, unlike great literature, there was a limit to what could be written about the detective novel. She left the door open to acknowledging that she had achieved some degree of accomplishment, however, when she added that the technical structuring of a detective novel may be "shamelessly contrived" but the style of writing and the characterizations need not be. Certainly her writing, with its fine descriptive passages, skillful dialogues, and wonderful humor, caught the eyes and ears of critics for decades. It is rather odd that Marsh dismissed her writing so cavalierly, and that she barely mentioned it in the first edition of her autobiography. Though she rejected and even mocked social pretensions through her characters, it was as if she had actually absorbed the intellectual pretensions of some of her New Zealand friends, who she felt liked her "in spite of" her fiction. Whatever embarrassment Marsh felt about her writing may have been partly mitigated when she was urged by her publishers—who were reacting to popular outcry—to reissue her autobiography with an added section on her career in fiction. It is from this chapter, albeit brief, and from some scattered thoughts and interviews that Marsh's view of her fiction can be ascertained.

Although Howard Haycraft calls her "more a novelist of manners than of character,"[4]Marsh reported that she began her novels with the characters alone. She conjured them up while vacuuming and then decided what kind of situation or crime best suited such people. Plot, mechanics, and technical details, she confessed, bored her, though she compiled a massive collection of reference books to check her details. Slip up on a detail, she warned, and "some babu in Pondicherry or a cock-a-hoop math's mistress in an establishment for middle-class maidens" will seize on it with glee (*BBH* rev.ed., 300). She made such a slip once, she confessed—ironically, in a reference to a battle in Shakespeare's *Henry V*—and it was noticed immediately by an eager reader.

Her choice of actors and artists as characters was, of course, a natural one because of her theatrical background, but she also insisted that they were perfectly appropriate for the drama of a murder story. They were not insincere, but they did feel everything in a most exaggerated fashion and there was nothing restrained in their reactions. This quality was attractive to the detective novelist who was writing about the most dramatic event of all: murder. Marsh wished to make her detective, Roderick Alleyn, as normal and uneccentric as possible. She eschewed the foppery of the earliest Peter Wimsey appearances and the heavily stylized Hercule Poirot. She never tired of Alleyn, nor of his wife Troy, and saved her sense of fun and the peculiarities of character for the eccentrics in each book. In her wisdom and restraint, Marsh not only wrote books that wear well but also created enduring men and women.

Critics frequently cite Marsh for the creativity of her murder methods. Marsh herself remarked that when people commented on her particularly grisly murders they were "inclined to take the line of wondering how a nice old dear like me could dream up such beastliness. . . . The idea being, I fancy, that perhaps the nice old dear is not so nice after all" (*BBH* rev.ed., 305). She offered no explanation for her imaginative murders, except to protest that she was not sublimating violence in her own character. Surely someone particularly drawn to Shakespeare's tragedies had become inured to mass stabbings, eye gougings, strangulations, poisonings, and mutilations. Marsh created murder methods that were inventive and dramatic, such as booby traps, meat skewers through the eye, suffocation by a wool press, and death by boiling mud. These death traps have about them an almost cinematic quality—very much in keeping with the theater's heightened effects. Marsh was and remained always a woman of the theater.

In addition to memorable characters and means of murder, Marsh's books contain a strong sense of place. Of course, when she described theater—from the front box office, the house stalls, boxes, and backstage to the back alleys—she became so explicit that her readers almost smelled the dust and greasepaint, felt the grime of windows sealed for decades, heard the swish of the ropes and the soft pad of footsteps on the grid. After her experiences with a variety of theaters, it was not surprising that Marsh managed to make each one she wrote about unique. Her sense of place extended to winter scenes in Dorset, where she created manor houses of very specific proportions and characteristics, with rooms whose details were chronicled with a former decorator's eye for style. She described one place so vividly and with such a loving hand that it became an integral part of the yarn she told: New Zealand. Five of her novels take place there—not an impressive percentage of her overall work, but in those novels the setting is of major importance in forwarding the story and solving the crime. Despite Marsh's obvious love for her homeland, questions remain about her decision to stay based there at such a very great distance from the majority of her reading public, most of the good Shakespearean productions, and the community that respected her writing as art.

To understand Marsh's loyalty to her remote homeland, it is necessary to consider the relations between England and the Commonwealth and to speculate about Marsh's own character. In the late nineteenth century, and especially in the twentieth, New Zealand and Australia, but especially the former, were regarded by the English—when they were considered at all—as boring and expensive properties necessary to the maintenance of a British global presence. Lacking the exotic qualities of India or the sense of new adventure of the African landscapes, the antipodes had generally been ignored both before and after the grant of dominion status gave them almost complete self-government. Ambitious young people in all the arts who sought to make their fortunes almost always left home to gain a wider audience. Her biographer maintains that Marsh's older contemporary, Katherine Mansfield, fled from New Zealand and changed her name to disguise her connection to a prominent New Zealand family. Mansfield's parents were wealthier and more prominent than Marsh's, but they were comparable in the middle-class values and Victorian/Edwardian assumptions they held.[5] Virginia Woolf illustrated these themes in *The Waves,* in which Louis carries a deep sense of shame through his entire life because his father was an Australian banker. Beatrice Webb commented in the 1890s that New Zealanders were the most provincial people on earth, always yearning for "home" in England twelve thousand miles away.

This kind of cultural insecurity might have been even more prominent in Christchurch, Marsh's home; she herself described the gently flowing river with its banks bedecked with flowers and willow trees in her "curiously English antipodean suburbs" (*BBH*, 38). Christchurch was founded in 1850 by settlers handpicked by the Church of England. They created as perfect a reproduction of an English city as they could muster, naming their winding river the Avon and priding themselves on being known as "the most English city outside England."[6] This strange phenomenon of scattered colonials who identified England as "home" and themselves as thoroughly English while being in radically different climates and circumstances was common throughout the British Empire, from the Ganges to the Mackenzie territory. The English people themselves, when not whipped into a frenzy of jingoism, were rather benignly indifferent to it all and regarded colonial enthusiasms as a bit of an embarrassment. How did Marsh, who had a foot in both worlds, regard them?

After several decades of traveling between England and New Zealand and coming to feel at home in both cultures, Marsh compared modern New Zealanders with the English of the eighteenth and nineteen centuries: "If you put a selection of people from the British Isles into antipodean coolstorage for a century and a half and then opened the door, we are what would emerge" (*BBH*, 267–68). New Zealanders, she added, were doubly insular in experience and attitude because their forefathers had left one island in the Northern Hemisphere for another island in the Southern Hemisphere. Their isolation from the monumental changes in European and English culture since the mid-nineteenth century had caused them to congeal in their Victorian ideas and become anachronisms in the modern world. Marsh's years in England gave her a distance and perspective on her native land that was often not appreciated in New Zealand.

Many colonials found their ideas about nationhood changing after World War II. In the crucible of that conflict they not only discovered their common purpose with the mother country but also confronted their differences from it. A new nationalism, based on a distinct perception of what a New Zealander is, began to emerge. At first it was negative—a rejection of British, or what were deemed to be British, characteristics. Gradually it moved toward a positive image that, as Marsh so clearly anticipated, needed to incorporate the Maori tradition as well. Marsh stood on the cusp of this movement—clearly a woman with a love for England and the English tradition, but with her native roots firmly planted in New Zealand.

Ngaio Marsh was a woman of deep loyalties—to friends and family, to her parents, and to her homeland. Though she had friends all over the world, the oldest were in New Zealand. Her father had built the cottage that she called home throughout her life and in which she ultimately died. Her homeland appealed to her with its emerging identity: awkward as an adolescent but full of promise. And the country needed her and her special talents; she participated fully as a leader in the cultural life of the nation. In England a detective novelist with a burning desire to direct Shakespearean plays would have been an eccentric; in New Zealand she was seized on as a rarity and came to be regarded by many as a national treasure. Others, less enthusiastic, resented Marsh because of her ties to a traditional and "proper" Britain, which she never tired of emphasizing, her unsentimental views of race relations in New Zealand, and her impatience with the truculence and narrow-mindedness that often passed for patriotism. Others resented her simply because she was a success, and they attacked her as a "mere" detective story writer who was never a real New Zealander in the first place. Those whose opinions Marsh surely valued more—her former students and others who discovered a love of Shakespeare through her efforts—speak of her in a different voice.

One of the most moving obituaries to appear after Marsh's death on 18 February 1982 was that by Bruce Mason, a former student and theatrical colleague. He called Marsh an "inspiration, confidant, vigorous galvanizer of scattered energies and a life-long friend of the purest integrity."[7] Indeed, all who knew her speak of her kindly manner, her delightful sense of humor, and her unselfishness. As for Marsh's choice to write detective fiction, Mason argued convincingly that "her chosen fictional *genre* . . . affirms the value of life, for it demonstrated that death has not the final say. Life goes on and the victim of a crime is avenged (at least in 'classical whodunits') by due process of law."[8] It is the sense of order and form that appealed to Marsh, like the regularity of a sonnet or the self-imposed confinements of the metaphysical poets. Within those limits she created narrative gems revealing life, death, love, and justice. Those were her themes; that she chose to develop them in detective fiction does not trivialize them. In her funeral service in Christchurch Cathedral, Shakespeare's poetry again said it all:

> Fear not slander, censure rash;
> Thou hast finish'd joy and moan. . . .
> Quiet consummation have,
> And renowned be thy grave.[9]

Chapter Two
Images of Commonwealth

Ngaio Marsh occupied a unique position among detective writers of the 1930s and 1940s because of her New Zealand background. She was the most popular dominion novelist of this period, continuing until well after the war; no Canadian, Australian, or South African came close to her achievement. In addition to writing detective fiction, Marsh promoted a view of New Zealand and the empire, its possibilities and its problems.

To many English readers New Zealand must have seemed a distant and exotic land. In the decades before commercial air travel, an ocean voyage of five weeks between the two countries must have discouraged all but the most curious tourists. Despite the distance, however, the English and New Zealanders shared several bonds: the heritage of English-speaking peoples, a Commonwealth commitment to the Allied cause in World War II, and the experience of being beleaguered island nations. According to Marsh, these mutual interests, so necessary for the war effort, would ultimately prove problematic for New Zealanders, who viewed their land and experiences as unique and quite distinct from the mother country. Certainly no one questioned New Zealand's loyalty in World War II, but in two novels, *Colour Scheme* and *Died in the Wool,* Marsh introduced enemy spies wreaking havoc with Allied shipping and special weapons development. Of her five New Zealand novels, four were written just before or during World War II. Marsh was in New Zealand at that time, so perhaps she turned quite naturally to her immediate surroundings. Beyond propinquity, however, this choice of subject matter may have been affected by other motives: Marsh may have been sounding an alarm to those who believed that New Zealand was too isolated or inconsequential to be in danger.

In *Colour Scheme* Dikon Bell finds it difficult to believe that enemy agents threaten his peaceful, isolated homeland.[1] He speculates that meddlesome old women and bored old men fantasized fears of enemy agents and secret plots to feed their gossip. In each book Marsh revealed that dangerous enemy activity did indeed threaten Allied successes and was responsible for the murders of two people who stumbled onto decisive evidence of the espionage. According to Marsh, any nation that believed itself to be immune from the war deluded itself.

In addition to her warnings, Marsh, having just returned from Britain, had become acutely aware of the Commonwealth tie between her two "native lands." Her cultural loyalty to England—its arts and Shakespeare, especially—combined with her deep familial ties to New Zealand made her an unwitting ambassador whose task was to increase each country's understanding of the other in those critical years. As she put it in her autobiography, upon her return she "began to think about the bloody pommy thing and to speculate on the kind of within-the-family friction that has developed" (*BBH*, 268–69). She pondered the state of imperial harmony, not just in her autobiography but also in her travel articles and her detective fiction. She took an exceptionally unsentimental look at her fellow New Zealanders, with their mixture of brass and bashfulness; the English, prejudged by New Zealanders as either class-conscious snobs or conversely, the refuse of that class-defined society; and the Maori, still clinging to tribal traditions, some savage, in the face of English domination. Even as Marsh wrote her three major New Zealand novels, the empire's contours were changing. Many foes—external and internal, war being the most immediate —threatened to shatter its unity.

"I have not become the King's First Minister in order to preside over the liquidation of the British Empire."[2] With these brave words, Winston Churchill in 1942 reaffirmed his defiance of enemies abroad and his implacable opposition to dissidents who sought to alter Britain's imperial destiny. Successful in repelling Germany's challenge, Churchill could not forestall the transformation of the British Empire from dependent colonies into the freely associated British Commonwealth of Nations. As the world watched, the empire on which the sun never set surrendered its hegemony —sometimes grudgingly, sometimes graciously—over nations around the globe.

With the successful experience in Canada as their only guide, British policymakers had granted dominion status to Australia, New Zealand, and South Africa in the first decade of the twentieth century, and to Ireland in the third. In 1926 the Balfour Declaration informally defined the nature of a dominion, and in 1931 this definition was written into English law as the Statute of Westminster. In the late 1940s India and Burma, after long campaigns by nationalist groups, became the first non-Caucasian or European dominated areas to achieve dominion status. For all their differences, however, Marsh believed that "just as children who have been energetically bickering with their parents will close the family ranks with a bang against an outsider," so would New Zealanders hasten to make common cause with the mother country (*BBH*, 270). It was unthinkable to Marsh that all Commonwealth peoples would not support Britain in a crisis, yet those peoples had to understand one another and their common bonds.

As a detective fiction writer Marsh had a unique opportunity to reflect and perhaps influence that exchange. Somerset Maugham comments that "when historians . . . come to discourse upon the fiction produced by the English-speaking peoples in the first half of the twentieth century, they will pass somewhat lightly over the compositions of the 'serious' novelists and turn their attention to the immense and varied achievements of the detective writers."[3] Part of the "immense" achievement was that detective stories appealed to everyone from "Oxbridge" dons to fishmongers. Any images and values promoted in detective stories could, conceivably, cross class, educational, and economic barriers. Those writers, like Marsh, who utilized themes of Commonwealth development offered some interesting perspectives on this issue and ultimately suggested how the British people viewed themselves and their great colonizing effort in a world where power was being transferred increasingly from older nations in Europe to newer ones in Asia and Africa.

In 1937 Marsh, in the earliest of her New Zealand books, *Vintage Murder,* introduced some of the major themes that she would reprise throughout the series.[4] She explored the unease that quivered just below the surface of New Zealander–British relationships; the ambiguous position of the Maori, native to the country but pressed to adapt to the dominant Caucasian civilization; and the beauty of the countryside. *Vintage Murder* also contains the ingredients that would become vintage Marsh—Alleyn, the theater, a bizarre murder, and a cast of flamboyant actors. She dedicated the book to Allan Wilkie, the actor-manager of her first theatrical tour, and to his wife, Frediswyde Hunter-Watts, the most memorable Ophelia of Marsh's career. The central couple in the story appear to have been based in part on some of the characteristics that Marsh admired in those two, such as their utter fidelity to each other and their rejection of theatrical cant.

In the novel Carolyn Dacres heads the company named for her and is, as Alleyn muses, a star but not a great actress. Her husband, Alfred Meyer, manages the business end of the company, and although he is a homely, plump fellow, they are a devoted couple. They travel through New Zealand with their troupe, ranging in type from the old character actress and ultimate professional, Susan Max, to the hysterical starlet whose father "bought" her a position in the company, Valerie Gaynes. The male cast includes leading man Hailey Hambleden, long in love with Miss Dacres;

Francis Liveridge, the randy, aging actor who enjoys Miss Gaynes's attentions; and George Mason, Meyer's partner in management. After a successful performance in Middleton, North Island, the company and its guests assemble backstage for a birthday banquet for Miss Dacres, organized by her husband. The grandest moment, as he has planned it, is to be a dramatic lowering of a jeroboam of champagne from the top gallery onto the table, with accompanying fanfare. The festivities turn to horror, however, when the champagne instead crashes down on the head of the unsuspecting host. Alleyn, who had met the company earlier on the train, is at the party and therefore involved in the initial inquiries; the New Zealand police ask him to stay involved. Within a day Alleyn's questions have stripped away the false bonhomie and bared secrets and past shame. He reveals the murderer to have been Meyer's business partner, Mason, and for the most prosaic and predictable of reasons—money. Mason's motives are ordinary, but his methods are not—the rigged booby trap was set by the victim. Marsh would utilize this gambit several times in other books and would also return to these characters. Susan Max had already appeared in *Enter A Murderer,* and all the rest, under different names and circumstances, would people Marsh's casts in subsequent theatrical murders. Marsh's achievement in *Vintage Murder* lay not in her creation of unique characters—though later she developed memorable ones similar to them—but in the book's setting and atmosphere, the complications of its plot, and the theme of imperial relations.

In *Vintage Murder,* as in all her novels that take place in New Zealand, the mystery played a secondary role as Marsh, in an almost somber mood and with a scientific eye, studied her compatriots under the microscope of a murder investigation. She analyzed what New Zealanders thought of themselves and their place in the world, and what illusions shaped their perceptions until that time when the riveting, unrelenting queries of her detective stripped them naked to reality. Carol Acheson comments that Marsh's novels incorporate "many of her responses as a returned expatriate, particularly her feeling for the land, sympathy for the Maoris, and dislike of defensive and self-limiting attitudes."[5] In discussing *Vintage Murder,* Acheson notes that

the problem of combining a serious commentary on New Zealand with the stylized format of a detective story is overcome largely by changing the character of Alleyn, and making him the central consciousness of the novel. His former flippancy is dropped: he is now serious and thoughtful, a sensitive observer with a police-trained eye for detail. His personal desire to understand New Zealand and its people is given impetus by the murder investigation, and the usual tension between detective and suspects gains additional depth and interest by the conflict of three cultures. As a result the New Zealand setting is no mere travelogue but a significant and well-integrated element of the story."[6]

By allowing the hybrid nature of her own background to shape her vision and purpose, Marsh achieved the status of a woman of letters, rather than of just another good detective novelist.

Marsh depicted Alleyn becoming educated about New Zealander sensitivity as he picks his way through the professional turf of the local police. After an embarrassing first encounter with Inspector Wade, Alleyn, diffident and courteous, wins him over with his modesty; he assures Wade that he recognizes he is in the inspector's bailiwick and offers himself as a witness, no more. Wade, whose manner has been a curious mixture of deference, awkwardness, and somewhat forced geniality, now thaws completely.

Although Alleyn enjoys the cooperation, he muses, both to himself and in letters to his friend Detective Inspector Fox of Scotland Yard, about the slang and characters of these colonials. He acknowledges that there is some merit to the New Zealander's defensiveness in the face of certain British attitudes toward those who settled the islands, because there is a "type of Englishman [who] still regards the dominions either as a waste-paper basket or a purge" (VM, 21). When New Zealand–born Susan Max is mistaken for an Australian, she responds that she is offended not by being taken for another nationality but by the ignorance of the average Englishperson about the antipodes. Marsh is clearly tweaking the English for some of their ignorance. She has Alleyn define what the colonial wants from the English: to be treated fairly, as an equal, with no English condescension. Alleyn knows that to reassure Wade and his colleagues that he is not patronizing he will have to bend over backward and maintain a "strenuous heartiness." He does not underestimate the difficulties in this situation of Anglo-colonial cooperation. He recognizes that, "if I don't remember to be frightfully hearty and friendly, he'll think I'm all English and superior. I know he will. I would myself, I suppose, in his shoes. He's been damn pleasant and generous, too, and he's a very decent fellow. Dear me, how difficult it all is" (VM, 79). Marsh examined, through Alleyn's sensitive perceptions, the barriers between these Commonwealth family members.

Marsh also paused to comment on the language barrier between Alleyn and the New Zealanders. (George Bernard Shaw remarked that England and America are two countries separated by a common language.) Alleyn is puzzled but not offended by the slang he hears as he eventually unravels the multiple meanings of *crook* and the variations in the local idiom of *corker,* a *fair nark,* a *fair con, dikkon,* and *good-oh.* In his entirely evenhanded way he remarks that aside from the difference in slang, the average New Zealander speaks more precise English than his British counterpart. In her autobiography Marsh made more severe comments on the subject of language definition, points she illustrated in her later novel *Colour Scheme.* In *Vintage Murder* she was content to treat this issue more gently. With superb tact Alleyn manages to overcome Wade's "colonial defensiveness" and works with him to solve the crime. To his credit, Wade overcomes his "bloody pommy" suspicions and reacts to Alleyn's success as graciously as any local English policeman who had watched the detective's wizardry. He compliments Alleyn on the speed and thoroughness of his investigation, although as a pride-saving device, Wade insists that the New Zealand police would have come to the same conclusions as Alleyn, whose assistance has merely quickened the process. With this extension of graciousness on both sides, the "within-the-family friction" is reduced considerably.

Marsh continued this theme, offering a variation on the family feud in *Colour Scheme.* In this 1943 wartime novel she acknowledges that the problems of Commonwealth integration varied with the levels of maturity of the members. In her autobiography she commented that, as in a family, the New Zealand–Britain ambivalence was marked by "spontaneous outbursts of irritation" (*BBH,* 270) while the colonies were maturing from infancy to adolescence and on to adulthood. *Colour Scheme* emphasizes the adolescent stage—the search for a unique identity by which to separate from the parents. With New Zealand's roots, branches, and struggles so similar to those of England, what made a New Zealander a New Zealander rather than an absentee Briton? In her novels Marsh insisted that simple political independence from Britain failed to create nationalism or a national identity. That task devolved on a group of often muddleheaded settlers standing with one foot firmly planted in England and the other in virgin soil. Some in *Colour Scheme,* like the Claires, clung to the illusion of their English selves; others, like Maurice Questing and Dikon Bell, had their English, New Zealand, and American influences confused and reflected no dominant culture. Those of the younger generation defined themselves by rejecting all that they were not—English, American, or Maori—in the vain hope that the residue might be undiluted New Zealander. Marsh examined all three types in probing but sympathetic portraits; every character in the novel reflects a phase of the developmental conflict.

The mystery centers on who has killed Maurice Questing, an obnoxious entrepreneur who promoted and planned to take over the Wai-ata-tapu

Hotel and Spa. The hotel's owners, Colonel and Mrs. Claire, run their establishment more by eccentric whim than by sound business principles. They are assisted by their children Barbara and Simon, the handyman Herbert Smith, and Mrs. Claire's brother, Dr. James Ackrington. It is the doctor who becomes suspicious of Questing's activities and writes to the Foreign Office requesting an investigation into possible espionage. The investigation coincides with a visit to the spa by Shakespearean actor Geoffrey Gaunt and his secretary, Dikon Bell. When Questing is shoved into one of the boiling mud pools, the search for his killer encompasses the spa's personnel and guests, as well as the population of a nearby Maori village. Alleyn, in one of his rare disguises, is Septimus Falls, a near-invalid taking the mud baths; he uncovers Smith as the spy and the murderer. This discovery is almost anticlimactic, for the real story centers upon the self-discovery of the major characters, and the real mystery lies in the land.

Each of these characters symbolizes a stage of national identity. For the elder Claires there is no conflict; they are English by origin, loyalty, and persuasion. The isolated, desolate area in which they live makes no difference. Their hotel feels like an English vicarage with its garden, its scenes from "home"—London posters, Anglo-Indian photographs, and "blameless" novels. Mrs. Claire sees herself as the village doyen of her strange community and welcomes Gaunt as if she were welcoming a bishop suffragan to a poor parish. She exhibits the poise, grace, and vagueness of a proper English rector's wife who intends to rear her children as good English children and instructs the awkward Barbara in the subtleties of class distinction. Class distinction, she maintains, can be measured on an intuitive scale based on breeding rather than money. It does not matter so much what one does; class will tell in the doing.

Mrs. Claire's qualities are not affectations but come as naturally to her as her husband's military bluff and distracted nature come to him. Marsh undoubtedly drew on colonial dames of her acquaintance, since this Anglocentric view was a feature of life in the Christchurch of her youth. She later confessed a strong affection for the Claires and was smiling just a bit at them when she placed them within an ornate silver frame, as if they were a proper Edwardian family with only a few eccentricities. Just as boiled shirts and teatime turned up in the tropics, so here in the remote, sulfurous backsludge, formal manners, class consciousness, and an ersatz Englishness were maintained.

The second sort of New Zealander appeared in Marsh's novels as a rather bland amalgam of influences—unable to decide which loyalty compelled him or her most. In *Colour Scheme* Maurice Questing, the mysterious victim, is despised by all for incorporating the most vulgar traits of England, New Zealand, and America: "His speech, both in accent and in choice of words, was an affair of mass production rather than selection. . . . His conversation was full of near-Americanisms that are part of the New Zealand dialect, but they, too, sounded dubious" (*CS*, 26). In the same novel Dikon Bell "ached" for England. He stares out of the Claires' hotel and sees an indifferent landscape, beautiful but remote, even as he is awed and intimidated by its ancient and profound majesty. Dikon resents his attraction to this land and resists its call back to his New Zealand roots. He wishes to return to the urban landscape of London, yet his homeland exercises its charm on him.

Despite our initially unfavorable impressions of them, by book's end both Questing and Bell are patriots. In his last letter before he is murdered, Questing declares, "I venerate the British Commonwealth of Nations and the idea of a spy in God's Own Little Country gets my goat good and proper" (*CS*, 260). Dikon rationally contemplates the possible invasion of New Zealand. As he thinks about it, his emotions are deeply stirred by a passionate surge of patriotic anger; he resolves to join the army.

Although it takes a war for Questing and Bell to find themselves as New Zealanders, Marsh recognized that many youngsters denied any ambivalence in their loyalties, defiantly rejecting English qualities and asserting a hearty virility that anticipated Florence Rubrick's patriotic bluff in *Died in the Wool.* In *Colour Scheme* Simon Claire has attended local schools and is torn between his family's proud English traditions and his schoolmates' disdain for English attitudes and characteristics. He becomes "truculently colonial, somewhat introverted and defiantly uncouth" (*CS*, 7). His obstinance veers into left-wing affiliations—though of a sort characterized by knee-jerk shibboleths more than by a true revolutionary's alienation. Simon reduces World War II's origins to greed and shouts that although big business started the war, it will be fought and won by "ordinary chaps" who mean to have a hand in the restructuring of society once it is over. Ironically, Simon is not in uniform, and his only battles are with his own gaucheries. As Dikon Bell's confidence grows throughout the novel, he finally confronts Simon's simpleminded stereotypes. Asked to defend his prejudices, Simon maintains that the English are weak sissies who are too tired to be assertive. Bell responds, " 'Like Winston Churchill?' 'Aw to hell!' roared Simon, and then grinned. 'All right, all right!' he said. 'You win, I apologize' " (*CS*, 103–14).

Marsh was convinced that neither of these extremes was sufficient to form a separate New Zealand identity—not the slavish devotion to reproducing little England, symbolized by the Claires, nor Simon's type of defiant rejection of all that is English. Dikon Bell, in his muddled loyalties, offers more promise as the personification of a separate culture than the others do because he is sensitive to New Zealand's unique physical qualities and lacks prejudice against the Maori, features Marsh believed critical for a legitimate and mature New Zealand nationalism. On the question of racial issues she insisted that cooperation and mutual pride had to develop between the races to ensure internal unity. She professed to be proud of her Maori name and reassured an American interviewer that had she possessed Maori blood she would have been proud of it—views undoubtedly regarded as radical when first publicized in 1961 (*BBH*, 271). In 1965 Marsh complained that none of the serious New Zealand novelists had addressed in depth the great racial problem that had to be resolved before New Zealanders could claim to have realized the dreams of their ancestors: "that the Maori and the Paheka [European] shall be as one people" (*BBH*, 271). Although Marsh credited the New Zealand founders with a remarkably modern vision, early settlers of all imperial lands with indigenous populations recognized that some sort of rapprochement would be necessary for peaceful coexistence. Beyond mere coexistence, however, building national loyalties did, as Marsh anticipated, present far more complicated challenges.

Marsh evoked a sense of Maori identity and tribal traditions in her first two New Zealand novels, *Vintage Murder* and *Colour Scheme*. Many other novels contained references to Maori weapons and superstitions, but those two examined in greater depth the nature of Maori culture and its adaptations to European ways. The best possibilities for misunderstandings as well as for the blending of New Zealand's twin heritages were along the boundaries of interracial contact.

In *Vintage Murder,* Maori physician Rangi Te Pokiha procures a greenstone tiki for Alleyn to present to Carolyn Dacres on her birthday. Te Pokiha attends the birthday party and explains to the guest of honor that the tiki brings good fortune, as it represents a human embryo and is a symbol of happiness and fertility. Although Miss Dacres reacts with delight and confusion, Te Pokiha is dismayed at the casual and disrespectful humor the tiki engenders among the other guests. Even the normally sympathetic Alfred Meyer mocks its powers and invokes the tiki to produce good audiences for their theatrical troupe. As the tiki is handed around, the guests' crude remarks and jests chagrin Alleyn who confesses to Te Pokiha that he regrets having given it in the presence of these insensitive people. " 'Oh,' said Te Pokiha pleasantly, 'it seems amusing to them naturally.' He paused and then added: 'So may my great grandparents have laughed over the first crucifix they saw' " (*VM,* 52). With her usual irony, Marsh was suggesting, as she did in later novels, that only the form differed. Both Maori and Paheka had their beliefs, sacred to one, mere superstition to the other; but for either to berate the other because of those beliefs was hypocrisy of the worst sort.

Fortunately, the friendship that has developed between the Maori doctor and the inspector does not suffer as a result of this insensitivity. As Acheson maintained in her article on Marsh's "cultural ambivalence," Alleyn is far too "serious and thoughtful," earnestly seeking to understand the New Zealanders—white and black. Inspector Wade, Alleyn's opposite number, modifies Alleyn's naive observation that there seems to be no racist sentiment in New Zealand: " 'Well, not in the way there is in India, for instance. Mind, there are Maoris and Maoris. Te Pokiha's high caste. His mother was a princess and his father a fine old chief. The doctor's had an English college education—he's ninety per cent civilized' " (*VM*, 79). Yet Wade warns Alleyn that the 10 percent of Te Pokiha remaining "uncivilized" can be formidable: contest the doctor's word in professional matters or demean a cause in which he believes and the fiery savage in him will erupt.

Alleyn has the opportunity to observe the truth in Wade's assessment when Te Pokiha is accused of murder. At this accusation the doctor's eyes flash and his face darkens. As the doctor snarls and snaps at his accusers, Alleyn thinks, "By Jove, . . . the odd twenty per cent of pure savage" (*VM*, 265). Baited beyond his endurance, Te Pokiha actually attacks his tormentor, who screams to get the "nigger" off him. The Caucasian characters do not endear themselves by their repeated assurances to one another that, after all, the murdered Alfred Meyer "was a white man," and that one of the suspects is a "white man." Marsh employed these sentiments and phrases not to state the obvious but to suggest that kind of racial sensibility that has left Alleyn with a hearty distaste for all who express it. Just below the surface of both races, Marsh suggested, lie the ugliest responses, suspicions, and hatreds. It is from such portrayals that Marsh earned a cautious reception by her Maori readers.

Despite imputing savagery in the Maori, Marsh treated them extraordinarily well in other parts of the story and emphasized the dignity of their race. But because she was a Paheka—albeit sensitive and liberal—describing and analyzing another race from the outside, she could not breach the gulf between the races, and her clear-eyed integrity would not permit her to idealize the Maori. She harbored no "noble savage" fantasies from her observation point on the European side. She studied the distinct shapes of a different people and portrayed them as fairly and evenhandedly as she could perceive them. In a letter to Fox, Alleyn records his impressions of the Maori deities he sees in museums as "wild grimacing abortions, with thrust-out tongues and glinting eyes" (*VM*, 177). They fascinate him as evidence of an ancient New Zealand—a people and a country imbued with the scents of forest and soil. Later on in that letter, however, Marsh can be accused of unconscious condescension when Alleyn comments that the Maori have adopted European clothing styles that, combined with their native jewelry, create a charming portrait of a lighthearted people. Such language sounds a bit like the comment, "they all have rhythm," which American blacks find so offensive.

Yet Marsh went to great lengths, interrupting the flow of her detective story rather significantly, to introduce an intelligent discussion of Maori customs and the difficulties this proud people face in attempting to survive in the dominant Caucasian culture with their racial integrity intact. Acheson noted that Marsh had sympathy for the Maori dilemma but did not back away from describing the degenerate condition of their life. Though Alleyn's visit to Dr. Te Pokiha's home provided the opportunity for Marsh to display her sympathies, that episode is blatantly expository; in later novels such background information was far more skillfully integrated. When Alleyn asks the doctor to speak of his homeland, Te Pokiha embarks on a rather lengthy explanation of Maori origins, myths, and present problems. As a medical man he treats the myths with skepticism; as a pure Maori he responds to their power. After explaining the background of the little greenstone tiki that Alfred Meyer mocked just moments before he was murdered, Te Pokiha declares that the tiki has been avenged. Alleyn questions the doctor about his own views of the revenge superstition, to which Te Pokiha responds, "Naturally . . . I do not feel exactly as a European would feel about the Tiki. What do your Gypsies say? 'You have to dig deep to bury your daddy' " (*VM*, 246).

Te Pokiha's personal contradictions run deep. He is Oxford-educated and trained at Thomas's Hospital in London, but he lives deep in the bush in a bungalow with a porch decorated with Maori carvings. The interior is furnished in standard English taste, with a photograph of Oxford undergraduates hanging next to a Maori feather cloak. His home symbolizes Te Pokiha's deeply conflicting blend of European and Maori influences. If he is ill at ease with European influences, they have been unrelentingly destructive to the Maori people. Te Pokiha, whose grandfather was a *rangitira* (similar to a Brahman), feels that the passing of the old order of Maori teaching is regrettable. But even more regrettable, according to Marsh, was the fact that the Maori had been unable to take from each civilization what it offered of value and form a higher culture. As Te Pokiha reflects "I have a kind of pride of race—shall we say a savage pride? The *paheka* has altered everything, of course. We have been unable to survive intact the fierce white light of his civilisation" (*VM*, 241). In adopting European ideas, the Maori lost some of their most important traditions, especially in their health care. As a result, the Maori had become "spiritually and physically obese" (*VM*, 242), according to Te Pokiha, who confesses a nostalgia for the old Maori civilization in spite of some of the so-called progress among his people.

Marsh was appealing to both races, through this friendship of Alleyn and Dr. Te Pokiha, to connect, to build a bridge of individual tolerance that might then expand to the two cultures. This passage repeated a theme that E. M. Forster had developed years before in the Dr. Aziz–Fielding friendship in *A Passage to India* (1924), and that George Orwell would suggest in the Flory–Dr. Veriswami alliance in *Burmese Days* (1945). But unlike Forster and Orwell, Marsh did not follow the relationship through to a disappointing conclusion. She had departed as far as she dared from the detective story plot; Alleyn had to return to his hotel and continue to detect a killer. Within its detective genre, *Vintage Murder* stands as a clear appeal for a biracial, open society in which color and caste are replaced by tolerance, in which the best attributes of all the races are combined. Such views defied the proud Anglocentric view of civilizing "lesser breeds without the law" as well as conversely, the back-to-origins nationalist movements such as Ghandi's. Against these formidable forces, Marsh's generous worldview could not survive.

Marsh continued to develop her Maori theme in *Colour Scheme*. The focus here, as in *Vintage Murder,* is on one particular object sacred to the Maori, in this case an ancient weapon, but the scope of Maori culture is more broadly portrayed. There are three prominent Maori characters in the book, each of whom represents different aspects of Maori life and Maori adaptation to European ways. Adjacent to the Wai-ata-tapu Springs Hotel and Spa is an entire Maori settlement whose inhabitants are more remote and less anglicized than Te Pokiha. The elderly chieftain, Rua Te Kahu, like Te Pokiha, is descended from a long line of chiefs and warriors and, also like the doctor, has witnessed with great sadness the changes wrought by "the white man's ways" (*CS*, 29). He has been a warrior, the editor of a native newspaper, and a member of Parliament, but in his extreme age he has renounced his European habits and returned to his own subtribe and to a way of life he remembers from his youth. Although a personal friendship does not develop between Alleyn and Te Kahu, it is clear that these two represent the least prejudiced or hysterical members of the book's cast. They are, on one level, each other's equal in their separate communities—lovers of justice and voices of reason. The second Maori in the book, a young serving girl at the Claires' hotel, is a perfect contrast to their daughter Barbara. Huia has natural grace and a lively spirit; "she seemed to be a part of the landscape compounded of the same dark medium, quiescent as the earth under the dominion of the sky" (CS, 17–18). In one of Marsh's humorous asides she refers to Huia "wearing cap, crackling apron, and stiff curls. She looked like a Polynesian goddess who had assumed, on a whim, some barbaric disguise" (CS, 13). Here, of course, the European clothes are the barbarous element. The third Maori character in this book, Eru Saul, a half-caste, flirts and quarrels with Huia throughout. Like so many of Somerset Maugham's Eurasian characters, Eru is only partly adapted to Maori ways. Te Kahu contemptuously calls him a bad Paheka and a bad Maori. Not fully accepted by either culture, he occupies a tragic fringe.

The Maori community, with Te Kahu as its leader, has enjoyed good relations with the Claires and their guests over the years, owing largely to Te Kahu's benign goodwill and to Colonel Claire's vagueness. Te Kahu's charitable nature is based on a perspective on and a patience with his people that Te Pokiha, a younger man, lacks. As Te Kahu explains, "In a century we have had to swallow the progress of nineteen hundred years. Do you wonder that we suffer a little from evolutionary dyspepsia? We are loyal members of the great commonwealth: your enemies are our enemies" (CS, 34). His loyalty to Britain and to Claire dates back to a violent outbreak of influenza in his village when he himself was too ill to attend to his duties. In their muddleheaded way the hoteliers saved the situation, with Mrs. Claire responding to the crisis as a rural vicar's wife would and rallying to help her villagers. The Claires turned their hotel into a hospital and nursed their charges, including Te Kahu, back to health. Colonel Claire, "whose absence-of-mind had inoculated him against the arrogance of Anglo-Indianism, and who by his very simplicity had fluked his way into a sort of understanding of native peoples" (CS, 55), had been accepted by the Maori as a person of breeding. Though the Claires profess neither great love nor hate for the Maori, the villagers regard them as essentially benevolent neighbors. It never occurs to them to interfere with Maori relics or customs, except in matters of religion; the indefatigable Mrs. Claire and the shy Barbara conduct a Christian Sunday School in the village. The notion of racial violence is foreign to their optimistic nature. When Dr. Ackrington expresses fear of an uprising, Colonel Claire snorts that the Maori concentrate on their own business and do not worry themselves with political matters. The only problem in relations with native peoples that Colonel Claire recognized was the suspicion created in the minds of the governed by the secrecy among the governing class. For the open-minded Claires, who lacked not only color prejudice or suspicion but also fear or duplicity, relations between the races worked smoothly. Marsh was again suggesting that, instead of suffering like the tormented souls of Te Pokiha, Aziz, and Veriswami, men and women of goodwill and tolerance could be peacefully integrated.

The greatest moment of that integration occurred in *Colour Scheme*—not surprisingly, at a benefit Shakespearean recitation. Geoffrey Gaunt, a professional actor visiting the spa for its curative powers, is invited by Te Kahu and his community to a party in Gaunt's honor. The private party expands into a public gathering at which the actor offers to render some of the memorable speeches from Shakespearean dramas, a type of performance for which he is famous. The Maori extend their full hospitality to him, decorating their meetinghouse and its Polynesian wooden god carvings with Union Jacks and colored prints of three kings of England. This was as close to an amalgam of cultures as Marsh ever came.

The Maori had been waiting all day, squatting on the floor, the steps, even the edge of a temporary stage. As their guests arrive, they have different ways of greeting other Maori and Paheka. Mrs. Te Papa, the oldest grande dame of the tribe, orders about young and old alike. She speaks only in Maori and refuses to acknowledge comments made in English—unlike other Maori who, as Marsh pointed out, had adopted a truncated version of English mixed with Maori phrases and idioms. Although they had forgotten the pure version of their own language, Marsh commented that they beautifully transformed English into a musical idiom with softened deep vowels.

Despite her appreciation of Maori culture, and even its mixture with English traditions, Marsh was well aware of all the prejudices that separated the races. Leaving aside rational conviction and liberal sentiments, the instincts of the races differed profoundly. If, as psychologists and biologists have repeatedly demonstrated, people are attracted to or repelled by others on the basis of atavistic animal clues, then the Maori and the Paheka encountered many obstacles in resolving their differences. Just as George Orwell insisted that the capitalist classes despised the workers because they "smelled," so also Marsh portrays a similar racial consciousness: as the crowd gathered in the Maori meetinghouse, "it became very hot and the Maori people thought indulgently that it smelt of *paheka,* while the *pahekas* thought a little less indulgently that it smelt of Maori" (*CS,* 143–44).

In *Colour Scheme,* Marsh again included the theme of Maori deterioration that Dr. Te Pokiha speaks of in *Vintage Murder.* Another medical man, Dr. Ackrington, Mrs. Claire's brother and the resident curmudgeon, expounds on race. His sentiments are not strictly bigoted, for he rails at length against both nationalities for their collusion in the tragedy: "The natives of this country have been ruined by their own inertia and the criminal imbecility of the white population." The Paheka had replaced Maori religious practices with Calvinist doctrines of sin and degradation and bribed the Maori with whiskey to surrender their land. As if this were not hypocritical enough, white settlers destroyed Maori communal farming and tribal structure and replaced them with government welfare and trade unions. "And for mating customs that agreed very well with them, we substituted, with a sanctimonious grimace, disease and holy matrimony" (CS, 46).

Ackrington is finally quieted by the others and exhorted to silence, after which he lapses into a self-righteous snit. As with Te Pokiha's sentiments, the Maori reader might take exception to Marsh's views; but her sentiments placed the blame rather evenly and did not patronize the Maori. Only a people believed capable of greatness will be encouraged to achieve it. Marsh's fair-minded assignment of responsibility to both sides avoided the kind of acrimonious name-calling that she so clearly despised. She argued throughout her work that mutual liability for the problem implied joint accountability for the solution to be worked out in an atmosphere of reciprocal respect.

Part of the mystery in *Colour Scheme* ultimately revolves around an object of Maori veneration. Like the tiki in *Vintage Murder,* Chief Rewi's adze, a weapon used in the Maori wars, is reputed to be invested with supernatural powers by the god Tane. According to Maori funeral traditions, certain chieftains were buried on the side of Rangi's Peak, and their weapons were entombed with them. No one, especially any white man, was permitted on this sacred Maori burial ground; to hunt for these weapons as collector's items was not only to steal but also to desecrate holy soil. When it is discovered that Maurice Questing and Eru Saul have stolen the adze for a visiting Englishman, Te Kahu's anger and his invocations for revenge know no bounds. In a scene reminiscent of Te Pokiha's outburst, Te Kahu clings to the adze and declares: "You will think it strange . . . that I, who have in my time led my people towards the culture of the *paheka,* should now grow quarrelsome over a silly savage notion. Perhaps in our old age we return to the paths of our forbears. The reason may put on new garments but the heart and blood are constant" (CS, 253). He believes that the adze has special powers—powers that only a full-blooded Maori would understand.

Marsh had again illustrated the hybrid personalities that empire has bred into indigenous peoples. The commonwealth bond must be made large enough to encompass Eru Saul's mixed blood and Te Kahu's mixed philosophic traditions. Certainly New Zealand, in Marsh's eyes, needed to have all of her heritage respected beneath the British-style umbrella of the Commonwealth.

In Marsh's third novel of New Zealand, *Died in the Wool,* published in 1945, questions of Commonwealth loyalty are central to the solution of the mystery and to identifying the murderer.[7] There are no Maori here, but questions of nationalism and commitment are raised in other ways. Like *Colour Scheme,* Marsh wrote it while the outcome of the war was still unpredictable, and it reflects some of the uneasiness and insecurity of the Allied side. Alleyn is summoned to the isolated Mount Moon sheep ranch in the remote plateau country to untangle the skein of murder threads—now tangled up for over a year. Florence Rubrick, a member of the New Zealand Parliament and wife of ranch owner Arthur Rubrick, has been asphyxiated and stuffed into a wool press; her body is discovered weeks later, to the horror of her husband and household, who had assumed that she was off attending to her parliamentary duties. The police investigate all who had lived or worked with her, to no avail. Among those questioned are her husband; Fabian Losse, a nephew of Florence's husband; Ursula Harme, the deceased's ward; Terence Lynne, her secretary; and Douglas Grace, her nephew. Those of the staff who fall under suspicion are Markins, a butler who, unbeknownst to the household, is an Allied agent sent to check up on some security problems; and Cliff Johns, a young man who works with his father on the sheep ranch but is also a promising pianist whom Florence Rubrick educated and sought to promote. With the exception of Markins, each of these characters has been thwarted in some way by Florence Rubrick's controlling personality. Each had a motive and an opportunity. Alleyn's problem, a year later, is to sort through their contradictory views of the victim, their accounts of the events preceding the crime, and the possible link with espionage against the secret research that Losse and Grace were conducting on a bomb fuse. He could no longer interrogate Arthur Rubrick, who had died of natural causes since his wife's murder. Alleyn's deductions eliminate the red herrings; he focuses on a central clue that narrows the list of real suspects and ultimately succeeds in his quest.

In *Colour Scheme,* in a most bizarre landscape of bubbling mud, the Claires had created an imaginary English setting. In *Died in the Wool,* Mount Moon, isolated on a distant plateau, also sports a deceptively English home and manner. Detective Alleyn notes the Victorian gables and the English architecture and furnishings of the house. Florence and Arthur Rubrick's attempts to establish a little piece of England here were as futile as the Claires': their garden was "a queer transformation of what had been originally an English conception of a well-planned garden. But beyond this unconvincing piece of *pastische*—what uncompromising vastness" (*DW*, 24). Even here, in an almost echoing emptiness, the world at war intrudes as Alleyn's murder investigation unearths a Nazi spy and murderer. Spies and the clash of arms haunt even remote New Zealand, as Marsh illustrates the vital position her country occupied in the war, despite its distance from the worst hostilities and its apparent preoccupation with prosaic pursuits.

The story is constructed in a series of flashbacks alternating with the present action. "Flossie" Rubrick emerges as a domineering woman with dreams roughly proportional to her ego. Yet Marsh found her interesting because she ventured beyond her anglicized cocoon to envision a separate nationalism. She stood as a member of New Zealand's Parliament, she tried to encourage a young New Zealander's musical career, and thought of herself as a blunt and beloved democrat amongst her hired hands. Her nephew tries to explain her appeal to Alleyn: "You don't understand the people in this country. . . . We like it straight from the shoulder and Aunt Floss gave it to us that way. She had them [her constituents] eating out of her hand" (*DW*, 34). As Alleyn ultimately discovers, much of her personality was merely a politician's pose, creating more effect than substance. Markins reiterates this view when he tells Alleyn: "She was great on talking Imperialism. You know. The brand that's not taken for granted quite so much, these days. She talked a lot about patriotism" (*DW*, 130). As Alleyn realizes, her great, well-intended schemes—the resettlement of veterans and the glorification of women in the back country, among others—sprang from a profound ignorance of other people's difficulties and complications. Even her family knew that she lifted cadences and borrowed rhetoric from Winston Churchill. Whatever pride Florence Rubrick took in her identity as a New Zealander was tainted with insincerity and plagiarism.

Even in absentia her personality dominates the novel; beside her all the other characters fade. Certainly her gentle, martyred husband, who composed her speeches (and, in secret, Elizabethan verse), does not stir passion, except in the heart of Terence Lynne. Her nephews and her ward exist only as commentary on her remarkable force. Standing separate from her family and instructing others in her service, Florence Rubrick fulfilled her surname, and it is tempting to attribute the name play, and others in the book, to Marsh's sardonic humor. Certainly Fabian Losse, or F. Losse, as he would have abbreviated it, is similar to Flossie. When Douglas Grace, her nephew, is discovered to be the villain and murderer, Flossie Rubrick suffers a Losse of Grace. If Leon Edel is right about authors choosing names that unconsciously reflect their convictions,[8] perhaps these observations are not too whimsical. Marsh indulged this same playfulness in several other novels.

The most interesting conflict that Marsh explored in *Died in the Wool* concerned not the murder but maternal Florence Rubrick's frustrated instinct. She proposed to send one of her sheep shearer's sons to the New Zealand equivalent of an English public school. The boy's father objected because he was an ardent trade unionist and feared that such a posh education "would make a class-conscious snob of the boy" (*DW*, 40). Schooling had the opposite effect on Cliff Johns, who comes to share Simon Claire's truculence and left-wing opinions, as well as Claire's youthful tendency to blunder. In explaining to Alleyn his reasons for rebelling against his patron, he storms, "I don't approve of the system, of course. Education ought to be the business of the state; not a lot of dessicated failures whose real object is to bolster up class consciousness. The teaching on the whole was merely comic." Then with one of the gestures that make him so appealing, Cliff smiles and says, "I suppose you're thinking I'm an insufferable young puppy, aren't you?" (*DW*, 157). Florence Rubrick had recognized his musical talent, as well as his vulnerability, and sought to shape him into her image of a cultured New Zealand youth. Influenced by a young English boy at his school, Cliff becomes an enthusiastic leftist and, as he maintains, "I realized pretty thoroughly how hopelessly wrong it was for me to play at being a little gentleman at her expense. I realized that if I couldn't get as my right, equally with other chaps, the things that she'd given me, then I shouldn't take them at all. I was admitting the right of one class to patronize another" (*DW*, 159). When he rebelled against her values and her Pygmalion fantasy and returned to his father's profession, she had erupted in anger and frustration. His return is awkward for, as Fabian Losse observes, the other men "were inclined at one time to look upon him as a freak. His schooling and tastes aroused their deepest suspicions, of course. In this country, young men are judged almost entirely on their ability to play games and do manual labor. . . . [But] when he came home a good whole-hog leftist, they were delighted" (*DW*, 113). Losse admits his fondness for Cliff and his eager young mind, and he frequently loans him his *New Statesman*. Like many young people with great dreams, Cliff builds governments and societies out of his fantasy of a new moral and ethical order that would challenge traditional economics, traditions that his employer and benefactor upheld. Lurking within Cliff Johns, a deeper sense of New Zealand patriotism struggles for expression. It is not enough for him merely to reject imported European art; he yearns to fulfill Florence Rubrick's dream on his own terms—not by grafting English culture onto a colonial stalk but by creating and nurturing a distinct species of New Zealand art. " 'That's what I wanted to do with music, I mean. Say something about this.' He jerked his head at the vastness beyond the window and added with an air of defiance: 'And I don't mean the introduction of native bird song and Maori *hakas* into an ersatz symphony' " (*DW,* 151). Marsh's novels explored Inspector Alleyn's difficulties in relating to these New Zealanders who are simultaneously complacent and uncertain. He succeeds in winning their respect and trust by adopting an attitude of bemused detachment that never becomes patronizing.

Florence Rubrick and the Claires were not the only memorable New Zealanders that Marsh created. In her most autobiographical novel, *Death of a Peer* (1940), she described with loving detail a family of zany eccentrics, the Lampreys.[9] She presented these characters, her lifelong friends, first as she met them in New Zealand. She traced their adventures and her own initial visit to London in *Death of a Peer;* ironically, this is the one novel for which Marsh has been criticized for making her characters' personalities too intrusive. Eccentrics they may have been, but they deliver some wry observations about themselves and their reasons for coming to New Zealand, providing Marsh with an opportunity to describe her impressions of English social classes and customs and the English view of New Zealand. In the novel a colonial girl, Roberta Grey, comes to England and is inadvertently involved in the rigors and embarrassment of a murder investigation as Marsh introduces a theme that will recur in her books: a naive youth undergoes rites of passage that will lead to a broader worldview.

Marsh gave Henry Lamprey, the eldest son, the most sensible view of the family. He explains to Roberta, their New Zealand friend and Marsh's persona, "We're museum pieces. Carry-overs from another age. Two generations ago we didn't bother about what we would do when we grew up. We went into regiments, or politics, and lived on large estates. . . . Our trouble is that we go on behaving in the grand leisured manner without the necessary backing. It's very dishonest of us, but we're conditioned to it. . . . A dreadful time is coming when we shall be obliged to do something to justify our existence" (*DP,* 14–15). Henry had just summarized the problems of the twentieth-century peerage. The Lampreys decide to emigrate to New Zealand to seek that "something" to justify their existence. Instead, as Henry puts it, they find themselves "strangers in a strange land and making pretty considerable fools of ourselves" (*DP,* 11). Bearing in mind Marsh's disgust for those who deem the colonies a "wastebasket" for wastrel Britons, as she expressed it in *Vintage Murder,* it is significant that the Lampreys invite none of her sarcasm. Their personal charm, their sincerity, and their utter lack of condescension earn them the trust and affection of many New

Zealanders who might have been more wary of others. As Henry sees his family, it would be the New Zealanders who might wish to laugh at them:

Poor Daddy! When we first got here he became so excessively New Zealand. I believe he used sheep-dip on his hair and shall I ever forget him with the dogs! He bought four—I think they cost twenty pounds each. He used to sit on his horse and whistle so unsuccessfully that even the horse couldn't have heard him and the dogs all lay down and went to sleep and the sheep stood in serried ranks and gazed at him in mild surprise. Then he tried swearing and screaming but he lost his voice in less than no time. (*DP,* 12–13)

No one laughed; instead, the Lampreys are regarded as "remarkable." As Marsh explained, "Titles are rare in New Zealand and the younger sons of marquises are practically non-existent" (*DP,* 4), but titles have nothing to do with Roberta's affection for them; she is quite simply absorbed into the family, falls in love with them all, and often joins in their capers—but always with a bit of distance. When the murder investigation begins, Roberta is convinced that none of the Lampreys were capable of skewering their elder brother/uncle through the eye, even though his death means the end of their financial difficulties. Yet she is appalled at the family's vague defense of itself and its incomprehensible lies to the police. Inspector Alleyn, already fond of New Zealanders and recognizing part of her dilemma, questions her gently after complimenting her homeland. When Alleyn expresses his surprise that the Lampreys had willingly left such a beautiful country, Roberta puts words to a conviction that she had not articulated previously. She realizes that "it was only a New Zealand adventure for them. A kind of interlude. They belong here" (*DP,* 256). For all her attraction to England and her love for the family, she realizes that for her it is different—she is excited and delighted by England.

As Marsh wrote, perhaps of her own experience of Piccadilly Circus, "It is here at the place which he learns, with a rare touch of insolence, to call the hub of the universe that the colonial wakes from the trance of arrival, finds his feet on London paving stones, and is suddenly happy" (*DP,* 53). Roberta Grey learns, as perhaps Marsh herself did, that she is, in spite of everything, a colonial. She also encounters her adult self—sensible and strong in the midst of the trauma, a character forged in part by her background in New Zealand. Roberta knows "that the Lampreys, persuaded perhaps by dim ideas of pioneering hardihood, were inclined to think of all colonials as less sheltered and more inured to nervous strain than their English contemporaries" (*DP,* 284). Roberta anticipates the other New Zealand youths—

Martyn Tarne in *Night at the Vulcan* (1951) and Peregrine Jay in *Killer Dolphin* (1966), who embrace their heritage and its strengths while acknowledging their love of England and their commitment to its arts.

In her next to last mystery, *Photo Finish* (1980), Marsh returned to a New Zealand locale, but with characters who reveal nothing of her feeling for her homeland and its particular position in world affairs.[10] Except for the Alleyns, there are few among the cast who even appreciate the fantastic beauty that surrounds them. Her last publication, *Light Thickens* (1982), which appeared the year of her death, dipped once again into Maori lore.[11] Rangi Western, Maori actor, whose very name suggests a mingling of cultures, has been solicited by Peregrine Jay of the Dolphin Theater to play one of the weird sisters in Shakespeare's *Macbeth*. A superb actor and a prize student at the London Academy of Music and Dramatic Art, he portrays the witch as a vengeful Polynesian god—grimacing, eyes glittering, and tongue whipping in and out. His fellow cast members smile at him and his people's lack of tolerance for alcohol, but they secretly fear a hidden ferocity in Rangi, which they attribute to his race. After the murder of the Macbeth actor, Rangi remarks to Alleyn that the deceased "made fun of things that are *tapu*—forbidden. My great-grandfather knew how to deal with that, he cut off the man's head . . . and ate him" (*LT,* 160). Rangi's remarks are indiscreet, since the victim in this story was decapitated.

Light Thickens was Marsh's last combination of her favorite elements and themes—a theater locale, a Shakespearean play directed by a New Zealand immigrant to London, a Maori, a dramatic killing, and Inspector Alleyn solving his last case. Through it all Marsh entwined the ideas of mystery and superstition. *Macbeth* is a play about mysterious creatures and murder; many in the theater regard it as an unlucky play from which to quote, as well as to perform. The murder weapon used for the fight scene between Macbeth and Macduff is a claidheamh-mor—a weapon that supposedly "demand[s] blood." All the actors in *Light Thickens* invoke their own particular rituals to ward off disaster. The Lady Macduff actress goes through an elaborate ritual of kissing crucifixes and reading psalms. Resounding through *Light Thickens* are echoes of Te Pokiha's remarks in *Vintage Murder* about the tiki being an object of veneration to its people and the crucifix a peculiar token to be wondered at. Marsh appeared to regard superstition as superstition, whether it was found in northern Europe or the South Seas—all humans were subject to it. It was not the exclusive province of Maori or Paheka, not a force separating peoples but a quality of human experience uniting them.

Light Thickens was Marsh's final effort to underline her themes of tolerance for diversity. Here, as in the first four New Zealand novels, she peopled her book with vivid black-and-white characters who maintain close emotional ties to their homeland—whether it be New Zealand or Britain—and to the British Commonwealth of Nations, in war and in peace. Although they may have their internal conflicts within New Zealand and within the larger family of nations, Marsh insisted that the links were strong enough to build a biracial nationalism that would strengthen the Commonwealth.

When Marsh acknowledged a multiracial Commonwealth, she knew that it was more than a matter of the Maori and the Paheka making their peace. In *Black as He's Painted* (1974)[12] she examined the sensitive Commonwealth bonds that had been strained and broken by many newly independent nations.[13] In Ng'ombwana, the president (and dictator), Bartholomew Opala is still loyal to the British connection. He attended Davidson's, the fictional "house" at Oxford that the young Roderick Alleyn attended, where the two young men became friends because, according to Opala, Alleyn was the first Englishman to be kind to him and treat him as an equal. They shared social hours and political debates in their university years. After Opala, or "the Boomer" as he was known at Davidson's, read law at the Temple, he returned to his homeland and entered politics, ultimately rising to the top.

The years between 1950 and 1970 were tumultuous for the Commonwealth; former colonies were dropping in and out of the association with impunity. At home the Boomer has enemies with diverse reasons for hating him and wishing him dead. Although by Western standards he is an educated and sensible man, he subscribes to African superstitions, tinged with egotism about his own invincibility. Alleyn is assigned to persuade him to cooperate with British security when he visits England and to assist in his protection. In the service of these duties Alleyn flies to Ng'ombwana to urge Opala to exercise caution while in England. Later he attends the grand embassy party on the occasion of Opala's visit to London. On both occasions Alleyn senses and comments on a deep channel of uneasiness running through the newly independent country and its officials. Indeed, his perceptions appear correct when, at the embassy party, the ambassador to England is slain by a spear employed in the protection of the Boomer. Opala himself was the apparent target, although he insists that his *milinzi* (spear carrier) was quite innocent of the crime.

Juxtaposed against this international intrigue, Marsh told a charming story of a retired Foreign Office expert on Ng'ombwana, Samuel Whipplestone, and his cat, Lucy Lockett, who live at Capricorn Walk in one of the lovely residential areas of London. Behind the neighborhood's pleasant exterior, however, a white racist group gathers and plots its own version of revenge against the Boomer. Whipplestone and Lucy discover this group and its purpose quite by accident and help to link it to the death of the ambassador. The interweavings of the two plots and the exchanges between blacks and whites gave Marsh her opportunity for commentary, without preaching or judgment, on the patience necessary to develop that family relationship in the Commonwealth that she talked about so much in her autobiography.

To Detective Inspector Fox when he sighs, "I get muddled . . . over these emergent nations," Alleyn offers reassurance that he is not alone. In explaining Ng'ombwana's status, he tells Fox, "They're still a Commonwealth country more or less. They're having it both ways. All the trappings and complete independence. All the ha'pence and none of the kicks. That's why they insist upon calling their man in London an Ambassador and setting him up in premises that wouldn't disgrace one of the great powers" (BHP, 27). To Alleyn the Boomer is all charm and smiles and friendship. When they meet again in Ng'ombwana, Opala reminisces extensively about their days together, wears the old school tie, and, Alleyn notices, keeps a framed photograph of their class with the two of them standing together. He has greyed and his body has thickened, but Alleyn can remember him as an insecure young man who had responded to his friendly overtures with the great enthusiasm of a lonely and homesick child.

Despite the claims of friendship, the Boomer resists Alleyn's insistence that he is in danger. Alleyn sees this denial clearly: "It was if a blind had been pulled down. For the first time, seeing the slackened jaw and now the hooded, lacklustre eyes, he thought, specifically: 'I am speaking to a Negro' " (BHP, 30). Lest this be thought a racist sentiment, Marsh had the Boomer himself argue with Alleyn that "this thing we discuss now belongs to my color and my race. My blackness. Please do not try to understand: try only, my dear Rory, to accept" (BHP, 33). Marsh also returned to the *Colour Scheme* commentary on smell when Alleyn notices "the indefinable alien scent of persons of a different color" (BHP, 80). When this same remark is placed in the mouth of a racist, it turns ugly: "I smelt him. If you've lived out there as we did, you can't mistake it." Alleyn defuses this sneer with agreement. "Yes? . . . I understand they notice the same phenomenon in us. An African friend of mine told me that it took him about a year before he left off feeling faint in lifts during the London rush hours" (BHP, 95). To the equally racist sentiment that all Negroes look alike, Marsh offered Troy Alleyn painting the Boomer's portrait, fascinated by his features.

It takes more than a clever put-down or Troy's talent to still the disgust toward blacks of some for whom racial hatred runs so deep that reconciliation is impossible. Alleyn calls them "fanatics,"—those who hate black because it's black; women who fantasize about a black rapist; fundamentalists who believe that the anti-Christ is black; or those of more prosaic concerns who fear black competition in the workplace. In addition, there are those who are literal-minded enough to interpret the phrases "black outlook, black record, black as it's painted, black villainy" as evidence of evil. Alleyn lamented that these racists have an absolute belief that "Black is Bad." To this catalog, Troy adds, "And the Black power lot are doing as much for 'white' aren't they? The war of their images" (*BHP,* 56). Reducing groups of people to images stifles communication, thereby allowing individuals to be objectified as "they." Marsh believed that such objectification made it almost impossible to forge the bonds of friendship essential for the Commonwealth.

Marsh found the difficulties within Ng'ombwana typical of those countries making the awkward transition from a colonial childhood, through a nationalist youth, to a mature, international-minded adult. British political analysts had warned of the danger inherent in these phases in numerous tracts advising that Britain guide her colonies to independence. In a cluster of monographs published just before and after World War I, colonial officials proffered advice based on their experiences of governing sub-Saharan Africa since the 1890s. Most prominent was Sir Frederick Lugard's *The Dual Mandate in British Tropical Africa* (1922). Lugard was responding, in part, to the enthusiasm for the "self determination of peoples" fanned by the Treaty of Paris that ended World War I. His plan called for British administrators to rule indirectly through existing tribal authorities, who were concurrently "developing" the tribe into modern nation-states. This dual mandate appeared to be an ideal program for bringing about the necessary transition without callously throwing the Africans on their own resources unprepared.

Yet what seemed in London to be an excellent and generous solution failed miserably in Africa, a failure many Britons found incomprehensible. As Samuel Whipplestone explains to the Alleyns, the maturing process and the parental assistance of British policy proved far more complicated than anyone anticipated. In the Boomer's Ng'ombwana, for instance, there are political opponents whom the new president succeeded in breaking and who wish him dead. Their families and their survivors nurse a special grudge that pays no heed to political or economic consequences—they simply wish to destroy his regime. Among his other African enemies are those extremists who disapprove of his moderation and his refusal to dismiss all his European advisers immediately. This strong antiwhite, anti-European element ultimately forces the Boomer to dismiss many of his Caucasian officials in favor of inexperienced Africans, thereby adding considerably to the internal confusion engendered by lack of expertise in operating a new nation's bureaucracy. Then, Mr. Whipplestone continues, there are the disaffected among those who have been dismissed. In Ng'ombwana, as in many other African nations, all foreign enterprise is nationalized and property owned by Europeans and Asians has been appropriated by the state. Among those Europeans and Asians are familiar figures from many Agatha Christie stories and other popular novels: the Anglo-Indian ex–civil servant, or the former military men who have grown totally unsuited to any other way of life, who regard India or Africa as their proper "home" and resent the adolescent nation's casting off their advice and past service. As different as the New Zealand and African heritages might be, Marsh, in several pages of exposition, outlined these difficulties indigenous to the emerging nations as only an ex-colonial could.

Although other detective writers touched upon the theme of empire and Britain's shifting role there, only Ngaio Marsh made it a central focus in so many books. Some of her compatriots expressed embarrassment that New Zealand's most famous author portrayed her native country in "mere" detective fiction. Despise it as they might, New Zealanders were well served by her fiction, even though it revealed their foibles and failings. Marsh unveiled the insecurities of the young nation, but she condemned equally the arrogance and the condescension of the old one. Such a view usually arose from ignorance, and Marsh informed the world that New Zealanders and other former colonials were but flesh and blood like the rest of humankind. A novelist of manners may exaggerate, of course, although not to the same extent as a satirist; but she must present a fundamentally honest appraisal if she is to maintain her credibility as an accurate observer. Marsh's eye for detail, her love of the land, and her unflinching indictment of narrow, provincial attitudes in whomever she found them makes her writing valuable to the historian who probes below the level of official policies into attitudes and prejudices.

Her work is a unique depiction of the environment of commonwealth precisely because it is popular literature. The detective story could even be regarded as the heir apparent to the old empire-building adventure yarns that were dying with their creators, Kipling and Haggard, or becoming significantly altered by their new practitioners, Cary, Buchan, and Orwell. Instead of brave men enduring harsh and unfamiliar territories and hostile natives to bring the benefits of British law and civilization to the benighted, the detective painstakingly eliminates distortions to bring order to chaos and produce justice in the midst of tragedy. Detective stories are modern adventures and morality plays. Ngaio Marsh ranks among the first order for her subtle insights and the social analysis that she brings to the genre.

Chapter Three
Country as Place and Character

In reviewing Marsh's *When in Rome* (1970), one critic noted that it moves away from the classic puzzle story so revered by the conventional golden-age writers. It has instead the style and emphasis of the novel of place. Marsh displayed her gift of setting throughout her books, whether that setting was New Zealand, England, or other European locales. With her keen director's eye, she knew just how to block her characters against sets that would heighten the reader's interest by contrasting or complementing the action. In her New Zealand novels—*Vintage Murder,* parts of *Death of a Peer, Colour Scheme, Died in the Wool,* and *Photo Finish*—the country is a major character in the plot. In those stories that feature the English countryside, especially *Death and the Dancing Footman* and *Tied up in Tinsel* (1972), the setting is more subtly drawn, like a charcoal sketch of the desolate winter scenes, outlining the starkness of landscape without and murder within. By contrast, the warmth of the temperate climes shines through in splashes of color in *When in Rome* and *Spinsters in Jeopardy* (1953), alternating with the sepia-colored caves and interiors where the crimes occur. In all her books Marsh created uniquely detailed environments; some of her descriptions rose to lush poetry, others were attenuated, but each represented Marsh's continuing departure from the classic precept for writing a detective story, that place and character are always of secondary importance.

Marsh's New Zealand novels contain some of her most vivid descriptive prose; the country is not just a place where murder occurs but a living participant in the characters' lives. Indeed, in all the New Zealand novels the different parts of the country contribute significant commentary on the characters, the plot, and the mystery. *Vintage Murder* takes place in a fictional town on the North Island near the forest; *Colour Scheme* is set in a thermal reserve; a remote sheep station is the stage for *Died in the Wool. Death of a Peer*'s New Zealand portion was familiar territory to Marsh—the foothills of the Southern Alps—and she staged *Photo Finish* on an island in the midst of a beautiful inland lake. A close examination of such settings reveals the diversity of New Zealand's beauty and its conspicuous role in each novel.

In *Vintage Murder* an exhausted Roderick Alleyn is on holiday from the rigors of his caseload at Scotland Yard. He has brought his battered psyche to New Zealand where, to his chagrin, he witnesses Alfred Meyer's death. Here Marsh's prose is a study in contrasts: between the hot, close feel of the train, where the first murder attempt is made, and the cold, rushing wind outside; between the dusty theater and the clear, clean outlines of the mountains that frame the town. After spending all night reviewing every sordid detail of the murder, a policeman casually mentions that in the back country there are reports of snow. Alleyn's ears perk up, and he is reminded that beyond this sordid murder case lies a new world as crisp and clear as the breath of a snowfall. Just the thought of the cool mountains restores him. Marsh repeatedly turned to words of refreshment and revitalization to describe New Zealand's beauty. The "clean lightness" of the sky and the "immaculate blue" mountains cleanse Alleyn from the taint of crime; the wearing experiences of the previous night slip away, and his soul finds peacefulness.

When the investigation becomes hopelessly convoluted, Alleyn turns to the forests to put his mind in order and to open up the spirit of his prime witness. He takes the widow, Carolyn Dacres, on a picnic into the mountains. Her first response to the setting is to remark on its clean smell, and out in the wild her emotions, grief mingled with fear, begin to surface. The effect is instantaneous: "And from the trees came the voice of a solitary bird, a slow cadence, deeper than any they had ever heard, ringing remote and cool, above the sound of water" (*VM*, 195). When she hears this beautifully melancholy cry, Carolyn's sincere grief overcomes her stoicism. As she selects a picnic site for them, she takes off her London hat, symbolically sloughing off the conventions and the formal, but false, dignity that she has maintained since her husband's death. Alleyn watches as she peels away the layers of her studied whimsicality and charm in the atmosphere created by air that is clear and heady and the wonderfully melodious mountain stream. She has no way of knowing that, for him, this place is renewing as well. As he fills the billy for tea and dips his hands into the icy cold stream, he listens to "innumerable labials all sounding together with a deep undertone that muttered among the boulders" (*VM*, 197). Here for both Alleyn and Carolyn Dacres lies a sensory tranquility—sound, sight, and smell that purge the squalid tastes and horrors of the murder from their minds.

Carolyn recognizes that she must also purge herself of the secrets that she holds, festering secrets that infect her honest grief and frustrate Alleyn's search for truth. He allows her to compose herself for this confessional by gracefully removing himself to take a walk in the forest. As he walks, the rush of sensual images overtakes him again, but this time with heightened effects—he experiences a transformation of his imagination, a mystical stimulation, as he listens to the bird song alternating with the deep quiet that transcends human silence. He thinks about the tiki and the generations of Maori who have treasured its spell. He fantasizes that it was to them that the token truly belongs; it should be worn next to "sweaty dark breasts" and held by the "dark fingers" of those mysterious people who have moved silently through this forest generation after generation. Before he has completely repopulated the forest with figures of his fancy, Carolyn Dacres comes after him, offering the truth at last. For both the widow and the jaded detective the purity, the immaculate air and water, and the mysterious mountains and forests have done their work. Exhausted, but liberated by their encounters with green nature and pure truth, they return to the city. The natural beauty of New Zealand as a force capable of healing human unrest was a theme to which Marsh would not return in quite this manner. It is significant that *Vintage Murder* was written before the outbreak of World War II, before battle statistics—beside which a simple murder investigation might seem fatuous—became the chief preoccupation of the empire.

The brief allusions to country in *Death of a Peer* were similar to but more personal than those in *Vintage Murder,* since, unlike Roberta Grey, neither Alleyn nor Dacres are New Zealand natives. When Roberta surveys the beauty of the mountains and plains, she "knew contentment. This was her country" (*DP,* 11). When Alleyn asks her if she knows the McKenzie Country, "the scent of sun-baked tussock, of wind from the tops of snow mountains, and the memory of an intense blue, visited Roberta's transplanted heart" (*DP,* 256). The physical beauty of her homeland ties her to her national origins in a far more seductive way than the excitement of London beckons to her. By 1940 war had touched New Zealand very little, and the world still had time for the lovingly etched, gentle details of a young girl's memory.

Within three years that had changed drastically: the fears of war had cut into the very bedrock of English and New Zealander security. With the publication of *Colour Scheme* in 1943, Marsh's focus shifted from the tranquil to the seismic, much as the world's had done. Beneath the surface the very ground was trembling, quivering, signaling all humans that their notions of a stable earth, a solid place upon which humanity lived and died, was an illusion. It was not just the Nazi threat that shook the foundations of the old guard's stability, but the new ideas of youth were shocking to many as well. Simon Claire's "red" thinking is presented in a slightly exaggerated and, therefore, humorous way in the novel, but Marsh certainly recognized

Bolshevism's implicit challenge to the old order. Dikon Bell, Marsh's voice of reason and balance in the novel, realizes that the dark mysterious boiling mud could shift and cause the ground to crumble around it, a sense of uneasiness further reflected in the dark Maori, with their mystery and superstitions. In the background the all-pervading, sulfurous stench is accompanied by a chorus of monotonous sound—the thermal mud boiling, bubbling, and belching, "plop, plop, plop, a monstrously domestic noise." Indeed, it is a landscape that Alleyn calls "alien" to whites, a landscape that belongs to dark nights and dark people who are attuned to its mysteries. While leaving the Maori reserve in the half-light on the night of the murder itself, Dikon notes that the moon's rising has brought the landscape into a strange relief: "Plumes of steam stood erect above the pools. Shadows were graved like caverns in the flanks of the hill. . . . The higher surfaces, as if drawn in wood by an engraver, were strongly marked in passages of silver and black. . . . As always in moonlight there was a feeling of secret expectancy in the air" (*CS*, 168). Much like in *Vintage Murder* the senses are assaulted by a New Zealand scene that demands attention. This landscape provides smells, sounds, and sights that provoke an almost spine-tingling effect. To Dikon's observation that the landscape seems malevolent and vindictive in a very personal way, Alleyn responds that the Maori believe the bubbling mud and heaving earth possess anthropomorphic qualities that were a warning as well as a threat to humans.

Dikon thinks that, "if [the ground] wasn't so infernally alive . . . it would be a lunar landscape. It is a lost world" (*CS*, 168). The next day the still quaking ulcers of thermal mud look only slightly less strange to him. In the daylight his feelings of uncertainty persist, perhaps as a reflection of a world at war, menaced by unpredictable, disastrous events, explosions, noises, and the smell of death. An analogous vision of fields pommeled into mud by shells, and the shell holes filling with water in the rains, may have been in Marsh's mind here. Though that picture would be more appropriate for the battles of World War I, it lingered on as a horror in the minds of those who were actually in the trenches or those who saw the photographs. The devastated city, the shells of buildings with their ghostly vacant eyes of shattered windows were images more befitting World War II, but the sense of vacancy, of land not fit for human habitation, was a common image in most modern warfare. Marsh contrived an atmosphere in *Colour Scheme* that was as malignant as the mountains and forests were benign in *Vintage Murder.*

Died in the Wool, written during the war and published just as the war ended, proffered an amalgamation of her three previous views of New Zealand. Once again Marsh provided her customary mix of aural and sensual images, creating an active, intrusive setting that weaves itself into the plot and plays on the emotions of the characters. When Alleyn arrives in New Zealand, he observes about this new world that "the air was clear, beyond belief, unbreathed, one would have said, newly poured out from the blue chalice of the sky" (*DW,* 11). As Alleyn and Fabian Losse drive to the remote plateau where the Mount Moon sheep ranch is located, Alleyn is struck repeatedly by the clearness—clean water and air, brooding, "desultory boulders and giant tussocks, colored like torches in sunlight" (*DW,* 16), and moving across the landscape were sheep bleating in a hypnotic drone. In the midst of this spacious plateau sits Mount Moon homestead, surrounded by Lombardy poplars that rise from the ground like exclamation points. The Rubricks had achieved a certain illusion of English country charm in and around the house, but the illusion disappeared as one gazed out the dining room windows and saw the great Southern Alps rising in bold relief against a rose-colored sky. The contrast between the expansive plateau and the constricted, choking conventions of those within the house creates a tension primed for murder. It is initially suggested that it was Florence Rubrick who had the greatest feel for her land, confirmed by her public service, her pugnacious nationalism, her friendly relations with her workers, and her interest in the details of wool sales in town. Her husband Arthur, a delicate semi-invalid who lives through his books and cherishes his library, appears to be the confined and narrow one. In a flash of irony borne out by her landscape themes, Marsh reveals that Mrs. Rubrick was even more limited than her husband—by her literal-mindedness and her manipulations of people and objects. She was no liberal visionary, as she liked to portray herself, but only a smart politician. It is Arthur who sees beyond the world of objects, but only to Terence Lynn, his wife's secretary, does he confide his thoughts. He sees that humanity's feeble attempts to tame this wild plateau country are "faintly comic"; he senses that people are simply moving across the surface of the land, like elaborate chess pieces. From earliest times to the present, the hills and plateau have dominated humans, rather than the other way around. Arthur's deep, instinctive sensitivity to the raw and primitive nature of the land is reminiscent of Alleyn's observation in *Vintage Murder* that human beings move about like parasites over the skin of the country. Arthur speculates about the proper literary idiom to catch this phenomenon. Modern writers have failed to capture it in free verse, he maintains, so what is needed is a disciplined form. He begins a series of experiments in writing about the plateau in the style of Hakluyt's *Voyages,* but he never discusses his efforts with his wife, whose prosaic and cliché-laden mind did not have the imagination to understand.

The only other character besides Alleyn and the posthumously quoted Arthur Rubrick who responds to the magnificent appeal of New Zealand's beauty is the rebellious boy Clifford Johns. Before Alleyn questions him about the terms of Florence Rubrick's patronage, his rejection of her plans, and the murder, he lays a common ground of understanding and trust with the boy. Alleyn is not an artist but is married to one, and his natural instincts for observation, combined with his wife's comments on shape and color, have trained his eye, if not his hand, to artistic sensibilities. He understands Cliff and his music more than anyone else in the book. In their discussions, as earnest as Arthur Rubrick's attempts at literature, they debate the possibility of translating the dramatic beauty of the plateau into the artistic medium of paint or music. Marsh sets a perspective and a stage for their interview: "Behind [Cliff], beyond open windows, glared a noonday garden, the plateau, blank with sunshine, and the mountains etherealized now by an intensity of light. . . . Their snows dazzled the eyes and seemed to be composed of light without substance" (*DW,* 150). Alleyn asks Cliff if he is interested in painting as well as music. Clearly surprised by this approach from a policeman, Cliff gapes as Alleyn muses that capturing the metaphysical effect of this landscape on canvas would be almost impossible. Alleyn inquires if music is the proper medium to capture its extraordinary moods, prompting Cliff to explain for the first time how deeply the vastness of the plateau affects him and how much he longs to express its beauty in music. He envisions not an artificial amalgam of Paheka tradition and Maori chants but rather a new, pure form—the only way, as he sees it, to do the plateau justice. Alleyn understands: "There is no forcing the growth of an art . . . no denying it when the moment is ripe" (*DW,* 151). Nagio Marsh, who was trained as a painter and then developed into a writer, was reemphasizing that fresh ideas and language, whether new or reborn, were necessary to describe with any degree of accuracy the verdant country of New Zealand and to comfort a world emerging from war. Just as the sepia-colored landscape of Wai-ata-tapu served her purposes for recording the desolation of war, so the Mount Moon plateau, fresh and clean, promised the imagination an infinite possibility of regeneration and rebirth, making it a suitable setting for the end of the war.

By the time she wrote *Photo Finish* in 1980, the wars had receded into memory but Marsh still preached her same creed of racial tolerance, strength through the bonds of Commonwealth, and the gifts of regeneration that the new world provided for the old. The physical presence of the landscape was a central agent for this story as well. Marsh detailed the wildlife, the sparkling water, and the local fauna, again appealing to the senses with sounds and

sights of intense beauty. As the Alleyns approach Waihoe Lodge near a lake in
Westland, New Zealand, they are astonished by the prospect. "The Lake was
perfectly unruffled and held the blazing image of an outrageous sunset. Fingers of land reached out bearing elegant trees that reversed themselves in the
water. The sunset came to its preposterous climax. Everything that could be
seen, near and far, was sharpened and gilded" (*PF,* 26–27). Dramatic as the
sights may be, Troy is almost as deeply impressed with the sounds of the wild
birds. "Outside a tui sang: a deep lucid phrase, uncivilized as snow water and
ending in a consequential clatter as if it cleared its throat" (*PF,* 183). The
bird's song provides an intermittent chorus for the opera that is to be performed at the lodge. Isabella Sommita, the diva whom Troy has been commissioned to paint while Alleyn quietly investigates ties between her
benefactor and the international drug scene, is murdered. Her murderer could
have been one of the paparazzi who specialize in photographing her in unflat-
tering poses, or almost any of the other characters who have been inflamed by
the Sommita's extraordinarily intense tantrums and careless seductions.
Alleyn unwinds the false threads from the true and discovers that the
Sommita was being plotted against by all her intimates, her servants, and her
patron, who was avenging an ancient Italian blood feud—surely an ending fit
for grand opera!

Just as the murder is discovered, nature throws a tantrum of her own.
Dwarfing any rage of the diva's, a storm sweeps the lake into furious lash-
ings of water and wind. As primitive in its power as the savage storm of
Verdi's *Rigoletto,* during which a young girl is murdered, the Rosser, as it is
locally known, provides the dual purpose of putting the Sommita's tantrums into perspective and cutting the house party off from the mainland.
The first purpose displays the hand of a subtle, symbolic novelist; the second obeys the conventions of detective novels, in which only a limited cast
of characters is eligible to be suspected of murder. This combination was
characteristic of Marsh's skill in her better works.

After the storm subsides, the world is purged and pure. "The sun shown,
the dark wet trees glittered, the Lake was spangled, and the mountains were
fresh, as if, it seemed, from creation's hand. The morning was alive with
bird songs, sounds that might have been the voice of the bush itself, its hidden waters, its coolness, its primordial detachment" (*PF,* 214). Alleyn and
Troy recall the legend that a Maori god-hero, Maui, had gone fishing,
caught the South Island, and dragged it up from the sea. The storm re-
minds them of the violence, the volcanic action that produced the land
upon which they stand. As in *Died in the Wool,* Alleyn returns to the question of how one could capture the violent beauty of the land in art. Neither

he nor Troy, in what would prove to be Marsh's last speculation on the subject, arrive at a satisfactory answer. In the last scene, Troy comments again on the wildness and the sense of primitive forces in New Zealand. This landscape belongs to birds, "not to men, not to animals: huge birds that have gone now, stalked about in it. Except for birds it's empty" (*PF,* 252). It is a bell-bird chiming in the bush that has caught her attention—a sad tribute to the "songbird" Sommita, whose voice was loved by many while the woman herself was lonely, spoiled, and despised.

Although Marsh, herself an inveterate world traveler, selected a number of countries for her mysteries, none of them carried quite as strong a sense of place as one city, the Eternal City, beloved by Marsh and captured in *When in Rome*.[1] No other novel was so explicitly influenced by a particular setting. In the second edition of *Black Beech and Honeydew,* Marsh noted that she wrote *When in Rome* shortly after leaving the city, and that she attempted to portray the wonders of the Eternal City in the book. Other than changing the name of the basilica from the actual San Clemente in Via di S. Giovanni in Laterano to the fictional San Tommaso, she remained faithful to the geography and the historical sites familiar to the informed reader. Marsh created in exquisite detail the piazzas and winding streets of classical Rome; her descriptions reflected and reinforced the mood of the characters in a more intimate fashion than her sketches of New Zealand's majestical emptiness and were rendered in just as much detail as most of her London mysteries.

When in Rome revolves around British author Barnaby Grant and his dealings with an unsavory British expatriate, Sebastian Mailer. Grant first sees Mailer in the Piazza Colonna just as a thunderstorm breaks. The atmosphere in the crowded curbside cafe is claustrophobic, the very air torpid. With dreadful anticipation Grant can hear distant thunder above the traffic noise, but no lightning is yet visible, "being masked by a black canopy of low and swollen clouds." (*WR,* 2). This is an appropriately evil atmosphere for an encounter that results in Mailer stealing the manuscript of Grant's latest novel, plagiarizing one of its themes, and twisting the story so that Grant appears to be the plagiarizer. As the price for his silence Mailer blackmails Grant into leading expensive Roman tours that are a front for his nefarious drug dealing. The blackguard then disappears in the course of the sightseeing and is later discovered dead. Roderick Alleyn is among the tourists, most of whom, it develops, are tied to Mailer through drugs or blackmail. It is a tortuous plot, well suited to the labyrinthine Roman streets and the deeply convoluted catacombs in which Mailer's body is found.

Grant's dilemma is accentuated by the oppressiveness of the weather when he meets Mailer. The thunderstorm over the Piazza Colonna and its "black canopy" suggest at the outset that the meeting is ominous. Later, at Mailer's insistence, Grant plunges into Roman nightlife, "into narrow streets past gloomy windows and pitch-dark entries, through groups of people who shouted and by-ways that were silent" (*WR*, 16). Grant does not know that Mailer is setting him up for blackmail, and when he finally comprehends Mailer's obscene proposal, he is seated in the small waiting room of his hotel. For the rest of his life Barnaby will be sickened by the memory of "that commonplace little room" with its terrible decor: cheap furniture, a garish carpet, and a mass-produced imitation of a fine tapestry depicting in bright, lurid colors the fall of Icarus. Marsh was emphasizing the choking feeling of this space with its false decor and, of course, the classic myth of the disaster that befell the boy who tried to fly too high. Every allusion builds the tension and emphasizes Grant's shock as he realizes his vulnerability. The narrow streets, small hotels, and shaded cafes offer no sense of intimacy or coziness—they are, instead, menacing.

How different some of these same images appear when Grant meets young Sophy Jason and begins to fall in love. Sitting at another curbside cafe with Grant in the Piazza Navona, Sophy reacts to the same narrow, crowded place with the wonder and absorption the scene deserves. Although their view of Navona is obstructed, Sophy does not care. She is elated to be in the *real* Rome of crowds and bustle rather than sitting on a tour bus or being steered around the antiquities to the rote recitations of adenoidal guides. It is worth taking risks, even being bamboozled in a tourist scam, to seize the moment while she is here in an exciting city, young and alive. Her spontaneous enjoyment begins to calm the nervous Barnaby Grant, who, in a far gentler manner than he has yet evinced, describes the square, its sculpture and its mythology. Later, at dinner, the pleasant mood continues while Grant and the odd collection of tourists dine alfresco and watch Rome in the distance come alive with its dramatic lighting. At these moments, ancient and modern Rome are one. When the ruin of the Colosseum is lit from within, it appears alive, ready to belch forth an ancient Roman crowd—excited, vulgar, sweating, stinking, and shouting to one another. Unbeknownst to the company watching the scene (except for the murderer), Mailer is now dead—quickly dispatched in excavations under San Tommaso.

Throughout the novel Marsh skillfully evoked the lush beauty of Rome when seen through the eyes of the innocent, contrasted with the city's sordid taint at moments such as those when Sebastian Mailer plies his odious trade of blackmail and drugs. As always, Alleyn is acutely responsive to his environment. Posing as a tourist, he joins Mailer's tour to sniff out drug dealing. As he has done often before, he serves as a voice of balance, sanity, and authority in a crisis. He is also a sensitive observer of the moods of the city, providing a vehicle through which the reader is able to view the beauty, the antique mysteries, and the squalor of Rome. Unaffected by Mailer's menace, Alleyn freely apostrophizes in a passage that is representative of the sensuality and lyricism of Marsh's prose in this novel:

Rome sparkled in the spring morning. The swallows had arrived, the markets were full of flowers, young greens and kaleidoscopic cheap-jackery. Dramatic facades presented themselves suddenly to the astonished gaze, lovely courtyards and galleries floated in shadow and little piazzas talked with the voices of their own fountains. Behind magnificent doorways the ages offered their history lessons in layers. Like the achievements of a Roman pastrycook, thought the tall man irreverently: modern, Renaissance, classic, Mithraic, each under another in one gorgeous stratified edifice. It would be an enchantment to walk up the Palatine Hill where the air would smell freshly of young grass and a kind of peace and order would come upon the rich encrustations of time. (*WR,* 30)

Alleyn returns repeatedly to his image of a "sparkling" city. Yet his tenure there is based on a serious mission: to investigate the drug market and, more unexpectedly, to uncover two murders and a murderer. As Alleyn goes about his grim task, searching for the two bodies he suspects are stashed in the dark, dramatic nether regions of the Church of San Tommaso, he is unexpectedly and incongruously aided by fluorescent lighting—merciless in its destruction of the theatrical setting. "It changed completely the atmosphere and character of the underworld, which had become a museum with no shadows and its exhibits remorselessly displayed. Nothing could reduce the liveliness, beauty, and strangeness of the Etruscan terra-cottas, but they no longer disconcerted" (*WR,* 118). Even with the murder quite literally coming to light, the excavations into Mithraic Rome remain fascinating and mysterious.

The same cannot be said for the seedy nightlife of Rome, offered by Mailer as an "option" for his tourists. Taken through the twisting streets to Toni's Pad, Alleyn and a few of the others are ushered into a darkened room and led to velvet cushions scattered around the walls. Marijuana smoke lies thick on the air as a fat and effeminate Toni, dressed in floral satin, steps into the mauve light and introduces the floor show, "Keenky Keeks." After ascertaining the nature of this "infamous" entertainment, Alleyn slips out of the room and makes a heroin purchase from the porter. With his evidence secure, Alleyn shakes himself free of the jaded, decadent establishment and returns to his hotel. After his taste of depraved nightlife, the hotel's quiet and tastefully luxurious lobby seems peaceful; only the soothing sound of a fountain interrupts the silence. Alleyn, in this book as in all the others, remains Marsh's eyes and ears, sensitive to place whether in glorious beauty or mean squalor.

Other characters respond to and comment on the city—especially Sophy Jason and Barnaby Grant as they fall in love with Rome and with each other. Sophy is most taken with the basilica of San Tommaso, which sits astride the tunnels of the ancient Mithraic temple. Through her eyes, Marsh portrayed her own painterly response to such beauty: "It was alive with colour: 'Mediterranean' red, clear pinks, blues and greens; ivory and crimson marble, tingling gold mosaic. And dominant in this concourse of colour the great vermillion that cries out in the backgrounds of Rome and Pompeii" (WR, 45).

When in Rome is unquestionably Marsh's most sensational European novel. Only in her New Zealand works did she turn so consistently to the rich descriptions of place and blend them so successfully with a spatial sense. From the lush and beautiful city—usually displayed in wide vistas from a distant prospect—to the rich colors and mysterious historical excavations, Marsh turned her pen into a paint brush, here laying on a thick patina of oils, and there dabbing a faint water-color shading. Her Rome could be intimate in its crowds, its traffic, its enclosed squares; or the same places could be as menacingly claustrophobic as the action dictated. She presented a Rome of heavy storms and a Rome that "sparkles" in the sunlight. Her skillful prose illuminated the contrasts of this city that obviously fascinated her—a trait unique to her detective writing, compared to that of her contemporaries.

Although New Zealand and Rome inspired some of her most colorful prose, they were not the only settings Marsh found attractive. England was her adopted country in which she would spend many years of her adult life, but which would never completely claim her. Indeed, the English locales in her novels read like a tourist brochure: London, Dorset, Devon, Kent, Buckinghamshire, and East Anglia. After World War II Marsh lived a part of each year in England, and she came to appreciate the country and to love it like a native. She owned a London home in the fashionable Brompton area just south of Hyde Park, and she wrote about it as well as other neighborhoods of the well heeled and socially prominent. She described the seedy areas of London as well—the warehouse districts and the poorer tenements—creating a city of extremes, from Sloane Square to the East End. She painted the English countryside in spare, charcoal line drawings as opposed to her lush oils of New Zealand. Frequently her country mysteries occurred in winter, when snow and rain reduce the colors to white, gray, and black. In none of the domestic novels did the country or the setting play the same type of role as in the New Zealand stories; setting was background in these works, important for tone, supporting the plot, but lacking the dramatic intrusiveness of the New Zealand countryside. Nowhere did the characters muse about the meaning of the landscape in England. Accordingly, its emotional impact is reduced, as if a theater set designer sometimes given to the sensualist rococo had suddenly turned minimalist. Like bone and skeletal tissue, however, the settings supported the shape of the plot and illuminated the mystery.

Examining Marsh's use of London as a setting reveals that in thirteen or more of her thirty-two novels she featured the city in at least a portion of the story. Curiously, this middle-class, respectable woman, whom one would not suppose to be acquainted with any but the best neighborhoods, frequently wrote of the more modest accommodations of London, tracing even the "mean streets" or back alleys and describing warehouses and slums. In the imaginary Knocklatcher's Row, Marsh created the meeting place for the cult of the Sacred Flame in *Death in Ecstasy* (1936).² As Nigel Bathgate ruminates, "Knocklatcher's Row seemed an exciting street. Its name sounded like a password to romance" (*DE*, 16). Despite his naive anticipation, Marsh penetrated the facade of such fantasy. "There are many strange places of worship in London, and many remarkable sects. The blank face of a Cockney Sunday masks a kind of activity, intermittent but intense. All sorts of queer little religions squeak, like mice in the wainscoting, behind its tedious facade" (*DE*, 13). From the tedious and bland to the romantic, Marsh mingled London's real and fictional streets with her legendary foul weather to set a stage for religious mysteries. Nigel is at first caught up in the sect's ritual, and during it he witnesses a murder. He is depressed by Alleyn's subsequent investigation and awakens the next morning with a "vague sense of disquietude as though he had been visited by nightmare" (*DE*, 149). But he finds stability and reassurance in the view from his window: "The rain still poured down on the roofs. Wet umbrellas bobbed up and down Chester Terrace. A milkman's cart with a dejected and irritated pony was drawn up at the corner of Knocklatcher's Row" (*DE*, 149).

The scene from Nigel Bathgate's flat is not always reassuring, for on the night of Alleyn's recreation of the crime "it was blowing a gale and the rain made diagonal streamers of tinsel against the wet black of the houses" (*DE*, 293). That evening, in fact, London and the weather cooperate to produce a scene that is such an exact reproduction of the night of the actual murder that Nigel feels suspended in time. The gale howls, the windows rattle, and grayness settles in around them as Alleyn performs a ritual of his own to discover the murderer. Finally, Knocklatcher's Row, London, and the fictional world are purged of the taint of crime and the exploitation practiced by bogus cults as Alleyn has the Sacred Flame's sign taken away. One of the mice in the wainscoating, in this case a murderer, has been trapped.

In *Artists in Crime* (1938) Marsh painted an even grimmer, grimier London.[3] The city shows her worst side and is made even more vivid by the contrasts to Suva, Fiji, and the lush countryside of Buckinghamshire, where the novel opens. Though the first murder occurs in Agatha Troy's rural studio, the second is discovered in the warehouse area of Brixton. As Alleyn pursues the lead to the Brixton prison area, "the sky was leaden, and already the light had begun to fade" (*AC*, 199). He picks his way through a tangle of dirty back streets, oppressed by the monochromatic gray sky reflected in the dingy puddles of stagnant rainwater and the drab, windowless walls of the huge warehouses. When he finds the one he has been looking for, he discovers a partially dismembered automobile chassis, wheels, engines, and menacing-looking wrecking equipment. Certainly a suggestive place for a prison, which might be described in much the same kind of language— with human parts strewn about. It is also an ideally stark setting in which to discover the brutal murder of a scruffy and disreputable man: Wolf Garcia would naturally have died in such a place. Just before he discovers the corpse, Alleyn unlocks the outside door, imagining himself in a scene from a "realistic" film, complete with darkly garbed actors set against the gloom, with the traffic noise as musical score. If not a film, he thinks, certainly a piece of Dostoyevski imagery.

The depiction of these sordid back streets and several scenes in an unfashionable Chelsea neighborhood are neatly sandwiched between two of Marsh's loveliest settings—settings that bracket the novel's subplot of Alleyn in love. In the opening pages of *Artists in Crime,* Alleyn first meets the painter Agatha Troy, who is painting a scene from shipboard of the dock at Suva in the Fiji Islands. Alleyn has been struck earlier by the same view of a colorful Fijan with outrageously dyed magenta hair and skin tones that are a mix of brown and blue highlights, standing beside a fresh pile of green bananas. As he observes this delightful riot of color, Alleyn listens to the sounds, catches the smells, and then gazes at the landscape. In a burst of lyricism that anticipates her New Zealand novels, Marsh wrote of the distant hills that appear purple at their base, are lost amid a cluster of "sulky" clouds, but emerge at their peak jagged, set in sharp relief against the still

and "somber" sky. The clouds are ringed with indigo edges and are heavy
with rain. Above looms the sky, dark and menacing, in contrast to earth's
"violence of color—it was a pattern of wet brown, acid green, magenta and
indigo" (*AC,* 1). Marsh used this tropical setting not merely to create local
color but to assail the senses and call Alleyn back to life and to love. Being
of a brooding nature, Alleyn needs these vibrant tweaks from the author to
relieve his emotional solemnity.

The book ends with Agatha Troy in Alleyn's arms in the midst of an English rose garden, the air redolent with scent, the trees and autumn sky
framing their embrace. Though Troy is too distraught to pledge Alleyn her
love, this scene marks the budding of their romance and ultimate marriage,
which would endure for forty-two years and through twenty-three more detective novels. She accompanies Alleyn on some of his travels and adventures and, showing no sign of middle or old age, is present in New Zealand
at his next-to-last case, in *Photo Finish.*

Marsh captured the rush of life in her orgy of the senses, integrating color
and beauty into Alleyn's world, despite the seamier aspects of his work. His
sensitivity to beautiful settings refreshes him during the more oppressive
moments of his murder investigations. Although *Artists in Crime* was an
early novel, its author was already skilled in portraying extraordinary
textures.

Between these earlier novels and the later *Black as He's Painted,* which
prominently features a London locale, Marsh punctuated other novels with
brief forays into a London of fashion and the arts. In both *Death in a White
Tie* (1938) and *A Wreath for Rivera* (1949), Marsh provided glimpses of
the Sloane Square society and debutante crowd.[4] In both cases the large Victorian townhouses of this area witness parties of jubilant merrymaking often
underscored by the quiet desperation of the revelers. The fog, like a smoth-
ering rag, hangs about the fashionable squares and walks, democratically
cloaking the murderers, the victims, and the police alike. In *Death of a Peer,*
Marsh captured the excitement of London for a young New Zealand girl
who was visiting London for the first time: "But to British colonials the
symbol of London is . . . homely. . . . It is a small figure perched slantways
above a roundabout, an elegant, Victorian god with a Grecian name—Eros
of Piccadilly Circus. When they come to London, colonials orientate themselves by Piccadilly Circus. All their adventures start from there. It is under
the bow of Eros that to many a colonial has come that first warmth of real-
ization that says to him: 'This is London' " (*DP,* 33). For the remainder of
the book, Marsh dwelt more on interiors—the apartment where the murder
occurs, for instance,—and less on the exterior sense of place. So it was with

most of her subsequent London settings, providing the occasional glimpse
of neighborhoods, street names, foggy rambles in famous squares in the city,
all accomplished with the deft touch of the artist who blended place and
plot rather than separating them. In *Killer Dolphin* Marsh moved her characters about London, giving various perspectives on the fictional Dolphin
Theater: its sad and seedy exterior, and from within, a shambles from neglect.[5] To the sensitive eye of Peregrine Jay, this wonderful, elaborate building (surely representing so many of the older Victorian structures that
Marsh would have seen) now surrounded by warehouses and wharfingers'
offices is like a fine old lady cast among her social inferiors. In the novel, as
he enters the tattered lobby and works his way to the stage, Marsh describes
in photographic detail the fine rococo work and the damages from the blitz
and from lack of upkeep. By the intervention of a mysterious stranger, the
Dolphin is restored to great splendor, and Jay, who has lovingly directed the
restoration, opens with a new dramatic production. As the Dolphin gleams
with renewed hope, so do Peregrine's spirits, his romantic life, and, by extension, his whole world. As he walks the streets of the city, he goes "into the
early morning sounds and sights of the river and of the lanes and steps and
streets. The day was fresh and sunny and would presently be warm" (*KD*,
87). He gazes on his restored theater from a distance and with utter delight
notices that the building itself glows so brightly it might be under stage
lights. The beleaguered dowager has resumed her proper place of sartorial
prominence just as the theater and, by extension, London and all of England
in the postwar world had been awaiting restoration—awaiting the chance to
shine pristine as a leader in world affairs. Marsh's novels sensed this
moment—as in the days of *Death of a Peer,* Piccadilly and London should
once again represent artistic, political, and economic leadership.

It is in *Black as He's Painted,* her 1974 novel, that Marsh returned to a
more completely realized London locale. The action takes place in a small
area imaginatively titled the Capricorns, located in the old postal code SW7
and possibly modeled after the Montpelier Square area where Marsh lived.
Depressed by his enforced retirement from the Foreign Office, Samuel
Whipplestone happens on the Capricorns on an early morning walk. "As he
entered the flowing cacophony of changing gears and revving engines, it occurred to him that he, himself, must now get into bottom gear and stay
there, until he was parked in some subfusc lay-by to await—and here the si-
mile became insufferable—a final towing off" (*BHP,* 12). In the midst of
these gloomy ruminations, Mr. Whipplestone meets a cat who will become
his pet and finds a house for sale that will become his home. "The London
Feeling," as he calls it, overcomes his natural caution the moment he enters

Capricorn Mews. He sees a pleasant street lined with trees and well-kept Georgian and Victorian homes, each bedecked with blooming flower boxes and surrounded by neat iron railings. He strolls through the streets in a trance, smelling the wafting odor of fresh coffee brewing and smiling at the cleaning ladies, the nannies, and the postman, who are all bustling about in their morning activities. They all conspire, albeit unconsciously, to lift Mr. Whipplestone's gloom.

Mr. Whipplestone observes that life in the Capricorns appears uneventful but not "tiresomely quaint" or picturesque and smug; the neighborhood is "pleasing rather" and has the distinctive quality "he could only think of as 'sparkling' " (*BHP,* 14). Beneath the surface, however, unperceived by his increasingly besotted viewpoint, lurks an evil, racist secret society that is plotting assassination and finally causes three murders, all within this beautiful, upper middle-class neighborhood. The murders and the secret society take Mr. Whipplestone very much by surprise; nothing in his environment prepares him for the tragic underside of his joyful move to the Capricorns. On his sun-dappled walks, and while reveling in the pleasures of his new home, Mr. Whipplestone meets unsavory neighbors who, it turns out, are the villains of the piece: alcoholic and murderous Colonel and Mrs. Corkburn-Montfort and the revolting brother and sister Sanskrit, Kenneth and Xenoclea. They curb Mr. Whipplestone's optimistic moods while London and the Capricorns remain beautifully serene. Gone are the "dark and stormy nights" and the desolate blandness that introduce villainy in *Death in Ecstasy* and other earlier novels. By *Black as He's Painted* Marsh's touch was more certain; she blended the light and dark hues with assurance and mixed atmosphere and personal eccentricities, being content to have them complement and contrast rather than exactly mirror the action.

Marsh explored various locales in her novels that feature the countryside, returning frequently to the southern counties and East Anglia, her favorite settings. In these stories she utilized some of the conventional devices of the country house mystery—a small group of suspects drawn from the squirearchy or the "smart set," isolation from cities or towns, illicit extramarital dallying that adds venom to the brew, and, of course, the murder, which is never performed by a servant or a social inferior of the victim, regardless of his class. In addition to honoring these traditions, Marsh added her uniquely eccentric characters and rich interior and exterior descriptions of place. Even in novels that occur in fictional counties, such as *Scales of Justice* (1955) and *Death of a Fool* (1956), Marsh evoked the actual geography and climate of the region. Though her first mystery, *A Man Lay Dead,* takes place in the country house of Frantock, the only clue to its location Marsh gave was that it is reached via Paddington Station.[6] Presumably, then, it is in the southwestern region of England. Her description of both the house and its environs was spare—well within the strictures of S. S. Van Dine. It could be any country house anywhere in England; although that adds a certain universality to its appeal, not to mention respectability to the book as a golden-age detective novel, the reader familiar with later Marsh novels is left rather unmoved. *A Man Lay Dead* was her closest attempt at a Christie-style book in which plot reigns supreme over character and place. In her sixth novel, *Artists in Crime,* she described Suva, Fiji, and seamy London in colorful particularity but seemed to be rather indifferent to the Buckinghamshire countryside and to details about Tatler's End, Agatha Troy's home, and even the Alleyn family home located nearby.

It is in *Overture to Death* (1939) that Marsh first created a textured environment in rural England.[7] In this novel she established location, themes, and techniques that recur in her fiction, while departing from the classical strictures of the country house murder. The setting includes a manor house and a vicarage, but the murder occurs in neither; instead, it takes place in the parish hall in full view of the villagers, accomplished by a bizarre booby trap. Alleyn eliminates the red herring of opportunity—everyone in the village had that—and looks instead for the motives of a twisted psyche. Meanwhile, a brooding Dorset sky and countryside keep watch over the goings and comings of police, villain, young lovers, and illicit lovers as they skirt the edge of discovery until the final resolution. Looking out over Pen Cuckoo estate, young Henry Jernigham sees "a darkling vale . . . an austere landscape, adamant beneath drifts of winter mist. The naked trees slept soundly, the fields were dumb with cold; the few stone cottages, with their comfortable signals of blue smoke, were the only waking things in the valley" (*OD,* 10). Other descriptions early in the story attest to the cold and the somnolence, hinting at the frigidity and sleeping murderous passions of the women who are central to the plot. The mystery revolves around an eruption, a sudden storm of jealous rage that shatters the peace, the predictability of events, and the head of the spinster victim.

In what became a characteristic of her rural mysteries, Marsh presaged murder with an ominous chill. As the victim and two friends arrive at Pen Cuckoo, Henry "opened the great front door [and] the upland air laid its cold hand on his face. He smelt frost, dank earth and dead leaves" (*OD,* 18). When Alleyn and Fox begin investigating the crime, "it was a dank and dreary morning, and so cloudy that only a mean thinning of the night, a grudging disclosure of vague, wet masses, gave evidence that somewhere beyond the vale there was dawnlight" (*OD*, 137). The half-light of a murder investigation and the groping dim awareness of the shape of truth or truths about a case are familiar conditions to Alleyn and are reflected in the Dorset countryside and weather. It is also notable that the dawn, the light, is absent; correspondingly, Alleyn remains unenlightened at this point in the mystery.

As Alleyn seeks perspective on his case and puzzles over suspects and motives, he visits the manor house, Pen Cuckoo, to interview Henry's father, the squire. Unbeknownst to them, the murderer is in the house, hidden away beneath the guise of nervous collapse. Alleyn has unwittingly come to the right place. Although the manor house sits on the Cloudyfold Rise above the vale, Alleyn notices that one of the lanes from the valley "led crookedly up to the Manor" (*OD*, 158)—as though the crime that has taken place below has sent its red tentacle to the source of the infection— Eleanor Prentice, the squire's cousin. As Alleyn approaches the house, the theme of coldness and isolation recurs: "It is not a tame landscape, either. The four winds meet on Cloudyfold, and in winter the small lake at Pen Cuckoo grounds holds its mask of ice for days together" (*OD*, 158). An icy mask is an apt image for a woman who has slain her best friend, in a particularly hideous manner, in a fit of jealous pique. Marsh also provided particulars about the location of the rectory and Pen Cuckoo; the first edition even features a map of the area. The imaginary towns of Winton and Chipping were described with such specificity that her return to the area and these characters three years later in another country house mystery seems like a second visit to a familiar spot. Some critics have judged this first Dorset novel as her best work, in part because of the skillful evocation of setting and its integration with character and plot.

Pen Cuckoo and Eleanor Prentice's crime so affected Marsh's imagination that three years later, in her novel *Death and the Dancing Footman*, she set another Dorset mystery in the Cloudyfold area.[8] As guests motor in for a weekend at Highfold Manor, two of them pass the shuttered Pen Cuckoo and one comments, "Two years ago it housed a homicidal lunatic, and her relatives have not returned since her trial" (*DDF*, 38). Rather sadly then, Henry Jernigham did not marry the rector's daughter, the woman for whom he defied his father and his homicidal aunt. Diana Copeland, his intended, is now a leading lady on the London stage, appearing in Aubrey Mandrake's play in the West End. This was a rather rare instance in Marsh's novels of young love, though sincerely felt, not prevailing. In the later novel, Diana visits her father, who is being painted by Agatha Troy, whose husband, the great detective, is conveniently in tow. The mystery in *Death and the Dancing Footman* revolves around a bizarre house party given by

Jonathan Royal, squire of Highfold Manor, who has deliberately gathered a disparate group of guests, each of whom not only bears a secret fear but has reason to hate another member of the company. For Royal it is an aesthetic experiment, with human psychology as his medium, until murder sends it awry. William, one of the Compline brothers, is killed by a booby trap in a closed-room-with-everyone-elsewhere scenario. In the course of the investigation, Aubrey Mandrake falls in love with William's fiancée, braves the vicissitudes of a Dorset blizzard to retrieve Alleyn, and matures beyond his great fear that others will discover his lower-class origins. As happens in *Overture to Death,* the murderer is discovered to be the character with the most obvious motive, William's brother Nicholas; also like its predecessor, this novel is built around the misconception that it is the murderer who was the intended victim.

Marsh's use of the Dorset countryside again played a strong supporting role for her plot and characters. The desolate land and weather introduce the themes of coldness and barrenness of the human heart. Although no map was provided this time, Marsh gave such specific references to Highfold Manor, Pen Cuckoo, Winton, and Chipping that readers could have pictured the community without difficulty. For instance, Marsh succeeded in combining specific location and weather details with a sense of forboding in the following description:

The wind had fallen and, as Jonathan opened his great outer doors, the quiet of an upland county at dusk entered the house and the smell of earth, still only lightly covered with snow. They walked out on the wide platform in front of Highfold. Far beneath them Cloudyfold village showed dimly through tree-tops and beyond it the few scattered houses down in the Vale, four miles away. In the southern skies the stars were out, but northward above Cloudyfold Top there was a well of blackness. And as Jonathan and his guest turned towards the north they received the sensation of an icy hand laid on their faces.
'That's a deathly cold air,' said Mandrake. (*DDF,* 21)

Remembering her references to icy masks in *Overture to Death,* Marsh wrote that on the night before the murder, "Harpies and warlocks [were] abroad" (*DDF,* 8). The pastoral setting—"Somewhere up on Cloudyfold a farmer was moving his sheep and the drowsy sound of their slow progress seemed uncannily near" (*DDF,* 23)—fails to reassure Mandrake, who "felt the house to be alive with anticipation, but whether of a storm without or within he was unable to decide" (*DDF,* 23). His estimation that "it's a grisly day" would prove all too accurate. Just before Highfold Manor and all the surrounding area are suffocated by a deep snowfall and the murder occurs, the stage was set for this gloom and doom: "Under clouds that hung like a pall from horizon to horizon, the scattered cottages of Dorset stone looked almost black, while their roofs glistened with a stealthy reflected light" (*DDF,* 39).

The storm that finally breaks both outside and inside Highfold Manor produces huge quantities of snow, a murder, and a suicide. Frustrating delays caused by the storm mean that the police cannot be summoned for several days. Finally, rain melts enough of the snow that a party made up of Aubrey Mandrake, Chloris Wynne, and a Highfold gardener successfully traverses the treacherous roads to Winton to fetch help in the person of Roderick Alleyn. During the delay the mother of the victim (and, as it is later revealed, of the murderer), Sandra Compline, commits suicide rather than acknowledge that the son she adores is a murderer. As these events occur in a frozen time frame of people trapped in a manor house, Marsh began to free them, using her setting to introduce the next stage of the plot: "Here in the uplands it was drilled with rain and all through the night hills and trees suffered a series of changes. In the depths of Jonathan's woods, branches, released from their burden of snow, jerked sharply upwards. From beneath battlements of snow, streams of water began to move and there were secret downward shiftings of white masses. With the diminution of snow the natural contours of the earth slowly returned" (*DDF,* 210–11).

As the thaw continues, Alleyn pursues, questions, and evaluates. Masks hiding the secret hatreds and fears are stripped away; the contours of lives are revealed in sharp relief. Jonathan Royal's experiment succeeds in creating a rather ugly psychological portrait of a murderer and a nest of jealous rivalries. The image of a mask of ice and snow is significant; two of the characters are beauty experts, and one is a plastic surgeon. Marsh's story suggested that no matter how skillfully arranged, or how plain and ugly the outside appearance might be, the heart requires more substance than these vanities.

From *Death and the Dancing Footman* until the end of her career, Marsh continued to select interesting locations that underscored the themes in her murder mysteries. Though she did not return to Dorset specifically, her setting in *Tied up in Tinsel* suggested a similarly desolate and frigid wasteland.[9] The house party that gathered at the country house, Halberds, is overseen by eccentric entrepreneur Hilary Bill-Tasman, who, upon restoring his family's fortunes, had bought back the ancestral home and begun its restoration. Agatha Troy is a guest, invited to Halberds to paint Bill-Tasman's portrait. They are joined for the Christmas celebration by his aunt and uncle, his fiancée, and an old family friend. When Bill-Tasman's aunt and uncle's manservant, Alf Moult, disappears, Alleyn is conveniently available to join his wife and assume a role in the investigation after Moult's body is discovered. Complicating everything is the fact that the staff of Halberd's consists of murderers, each convicted for one specific crime of passion and subsequently paroled for good behavior. The very prison from whence they came is nearby. Referred to only as the Vale, Troy remembers that her husband calls it Heartbreak House and had taken part in dispatching several of the staff to it. Following the detective story formula, the crime is not committed by a servant but by the future chatelaine, Cressida Tottenham, who acted out of fear that Moult would reveal that he was her father. She knew that revelation of such dubious parentage would have reduced her chances of marrying the snobbish Bill-Tasman.

Bill-Tasman's ambitions and his exaggerated family pride are captured in Marsh's description of Halberds and its setting. As Troy climbs a slope to the moors and, remembering an eighteenth-century sketch of the house and its gardens, contemplates her host's restoration, "she was able to replace the desolation that surrounded the house with the terraces, walks and artificial hill, lake and vistas created, so Hilary had told her, by Capability Brown. . . . In the background a hill dozer slowly laid out preliminaries for Hilary's restorations . . . scooping out a new lake and heaping the spoil into what would become a hillock. And a 'Hilary's Folly' no doubt would ultimately crown the summit" (*TT,* 23). Like the plastic surgeon and beauty expert in *Death and the Dancing Footman,* Hilary is trying to rearrange the reality of a house and grounds almost destroyed by bombs and neglect. Like the beauty expert, he indulges his fantasy that he can control the perceptions of who he is by subscribing to that particularly English delusion that the home makes the gentleman. Troy instinctively realizes his self-deception and its inherent link to the house: "And no doubt, Troy thought, it will be very, very beautiful but there's an intrinsic difference between 'How it still is' and 'This is how it was,' all the monstrous accumulation of his superscrap markets, high antiques and football pools won't do the trick for him" (*TT,* 23). As she thinks about Bill-Tasman's pretensions and their source in his humble merchandising background, she turns in another direction. "It was as if a slide had clicked over in a projector and an entirely dissociated subject thrown on the screen. Troy now looked down into the Vale, as it was locally called, and her first thought was of the hopeless incongruity of this gentle wood, for it stood not only for the valley but for the prison, whose dry moats, barriers, watchtowers, yards, barracks and chimney stacks were set down below like a scale model of themselves for her to shudder at" (*TT,*

23). It is the prison in juxtaposition with the partially restored house that dominates the atmosphere of the novel. As in so many of her mysteries, Marsh also used the peculiarities of local weather, the extreme, damp cold of English country winters, to introduce and accentuate the coldness of murder—in this case, patricide. The body is hidden beneath an ice effigy in a mock catafalque as an icy mask descends over murder perpetrated by a perfectly groomed if especially shallow-minded and mean-spirited woman.

In contrast to the stark disparity between the restoration of Halberds and the Vale's desolation, Marsh softened her palette to evoke England's "green and pleasant land." The two novels that best illustrate this aspect of Marsh's sense of place are *Scales of Justice* and *A Clutch of Constables* (1968).[10] In the former, her lush prose creates verdant meadows cut by a winding trout stream, with spinneys, old stone bridges, and grassy banks, in imaginary Swevenings of her fictional county, Barfordshire. The effect is one of a watercolor or gouache overlaid with a filmy green finish. In the later novel she used her technique of contrasts: a pleasant and navigable river spoiled in places by industrial effluence, and villages of tourist-attraction perfection marred by dim and dingy alleyways. The novels have two characteristics in common. First, like so much of English life, each revolves around a river, the line of demarkation defining and marking much of the open space. Second, both novels contain such exact descriptions that during the course of the action a picture map is actually made, marking all the appropriate landmarks and people. The map provides an enumeration, an orderly placing of objects in their surroundings, a sort of spatial summing-up.

The opening paragraphs of *Scales of Justice* immediately set the tone for the role of landscape in reflecting the characters' social arrangements and attitudes: "She looked down on the village of Swevenings. Smoke rose in cosy plumes from one or two chimneys; roofs cuddled into surrounding greenery. The Chyne, a trout stream, meandered through meadow and coppice and slid blamelessly under two bridges. It was circumspect landscape. Not a faux-pas, architectural or horticultural, marred the seemliness of the prospect" (*SJ*, 1). From Nurse Kettle's point of view, all is as it should be. She believes in degree in the Elizabethan sense—a hierarchy, an order, is divinely ordained. This beautiful valley with its country society suits her sense of proportion admirably. Alleyn's response to Swevenings' physical beauty is quite different: "It's superficially pretty and fundamentally beautiful. . . . Quaint as hell, but take a walk after dusk and you wouldn't be surprised at anything you met. It's one of the oldest in England" (*SJ*, 71). Alleyn also recalls the violence that this area has seen: "There was some near-prehistoric set-to in the valley, I forget what, and another during Bolingbroke's rebellion and yet another in the Civil Wars. This Colonel's blood is not the first soldier's, by a long chalk, to be spilt at Swevenings" (*SJ*, 71). Marsh utilized one of her familiar themes to introduce the murder—the smell of earth and a chill. Nurse Kettle notes the evening vapor off of the Chyne, and she smells the "willow leaves and wet soil. . . . 'It's turned much cooler,' she thought" (*SJ*, 58). Just then she discovers the very dead body of Colonel Cartarette, whose spaniel had begun his howlings of grief.

The colonel, his daughter, and his new and unsuitable wife, Kitty, are among the community's leading figures. The murder victim, contrary to many detective story conventions, is a likable man, a warm father, and an integral part of Swevenings' society of ex-military men, colonial bureaucrats, and diplomatic corps retirees. In Nurse Kettle's view, all these characters, aside from Kitty Cartarette, "fit" in Swevenings. The colonel is even described, when he emerges in the evening light against the grass lawn and flowers of the valley, "as if he were an expression both of its substance and its spirit. It was as if from the remote past, through a quiet progression of dusks, his figure had come up from the valley of the Chyne" (*SJ*, 17). It is entirely satisfying to discover that the one misfit—the one discordant note in this symphony of landscape and social order—is indeed the murderer. Toward the end of the book, like in a Shakespearean tragedy, the world has been purged of its chaos and returned to a pure and predictable order. It is at this moment, as if to freeze this arrangement of nature and natures, that Commander Syce presents Nurse Kettle with a picture map upon which are marked all the geographic features of the Chyne Valley and the characters who inhabit it. Each is in his or her place, represented by caricature of status or profession, an apt device to signal the restoration of harmony and certainty among these conservative folk.

Marsh also utilized a river and a picture map in *A Clutch of Constables*. In this later novel, unique in its narrative device of a tale within a tale, Roderick Alleyn is recounting his wife Troy's impulsive decision to book a passage on a canal boat voyage in an undisclosed section of East Anglia. From this modest beginning Marsh developed a tale of international intrigue in drug dealing and murder. Unbeknownst to Troy, her little boat is the prearranged rendezvous of a gang of criminals. On the peaceful river voyage, awkward spinster Hazel Rickerby-Carrick stumbles onto the suspicious goings-on and is murdered, robbed, dumped overboard, and discovered days later on the return voyage upriver. Previously, Troy had found that the river and the slow pace induce a dreamlike state, a journey back into time. "Spires, fins, individual trees, locks; even a clod of tuffed earth that had fallen away from a bank and was half drowned or a broken branch that dipped into the stream and moved with its flow: these were familiar land-marks that they might have passed, not once, but many times before" (*CC,* 123). This passage occurs just prior to Troy's horrifying discovery of the body, "broken" and "half drowned." Though the body was in the water, it is not of it—death actually occurred from strangulation. The characters in *A Clutch of Constables,* unlike those in *Scales of Justice,* are always on the water—there is no integration of figures and landscape here, only observers caught, albeit briefly, in the place, pace, and time of the river.

The world away from the river takes on an increasingly unreal aspect. The acres of East Anglia melt into one another as uninterrupted flatland, but the twentieth century occasionally intrudes in the landscape—powerhouses stretch out along the general line of the river. Here Marsh created a slow-motion world where the past is far more intense than the present. As Troy muses in a letter to her husband, "The country beyond the River is about as empty as anywhere in England: flat, flat, flat and according to the Skipper almost hammered so by the passage of history. Red roses and white. Cava-liers and Roundheads. Priests and barons. The Percies of the North. The Jockeys of Norfolk. The lot: all galumphing over the landscape through the centuries. Did you know that Constable stayed here one summer and painted? Church spires turn up with minimal villages and of course, the locks" (*CC,* 38). This emptiness is only partially limited and defined by the river; otherwise, it is the nearest thing to wide-open space in Marsh's work except, possibly, for the New Zealand plateau in *Died in the Wool.* To limit her list of suspects and remain true to detective fiction conventions, she con-trasted these external spaces with the confinement, bordering upon claus-trophobia, of a riverboat's cabins or a sheep station's compound.

Underlining the closed nature of this river society, Troy sketches a carica-ture of her fellow passengers in a mock zodiac, with the signs representing a vivid personification of each of them. Troy instinctively provides clues to character in her drawing, in which she unwittingly designates as the Scor-pion, the murderer, who is an international crook long pursued by her hus-band. The poem included at the center of the zodiac commences, "The Hunt of the Heavenly host begins. . . ." (*CC,* 73). Indeed, the hunt is up, and Alleyn eventually traps his scorpion.

The landscape itself is similarly defined by Dr. Natouche, another of the passengers, who draws a fine pen-and-ink map of the river's windings. Alleyn evaluates it "with its tentative insets and its meticulous lettering . . . as indeed the work of a devoted amateur. It was so fine and so detailed that he almost needed a lens to examine it" (*CC,* 195). This precise map, com-bined with the impressionist zodiac rendered by Troy, serves almost the

same purpose as the picture map in *Scales of Justice,* for each pinpoints the
action to scale in specific locales. These places in turn reflect aspects of character and create a set for the action.

Marsh's bleakest mystery is *Death of a Fool,* set in fictional South
Mardian during the depth of winter at the solstice.[11] There is a physical
darkness in this mystery, a setting appropriate for a suspected patricide.
The action centers on a folk dance traditionally held at Mardian Hall, an
almost ruined Norman-Victorian manor house, and performed by a local
blacksmith and his five sons. In the course of the performance, William
Andersen, the father and lead dancer, is decapitated, apparently in full
view of his village audience. Alleyn and Fox must sort out the conflicting
passions and jealousies of the community, including innocent lovers and a
folklore enthusiast who is determined to spy and record the secret
dances. The novel is tinged with blacks, grays, and the flicker of firelight
throwing a rust-colored glow over it all. Though fire is often mentioned,
nothing seems to offset the cold and gloom of South Mardian in winter,
nor is there anything more than a pale shaft of sunlight to relieve the unrelenting darkness. This book illustrates the artistic unity of Marsh's writing
at its best—every description of place and space underlines the pinched,
cramped, isolated lives thrown into bold relief by the piercing beam of
light from a murder investigation.

Marsh's opening sentence established the tone of the novel: the bitter
chill of internecine jealousies discernible in the spare country: "Over that
part of England the winter solstice came down with a bitter antiphony of
snow and frost. Trees minutely articulate shuddered in the north wind" (*DF,*
13). The village itself has no redeeming architectural features to charm the
visitor, appearing to Alleyn to be "squat, unpicturesque, unremarkable"
(*DF,* 86). It is tempting to conclude that the only thing that saves South
Mardian from overt ugliness is its bland lack of character. It is this quality
more than any other that has enabled it to preserve rural folk traditions,
unhampered by what Nurse Kettle in *Scales of Justice* would have despised
as false antiquity; in South Mardian, as in Swevenings, there are "no Olde
Bunne Shoppes . . . no spurious half-timbering" (*SJ,* 3). But whereas this
purity has preserved the beauty of Swevenings, it has left South Mardian in
its virginal homeliness.

The manor house that dominates the village, and in whose courtyard the
dance traditionally occurred around a prehistoric dolmen, is equally awkward of prospect. The first view of it reveals "the shell of a Norman Castle,
theatrically executed against a leaden sky. Partly encircled by this ruin was a
hideous Victorian mansion" (*DF,* 13). The viewer moves through the

Norman archway and onto the dance site, scarcely prepared for the neglect. The courtyard is marked with piles of rubble, geese and their droppings, and weeds growing through the stones. In the middle is the dolmen, a stark remnant of early man's inexplicable urge to top a vertical standing stone with a horizontal slab, thereby causing future generations to ponder its meaning. This dolmen appears to be slightly disreputable, standing in a puddle of melting gritty snow as if it had publicly relieved itself.

For the dance the area is cleared of its obstreperous geese and exudes a distinctly festive air and a bold theatricality. Large torches stand about the courtyard, and the nearby bonfire gives the battlements of the old house an eerie effect. "Flames danced on the snow and sparks exploded in the frosty air" (*DF,* 71). With all the authority of a Maori tiki, the Mardian stone stands, mute, imposing, and shining in the torchlight. It is behind the stone (which, according to ancient legend, had been an altar for sacrifice) that Andersen's body is discovered. Yet far from enhancing the mystery of the place, the murder and the subsequent painstaking investigation, together with the daylight, reveal its dismal shabbiness: "The swept-up snow, running away into dirty water, was much trampled, the courtyard itself was greasy and the Mardian dolmen a lump of wet rock standing on two other lumps. Stone and mud glistened alike in sunlight that merely lent a kind of pallor to the day and an additional emphasis to the north wind" (*DF,* 94). Marsh's descriptions of the Mardian village and the manor courtyard are among her most potent, second only to the New Zealand novels in which landscape and place are as powerfully present as a character, and therefore directly concerned with the destiny afoot.

Although the village and the castle provide the most vivid displays of Marsh's colors, descriptions, and atmosphere, other locations in South Mardian reinforce the sense of depression. Copse Forge, where William Andersen and his five sons labor, first appears through "twilight and desolation"—the nearby trees and hills covered with a monotonous blanket of snow. The red glow from the forge "pulsed on the walls," creating a "deceptive welcome" (*DF,* 24), but the cold, hostile reception given the visitor by William Andersen more accurately mirrors the exterior chill. When William dies and his sons gather to lay out their murdered father's body and search for his will and his wealth, the forge becomes claustrophobic. The sons are "crammed together in a tiny kitchen-living-room in the cottage. . . It was a dark room." Later they are "bunched together in their cold smithy redolent with cold iron, stale sweat and old tobacco" (*DF,* 147). William Andersen's room likewise reflects the sense of closeness and "oppressive clutter." The walk to it is carved out between piles of litter, and the

room, itself, is tiny and heaped up with junk, especially old newspapers and
smelly boxes. Here Marsh combined her geographic awareness of place with
such a palpable sense of space that the very air feels heavily laden with snow,
odors, and suspicion. Even the village pub fails to dispel the heavy
blackness—Marsh describes it as "a singularly unpretentious affair, lacking
any display of horse-brasses, warming-pans or sporting prints" (*DF,* 31).
There is little of comfort or coziness here, despite the presence of the most
likable character in the novel, Trixie Plowman, the publican's daughter. Her
easy sensuality offers a pleasant counterpoint to the repressed propriety, stiff
class consciousness, and addle-brained and twisted familial loyalties of the
other characters. But even Trixie's natural warmth fails to thaw the frozen
landscape and the characters' dispositions.

As Alleyn travels to South Mardian, he compares a murder investigation
to a thaw. When the police first consider a case, "everything's covered with a
layer of cagey blamelessness. No sharp outlines anywhere. The job itself
sticks up like that partial ruin on the skyline over there, but even the job
tends to look different under snow. Blurred" (*DF,* 84). It is the policeman's
job, he continues, to produce the thaw. Alleyn, Fox, Thompson, and Bailey
step out into South Mardian in "grey slush. . . . They were left with a still-
ness broken by the drip of melting snow." Alleyn and his minions do not
produce the thaw in the murder case quite so quickly, but as they uncover
more and more information, they do so against the counterpoint of the
thaw. The murder scene, previously so frightening by torchlight, is now
simply wounded ground with a "tang of dead fire" on the air and a "patch
of scarred earth, damp now, but bearing the scar of heat" (*DF,* 98). The
characters gloomily contemplate the "dripping landscape." For the episode
when Alleyn meets the man who happens to be the murderer, Marsh returned to her references to cold and added some nice reprises of claustro-
phobia. At Simon Begg's garage Alleyn notes that, "in spite of the thaw, the
afternoon had grown deadly cold. Yowford Lane dripped greyly between its
hedgerows and was choked with mud and slush" (*DF,* 130). The garage itself is a "disheartened-looking shack," and Begg leads them inside to a
"choked-up cubby hole that served as his office" (*DF,* 173). It is at this interview that Alleyn begins to sense the truth.

To test his hypothesis, he calls for a reconstruction of the dance program,
including all the performers and essential witnesses. Marsh's images were
still bleak but with some subtle changes. On the day of the reconstruction,
"the mid-winter sun smiled faint as an invalid over South and East
Mardian" (*DF,* 217). This invalid's smile, however, lifts the spirits of the
characters and gives them an odd sense of resurrection. That evening at

Mardian courtyard, as Ernie Andersen lights the torches again, the firelight "dramatize[d] the attentive focus of the onlookers" (*DF,* 252), those very folk who had earlier been heartened by the pale sunlight. The sky is clear, and the "stars exploded into a wintry glitter. There was frost in the air" (*DF,* 253). It is the most beautiful and active description of winter landscape in the book. When the dance resumes, Marsh, as director/producer, sets her stage and light cues: "The archway gaped enigmatically upon the night. Smoke from the bonfire drifted across the background and occasional sparks crossed it like fireflies. It had an air of expectancy"(*DF,* 269). Through this personification, landscape, architectural space, and fire become characters either "gaping enigmatically" or waiting expectantly for the final revelation—the murderer's identity. Marsh did not disappoint; she stripped away his disguise, unveiling answers to the enigmas of who, when, and how in the murder of William Andersen. In *Death of a Fool* Marsh displayed a new mastery of her medium. Though in *Scales of Justice, Clutch of Constables,* and her other rural English mysteries, landscape is a valuable ally in setting the tone and pace, the characters always move through place without actually engaging it or uniting with it. In *Death of a Fool* place and space are characters fully integrated into the action. Marsh did indeed go beyond Dickens's plea "Make me see!" to make her readers feel and smell and hear and touch this winter landscape. *Death of a Fool* is as sensory an experience as the New Zealand novels.

Chapter Four
Characters: The Dress Circle

In *Murder for Pleasure* Howard Haycraft comments that Marsh's "power of characterization is excellent," but he believes her to be more powerful in her social analysis of contemporary manners.[1] Although one can agree with his evaluation of Marsh's skill, one can also argue that his distinction between novels of manners and character is artificial. Other critics analyzing Marsh's work have lamented that she sacrificed her substantial talent as a novelist to the rigors of formulaic detective fiction. In her best novels, however, Marsh transcended those categories to which the critics assigned her and blended colorful personalities with a precise sense of place to produce a detective novel of manners. Her characters and plots, which were revealed almost exclusively in lively dialogue, portrayed many segments of English society, from its sophisticated London "season" to its rural working-class roots. As she led Alleyn through his list of suspects, she created few "stock" characters; rather, she explored behavior and motive through close attention to individual qualities. She never forgot, however, that her characters, some of them certified eccentrics, operate within the boundaries of social pressures, and that a murder investigation heightens such stresses and reflects them, often revealing distortions in personalities and social mores. Marsh so successfully joined the elements of character and manners with the detective yarn that she provided a link between the older traditions of Charles Dickens and Wilkie Collins and the more recent writing of Agatha Christie.

Of all of the characters Marsh created, none was as important as her detective, Roderick Alleyn, through whose eyes others are measured and tested. He was her central consciousness in thirty-two novels, and she never wearied of him. She set out to create as "normal" a man as possible to feature as her detective. She never changed his personality and never found him boring. By adopting this approach, she avoided Conan Doyle's famous feud with the public over Sherlock Holmes, or more modestly, Agatha Christie's confession that Hercule Poirot grew tedious. Alleyn contrasted distinctly with Margery Allingham's Albert Campion, who was a strange young man for a hero, and Dorothy Sayers's dashing Peter Wimsey (with whom Sayers is reputed to have fallen in love). Marsh's Alleyn, though certainly not an "average" man and not without his quirks, has a personality and a life that ressemble the life of an upper middle–class professional. Despite Jessica Mann's contention in *Deadlier Than the Male* that Alleyn does not change, develop, or indeed age very much in the series of novels, it can be said that Marsh presented a man in whom many different aspects of character are revealed.[2] She employed facets of his personality to make subtle observations and commentary on the social milieu.

It was immediately apparent in Chief Detective Inspector Alleyn's first appearance in *A Man Lay Dead* that he was a man with a sardonic wit bordering on the fatuous. Asked by an underling why he is excited, Alleyn responds, "You've guessed my boyish secret, I've been given a murder to solve—aren't I a lucky little detective?" (*MLD*, 60). His wit endures throughout the novels, growing more gentle after his marriage to Troy. Readers of the earlier novels might, however, envision him as a bit of a nervous oddity when he confesses a distaste for asking suspects for fingerprints because it makes him feel "self conscious." In *Enter a Murderer* he leaves headquarters asking, "Am I tidy? . . . It looks so bad not to be tidy for an arrest." (*EM*, 145) When one of his chief suspects sarcastically asks, "What sort of breed are you? . . . Gentleman 'tec or the comedian of the Yard or what?" Alleyn responds, "My dear Mr. Saint, you make me feel quite shy." " 'Ow you-you-you,' Saint echoed the inspector's pleasant voice with the exasperated facetiousness of a street worker. 'All Oxford and Cambridge and hot air,' he added savagely. 'Only Oxford, and that's nothing nowadays,' said Alleyn apologetically" (*EM*, 51). Ask forgiveness as he may, Alleyn is at times unbearably smug and supercilious in his earlier incarnations.

At the same time, however, Marsh insisted that he be a dedicated detective and a healthy, virile male. He is the only active professional policeman among the creations of the "Big Four" mystery writers of the golden age. Wimsey and Campion, though brilliant and eccentric, are amateur sleuths, and Hercule Poirot is retired; only Alleyn earns his living, at least in part, by "teckery," as he calls it. As a working police officer, he has access to technical assistance in the persons of Inspector Bailey, the fingerprint expert, Inspector Thompson, the police photographer, and his greatest friend and colleague, Inspector Fox.

Before the relationship with Fox was truly developed, Marsh teamed Alleyn with another kind of Watson—the young journalist Nigel Bathgate. It was through his impressions that Alleyn's professional personality and skills were initially introduced, with Bathgate's exposure to a murder and to Alleyn occurring in the very first novel, *A Man Lay Dead*. In that novel Bathgate's cousin Charles Rankin is stabbed to death during a "murder

game." Rankin, a wealthy ne'er-do-well and roué, is done in by his lover's
husband, both for his successful cuckolding and for his brutality dating
back to college hazing. In answer to the predictable question early in the investigation, "Who stands to gain by this murder?" Bathgate, in an excess of
adolescent melodrama, confesses to Alleyn that he killed his cousin for his
inheritance: "My good young man," Alleyn darkly responds, "please don't
muddle me with startling announcements of that sort. It's incredibly silly.
Here are two witnesses to your theatricality. Pull yourself together and leave
me to do my detecting. It's tricky enough as it is, Lord knows" (*MLD*, 75).
The rebuke sobers Nigel, who apologizes. Later, however, observing
Alleyn's painstaking questioning, Nigel opines that he is "slow." He would
learn in the course of this and subsequent novels that the inconsistencies in
Alleyn's character—a heightened sensitivity combined with a disciplined
policeman's mind—are the very keys to his success in solving murders. At
the end of *A Man Lay Dead*, Nigel says to him, "You are an extraordinary
creature. . . . You struck me as being as sensitive as any of us just before you
made the arrest. I should have said you hated the whole game. And now, an
hour later, you utter inhuman platitudes about types. You are a rum'un"
(*MLD*, 284).

Indeed, Marsh did create a "rum-un": a facetious professional detective
with a quotable knowledge of Shakespeare, an Oxford degree, high social
standing, and an intermittent nervous insecurity about his work. In the
interwar years, England was still a nation where birth and class determined
one's accent, status, and opportunities, an era in which "gentlemen," as a
rule, did not enter the police force. Marsh has been accused of creating a totally contradictory background and profession for Roderick Alleyn, yet in
the contradictions lie much of the depth and many of the facets of his character. When Alleyn is introduced in *A Man Lay Dead*, young socialite
Angela North reflects, "Alleyn did not resemble a plain-clothes policeman
she felt sure, nor was he in the romantic manner—white faced and gimlet
eyed. He looked like one of her Uncle Hubert's friends, the sort that they
knew would 'do' for house parties. He was very tall, and lean, his hair was
dark, and his eyes grey with corners that turned down. They looked as if
they would smile easily but his mouth didn't." Angela notices that "His
hands and his voice are grand" (*MLD*, 67). Alleyn becomes friendly with
Angela North and her future fiancé, Nigel Bathgate. In subsequent novels
the young lovers and Alleyn socialize, and though Alleyn treats them with a
certain older-brother type of affection, they all become deeply attached to
each other. Bathgate also involved Angela in murder investigations in *Enter
a Murderer* and *Death in Ecstasy*.

The next time Alleyn's pedigree becomes critical is in *Artists in Crime,* when Agatha Troy meets him and writes to a friend in England: "The subject is a detective and looks like a grandee. Sounds like it, too—very old world and chivalrous and so on. . . . I'm rather on the defensive about this sleuth—I was filthily rude to him, and he took it like a gent and made me feel like a bounder. Very awkward" (*AC,* 12). Indeed, Alleyn is a gent, as the reader discovers in this book; he is the younger son of a baronet whose older brother, George, inherited the title and went on to become a member of Parliament, finally occupying an ambassadorial post. His mother, Lady Alleyn, is an intelligent woman of far-ranging interests who occupies the family estate in Buckinghamshire. Alleyn is slightly embarrassed when his high breeding becomes an issue in a case, even when it enables him to have the insider's view of murder among the elite. He makes light of his connections in a letter to his mother describing a predatory American female who pursues him on the same voyage where he met Troy. He characterizes the lady as "an American beauty who looks people up in Kelly's and collects scalps. She looked me up and . . . seemed inclined to collect ours" (*AC,* 16).

Discomfit him as it might, his social standing benefits Alleyn far more than it inhibits him. In *Death in a White Tie* he is called on to investigate murder among the highest social circles; without the proper calling card his work would have been much more difficult. On interviewing one of his vital witnesses, Mrs. Halcut-Hackett, she gushes to him, "I never realized . . . that I was speaking to Lady Alleyn's famous son" (*DWT,* 225). Though Alleyn utilizes this entry to question her, he writhes inwardly "under his blatant recognition of his snob-value" (*DWT,* 225–26). In *Death of a Fool* Dame Alice Mardian, after ascertaining his social status, provides him with vital clues, having been assured that he is a gentleman. Furthermore, though Agatha Troy is no ordinary snob, it is doubtful that he would have married her, or even met her, without the social distinction that he enjoys.

Marsh used the contradiction of background and profession to comment in subtle ways about the English class system. Unlike Lord Peter Wimsey, who, at the opening of many Sayers novels, is provided with a brief social description that sounds like an excerpt from *Burke's Peerage,* Alleyn leaves his social registry in his repertoire, there to be utilized, if necessary, but never automatically played for effect. He and Fox make a fine team, for Fox, like Wimsey's manservant Bunter, covers the "other" nation, the servants, village folk, and working class who play their part in a murder investigation. By examining the rather subtle tensions along the class boundaries, Marsh portrayed a well-ordered world, with only some gentle jostling of the class issue. This treatment was certainly consistent with that of her fellow golden-age writers, whose protagonists' calling is to investigate wrongdoing, not diagnose social ills. It was also congruous with the spirit of Van Dine's injunctions about keeping the focus on the crime. Yet Marsh pointed up some of the hypocrisy and false pretense that haunted English social manners between the wars—when the comfortable, insular world of the aristocracy and the upper middle class was changing rapidly as a result of mysterious economic factors that were incomprehensible to a nation accustomed to leadership from its landed gentry and great manufacturing interests.

Marsh never made it clear why Roderick Alleyn chose the police force over other more "elevated," or at least more appropriate, professions for his class. Alleyn, himself, offers no explanation. Lady Alleyn refers to it only in passing in letters to her son: "I always feel, darling, that you should not have left the Foreign Office, but at the same time, I am a great believer in everybody doing what he wants to, and I *do* enjoy hearing about your cases" (*AC,* 17). One of the reasons for her concern appears to be Alleyn's excessively sensitive nature. Because his social background prepared him to deal with nothing more serious than a breach of social etiquette, and because his sensibilities and education lead him to oppose the death penalty, the police force appears to be a peculiar choice. It is possible that Marsh, who never dreamed of producing thirty-two Alleyn novels in the course of writing this first group, simply enjoyed her gentleman detective and gave little thought to constructing characteristics that would endure. Like Conan Doyle, who regretted some of Holmes's extremes, and Agatha Christie, who confessed that she created Hercule Poirot much too old, Marsh began with an Alleyn who required modification as time passed and the novels progressed.

Alleyn's affection for detective work fluctuates in the course of the stories. In *A Man Lay Dead* he goes about his work mechanically but with the occasional attack of nerves to which Bathgate refers at the end of the novel. By the finale of *Enter a Murderer,* when he has just charged one of Bathgate's old school chums with murder, Alleyn remarks almost apologetically, "Well Bathgate . . . never make friends with a policeman" (*EM,* 183). By *Vintage Murder* it is clear that Alleyn's nerves are causing him to doubt his chosen profession. He has taken some time off to travel to New Zealand for relaxation; but there he witnesses a murder and, to his initial dismay, finds himself energetically involved in the chase to catch the murderer. In a letter to his faithful subordinate Fox, asking his cooperation in checking out some London leads, he remarks that he could have made his excuses and avoided any contact with the investigation, but "I confess I am surprised at myself and can only suppose that I must *like* 'teckery'—an amazing discovery" (*VM,* 173). At the book's end he also writes to Fox, "Good-bye, you old devil. It must be so exciting to be a detective" (*VM*, 271).

For all his mild discomfiture over detective work, the worst consequences of Alleyn's self-imposed split personality were still to come. In the next two novels, *Artists in Crime* and *Death in a White Tie,* he experiences the strain of conducting an investigation while simultaneously falling in love; in the latter book he is tormented by his apparently unrequited adoration for Troy *and* by having to investigate the murder of a friend. Each of these circumstances intensifies his soul-searching—now his work not only threatens his friend Bathgate's naivete but also his beloved's peace of mind. This is why Van Dine cautioned against love in the detective's life—the distraction, the preoccupation, and the general dottiness of falling in love take away from the pure, cold analysis of the classic detective tale. Marsh may indeed have cast herself in the quasi-romantic tradition in these novels, but by doing so she enriched her books, provided depth in her detective, and entered the realm of the novel of character. Her dialogue stripped away layers of pretense to reveal conflicting emotions, great loyalties, and great motives for murder. In his role as a detective, Alleyn is the provocateur for these revelations, as well as the director of an odd assortment of characters caught in the harsh glare of criminal investigations. His belief in justice carries him through the unnerving task of unraveling testimony by his beloved Troy and members of the social set to which he himself belongs. No matter how unpleasant the task or how offended his sensibilities, he proves his mettle by successfully completing both cases.

Alleyn views himself as a loner and as socially inept with the one woman he wants to impress. When he must investigate a murder that occurred in her artist's studio, he is rigorously efficient as a detective, but his pride and nerves betray him as a suitor. Their first evening together at her home, Alleyn must question Troy about the murder: "They treated each other to displays of frigid courtesy. . . . He thought she was very stiff with him and supposed she resented the very sight of him and everything he stood for." Later, when Alleyn has confessed his love and been refused immediate reciprocity, he tells her: "I think that if we had met again in a different way you might have loved me" (*AC*, 245). Here again, Alleyn is being overly sensitive and wrongheaded about what he assumes is Troy's revulsion toward detective work.

In *Death in a White Tie* Alleyn grows even more morbidly self-deprecating in front of Troy: "If you painted a surrealist picture of me I would be made of Metropolitan Police notebooks, one eye would be set in a keyhole, my hands would be occupied with somebody else's private correspondence. The background would be a morgue and the whole pretty conceit wreathed with festoons of blue tape and hangman's rope. What?" (*DWT*, 245). Troy dismisses his exaggerations and fears about her impressions of him and does gradually fall in love with him. After they are married, he continually assures her and anyone who will listen that he will never allow his work to interfere with her art. This resolve is put to the test several times, since Troy is often present at the scene, perhaps nowhere so directly as in *Black as He's Painted*. Her portrait subject is Bartholomew Opala, an old school chum of Alleyn's who is president of Ng'ombwana, an emerging African nation. Opala's sittings for Troy turn into highly publicized excursions fraught with danger and intrigue and inspire tabloid gossip. The loyal Alleyn snaps: "Look here, Br'er Fox . . . I've done my bloody best to keep my job out of sight of my wife and by and large I've made a hash of it. But I'll tell you what: if ever my job looks so much as coming between one dot of her brush and the surface of her canvas, I'll chuck it and set up a prep school for detectives" (*BHP*, 185). His devotion to Troy and to her art is genuine, as is her devotion to him. Fortunately, Alleyn is never called on to make the choice, even though Marsh paired her "odd couple" on a case together in several novels. Ironically, Troy's art brings Alleyn into the scene of crime far more often than Alleyn's work elicits Troy's direct participation.

For all his sensitivity, Roderick Alleyn is impelled to do his work by his sense of justice. It is that dedication that carries him past his squeamishness, his nervous reactions, and his protectiveness toward Troy. He does not pontificate about his deep convictions—they are left unspoken but tacitly understood. One of his very few references to the dedication required for detective work is made during his investigation of the murder of his personal friend Lord Robert Gospell, an elderly gentleman:

The hunt is up. . . . Have you ever read in the crime books about the relentless detective who swears he'll get his man if it takes him the rest of his life? That's me, Troy, and I always thought it rather a bogus idea. It is bogus in a way, too. The real heroes of criminal investigation are Detective Constables X, Y, and Z—the men in the ranks who follow up all the dreary threads of routine without any personal feeling or interest, who swear no full round oaths, but who nevertheless, do get their men in the end; with a bit of luck and the infinite capacity for taking pains. (*DWT*, 97)

All this dedication is sincere, despite his reference to himself as a "filthy crime dentist" who probes until he causes pain and hauls in someone "wriggling like a nerve on the end of a wire" (*DWT*, 112). He is the ultimate professional—dedicated and exacting. Whether his personal feelings are engaged or not he never allows his passion, or lack of it, to interfere with his job.

It is Alleyn's role as a suitor and married man that most offends detective-story conventions. Van Dine insisted rather firmly that the purpose of an investigation is to lead a criminal to justice, not to lead a couple to the hymeneal altar. Yet lead on Marsh does: Alleyn yearns after Agatha Troy, enduring her snubs with forbearance and finally winning over his lady with kisses in the rose garden of his mother's country house. He is a considerate and patient lover. When Troy shyly submits to his embraces, he restrains himself; with his gentleman's code of behavior, it would have been taking advantage of her vulnerability to press his suit. He wants Troy to come to him by her own, considered, free choice. In *Death in a White Tie* he comforts her when she confesses to a fear of the physical side of love. But Alleyn finally asserts himself with definitive kisses and tells her that he is her mate, and she knows it by the novel's end.

In subsequent novels, Troy is mentioned only briefly, and with the outbreak of World War II, Alleyn is sent away from her to New Zealand. Marsh used the device of repeating and summarizing evidence in Alleyn and Troy's correspondence, allowing him to soliloquize in his letters home much as he does in *Vintage Murder* in letters to Fox. In the absence of a Bathgate or a confidant of some sort, these letters are essential to Marsh's plots and to obeying Van Dine's injunction that the reader be informed of all evidence and peculiarities of character among the suspects. Since Alleyn's work takes him away from home and hearth with rather predictable frequency, Marsh used both the letter device and Alleyn's ruminations to Fox as means of reviewing the facts and thereby advancing the investigation.

Alleyn and Troy, like many husbands and wives, are apprehensive when they are reunited after a long wartime separation. In *Final Curtain* (1947) Marsh secured the future of their marriage, and by *Spinsters in Jeopardy* they have had a son.[3] In thoughts that Van Dine would have abhorred, Alleyn reveals human flesh and a tender heart: as he is reunited with his wife, he reflects on her and his past doubts about whether or not they could recapture the spirit of their love, his fear that the separation would drop between them like a transparent barrier through which they could only stare at each other, feeling love no longer. Upon first seeing her as his ship docks, "his physical reaction had been so sharp that it had blotted out his thoughts. It was only when she gave him the look of intimacy . . . that he knew, without question, he was to love her again" (*FC,* 142).

From this love they produce a child, Ricky, who appears in *Spinsters in*

Jeopardy, set in southern France. The 1952 novel opens with a happy domestic scene—Ricky is sitting for his portrait. Ricky speaks as a precocious
only child might speak; indeed, Alleyn, who is a devoted and gentle father,
wonders "if Ricky was really as pedantically mannered a child as some of
their friends seemed to think" (*SJ,* 24). The child has some exaggerated
fears, and here Marsh may have drawn on her own experience as an only
child who had clung to her parents rather timidly, as she recounted in her
autobiography. She placed Ricky in danger in this novel: he is kidnapped.
In response, Troy is the anxious, almost hysterical mother who contains her
emotions with every ounce of control that she can muster. Alleyn becomes
even more efficiently policelike, controlling his fears through iron discipline.
When they recover Ricky (and Marsh does not leave us in doubt about this
too long since it would have brought the other aspects of the mystery to a
dead halt), Alleyn and Troy act as calm as possible, but beneath their "mature" pose one senses the relief and fear flooding through them. Alleyn
makes light of the fact that he, a professional, has allowed his son to become
caught up in such nefarious goings-on. He banters, " 'Be kind enough, both
of you, to look upon me as a tower of dubious strength.' Troy managed to
grin at him. 'We have every confidence,' she said, 'in our wonderful police' " (*SJ,* 135). Fatherhood brings out in him the same protective air that
would have choked S. S. Van Dine.

   Marsh *was* breaking the rules here. She had given Alleyn not one love interest but two. Both Marsh and Sayers invested their detectives' romances
with a chumlike quality. Sayers's Harriet Vane is portrayed throughout as
rather a gallant young woman with appealing daubs of independence and
vulnerability added to the picture. Similarly, Alleyn comments in several
places about Troy's forelock falling onto her face like a schoolboy's. He frequently observes that Troy has a boyish build, and much of the same inde-
pendence/vulnerability mix is found in her. Even the use of her last name,
Troy, reinforces her androgyny. These characterizations do not suggest sexual peculiarities on the part of the detectives but rather promote the ideal of
male/female equality and kinship. Both Wimsey and Alleyn express great
respect for their mates' courage and strength: each encourages his mates'
separate career; each is tender in falling in love yet mature enough to recognize that a union between equals is the only route to marriage. Marsh, curiously enough, forced her readers to acknowledge the sexual aspects of
Alleyn's union by giving him a son. Although the sole unmarried woman of
the "Big Four" detective novelists, she was the only one to portray the detective's family so prominently in her fiction.

   Several critics have noted that Marsh put much of herself in her creation of Agatha Troy. Physically the two women resembled each other—taller than average, with short, cropped dark hair. Most important, however, both were painters, although Marsh had largely forsaken her painting when she discovered the theater and detective fiction. Marsh spent more time describing Troy's painting, the process by which she creates her canvases, the colors on her palette, and the frustrations inherent in artistic perfectionism, than any other activity outside of the detective work itself. Troy's art plays a role in all her more prominent appearances in nine of the thirty-two novels. It would be difficult to ascribe membership in an artistic school to Troy—she paints landscapes and portraits of those who interest her. At times she apparently follows a more representational style; at others, she seems to rely on an impressionistic use of light. She is recognized as a genius—characters comment throughout the novels about their affection for her work, and a "Troy" is a collector's piece. She has one-woman shows quite often, suggesting that she is prolific. Students, from the early *Artists in Crime* to the later *Last Ditch* (1977), recognize her genius and wish to study with her.[4] She seems to teach as much by inspiration as by instruction, and her students at her country house, Tatler's End, find her kindly but firm. She encourages her fellow strugglers—especially those just beginning. When an unsophisticated young Australian begins to paint like a fellow student, Troy cautions him, "You stick to your own ways for a bit. . . . You're a beginner still, you know. Don't try to acquire a manner till you've got a little more method. . . . Don't choke the pores of your canvas with paint till you've got the big things settled. Correct your drawing and scrape it down" (*AC*, 26). Not only is this good evenhanded advice, it is delivered without pedantry. It sounds like the art teacher–student relations that Marsh would have observed and enjoyed as a student at the Canterbury University College of Art.

For all her skill in communicating with fellow artists, Troy becomes extraordinarily reticent about her own work. In their first encounter it is Alleyn's impression of her art that is recorded: "The sketch was an almost painfully explicit statement of the feeling of that scene. It was painted very directly with crisp, nervous touches. The pattern of blue-pinks and sharp greens fell across it like the linked syllables of a perfect phrase. It was very simply done, but to Alleyn it was profoundly satisfying—an expression of an emotion, rather than a record of a visual impression" (*AC*, 3). When he ventures to compliment it, "she hunched up one shoulder as if his voice was a piercing draught in her ear, muttered something and crawled back to her work" (*AC*, 4). It takes him a good deal of effort simply to get her attention, though he finds himself immediately and intimately drawn to her. Troy, who is rather uncivil to him (though whether she senses the intimacy right away is not revealed until later), is equally ill at ease with her appreciative public:

It always embarrassed her intensely to put in these duty appearances at her exhibitions. People felt they had to say something to her about her pictures and they never knew what to say and she never knew how to reply. She became gruff with shyness and her incoherence was mistaken for intellectual snobbishness. Like most painters, she was singularly inarticulate on the subject of her work. The careful phrases of literary appreciation showered upon her by highbrow critics threw Troy into an agony of embarrassment. She minded less the bland commonplaces of the philistines though for these also she had great difficulties finding suitable replies. (*DWT*, 25)

Through all the novels Marsh emphasized Troy's shy manner, whether in regard to her art or her deepest emotions. The only time she responds unambiguously to her husband is in *A Clutch of Constables* when, unnerved by murder conspiracies while she had been on holiday alone, she runs joyfully into his arms when they are reunited. In her other appearances one senses that Troy is always a bit emotionally distant—not cold-hearted, but preoccupied with her art or her stiff upper lip. She is an interesting character in the historical context—a woman of inherited wealth who nevertheless earns a living, albeit in a rather rarefied profession. She is independent, an example of the "new" woman in many ways; she does not collapse in the throes of a strong love—either before or after marriage. She has a sense of humor similar to Alleyn's but lacks his facetiousness. She knows her Shakespeare and classical allusions and is every bit Alleyn's intellectual equal. She is a gracious person, but not a self-revealing one. Throughout the novels, Troy remains intensely loyal—with only one or two harmless flirtations. She is, above all else, a private person. Though Marsh created many memorable female characters, none of them approaches the interesting complexity of Troy Alleyn.

Troy's most vivid emotional reactions occur almost totally around the danger to her son, in both *Spinsters in Jeopardy* and *Last Ditch*. In the former, Ricky is a small boy doted upon by both his parents but possessing a special bond with his mother. It is his mother to whom he turns when frightened, and it is his mother who comforts him. With his father Ricky enjoys an affectionate, bantering relationship, and it appears to be a good balance for the child. When Ricky is kidnapped, Troy leans on Alleyn in ways that he finds surprising: "Troy stood in the hotel courtyard with her clasped hands at her lips and a look on her face that he had never seen there before. When he took her arms in his hands he felt her whole body trem-

bling. . . . 'He's gone,' she said, 'they've taken him. They've taken Ricky' "
(*SJ*, 89). As Troy tells Alleyn the circumstances of their son's disappearance,
emotions, heretofore unsuspected in her, surge to the surface. "She made a
great effort to be lucid . . . but every word was shadowed by a multitude of
unspoken terrors." Her terror is so great "that it was accompanied by physical pain. . . . Her heart rammed against her ribs and she suffered a disgust-
ing sense of constriction in her throat. Sweat poured between her shoulder
blades and ran down her forehead into her eyes. She was in a nightmare"
(*SJ*, 90). In many ways this would be the normal response to so great a fear
and shock, but it was highly unusual for Troy, in whom Marsh had created
such emotionally muted reactions. In a much later novel, *Last Ditch,* Troy's
deepest instincts are again touched when Ricky is injured. Alleyn breaks the
news to her in as calm and positive a manner as possible, but despite his re-
assurances she immediately books a flight and leaves to care for her son. It is
as though her tenderest feelings, which she does not allow herself to experience for any adult, even her husband, become activated by her child.

Ricky Alleyn merits such love from his parents, and though they worry
about his formalness and his shyness as a child, they also recognize that he is
quite precocious. Were it not for his flashes of childlike spontaneity, it
would be tempting to accuse Marsh of having created merely a little adult;
though she portrayed Ricky as extremely well mannered, she allowed the
little boy in him to come through. After reading Marsh's account of her own
life as an only child, it is tempting to see some of her fears and fantasies
transferred to Ricky. In *Last Ditch* other characters allude to Ricky's just
completed, brilliant career at Oxford. He has set out to be an author, and
here we see the pain and pleasure of Marsh's writing career mirrored in
Ricky's struggles. Despite his artistic bent, Ricky cannot resist a little amateur sleuthing when a mystery presents itself, in the process providing
Alleyn's cue to appear with Fox and rescue his son from foul play. Ricky is
successful at sniffing out wrongdoing but is far too unskilled to protect
himself from harm. Just as he is seduced by mystery, he is also bewitched by
an intriguing married woman. Although all is very proper between them,
the situation presents Marsh with the opportunity to explore all the obsessive mania of a naive young man's attractions.

One critic has remarked that Marsh allowed the action in her novels to
grow from psychological tensions. Surely there are no human connections
more tenuous and more tense than those generated by intimates—family
members especially. Of the "Big Four" women detective novelists of the
golden age, Marsh created this relationship most completely in Roderick
and Troy Allen and their son. A great irony, which she toyed with through-

out the novels, is that though Alleyn worries quite openly that his work will
interfere with Troy's art and constantly tries to keep his family away from his
implicitly distasteful profession, it is far more common for them to draw
him into a case. In six of the nine novels in which she plays a major role,
Troy's connections and her art take her into a world where Alleyn must then
follow and solve a murder. In Ricky's two novels he becomes enmeshed in a
mystery, and in *Last Ditch* he is responsible for his father's appearance and
for official police action. Alleyn's family provided Marsh with the solution
to a nagging structural problem—how to involve him in solving crimes
among his own social circle and how to bring him on the scene to witness
the crime before an official policeman would normally have been summoned. Often it is the information and impressions gained before the murder that later bear a direct influence on solving it. Beyond mere devices,
however, Troy and Ricky add another dimension to Alleyn's character. Had
he remained the brittle, sardonic man Marsh created in her first five books,
the man who lacked the leavening experiences that would have evoked his
gentler instincts, he would have been far less interesting over the course of
thirty-two novels. It was, indeed, Marsh's gift for endowing her creations
with lively qualities, from their manner of dress to their mannerisms of
speech, that ensured for her a reputation as a novelist of manners and not
merely as a writer of clever puzzles.

In addition to his family, Alleyn has another group of intimates who provide comradeship in his early single days and assistance in solving his murders. The first of these is a young journalist, Nigel Bathgate. Bathgate is
featured prominently in three of the earliest novels and remains a valuable
ally and source of information in several others. Like Troy and Ricky,
Bathgate involves Alleyn in solving the crime in *Enter a Murderer* and
Death in Ecstasy. In Bathgate's first appearance, in *A Man Lay Dead,* he is
a guest at the house party where his cousin is murdered. Nigel is twenty-
five-years-old, fresh out of Oxford and ambitious to succeed on Fleet Street.
He is callow and inexperienced in worldly affairs and yet ideal for the role of
a Watson for the same reason Watson was—he is intelligent and honest.
Bathgate sees events and draws conclusions that the average observer would
have drawn, thus allowing the genius/detective to use him as a foil. He is
first described to Angela North, whom he will later marry, as a "fine, clean-
limbed young Britisher" (MLD, 15–16). When Alleyn appears at the party
after the murder, his first impression of Nigel is of a conventional and even
foolish young man who, in exasperation, confesses to the murder while
overlooking his own ironclad alibi. Bathgate's impression of Alleyn is of a
foppish aristocrat whose painstaking and detailed questions bore the nimble

and impulsive younger man. It is not until they encounter each other seeking to rescue the same bit of evidence that some mutual respect begins to build. Alleyn makes the first overture when he asks Bathgate, "How would you like to be a detective, the lousiest job in creation?" and adds, "Well, you can have a start at it since you're so eager. Every sleuth ought to have a tame half-wit, to make him feel clever. I offer you the job, Mr. Bathgate—no salary, but a percentage of the honor and glory" (MLD, 167–68). By the close of the book they are becoming friends.

Bathgate's role might have developed along different lines had Marsh followed the design she created in *Enter a Murderer.* She began with the narrative concept that Bathgate had written this book as an account of Alleyn's adventures in capturing a murderer. The device of a Watson recording the ruminations of the great detective may have been tempting to pursue, but she never repeated this strategy. In the succeeding books Bathgate and Alleyn continue to spar a bit; the latter is still being portrayed at his most facetious. Bathgate is no match for Alleyn, however, because he has simpler loyalties and a less complicated psyche. He assists Alleyn in the murder investigation, which results in an old college chum of his being indicted for two homicides.

Actually, Bathgate is grateful for his friendship with the famous Roderick Alleyn. In *Death in Ecstasy,* when he calls Alleyn in on another murder that he witnessed himself, he gets a scoop from his friend, only partially censored to suit the Yard. Still, Alleyn twits him a bit over the youthful naivete and open-eyed wonder that had prompted Nigel to venture into the bowels of the "House of the Sacred Flame," where the murder occurred. In their conversations during the investigation, when Alleyn gives Bathgate certain privileges by allowing him to tag along, they parry: " 'I feel like a form master who goes in for favorites.' 'Oh sir, thanks most horribly, sir. It's frightfully decent of you, sir,' bleated Nigel. 'For the honor of the Big Dorm, Bathgate.' 'You bet, sir' " (*DE,* 151). Despite the easy bantering, Bathgate is always evaluating Alleyn. He watches his friend and thinks: "He isn't in the least like a detective. . . . He looks like an athletic don with a hint of the army somewhere. No, that's not right: it's too commonplace. He's faunish. And yet he's got all the right things for 'teckery.' Dark, thin, long. Deep set eyes—" (*DE,* 153). Nigel and Angela North give the most complete descriptions of Alleyn that Marsh allowed in these first four books. They emphasize his aristocratic background, his unusual but striking good looks, his facetious side, and his grim determination to solve the crimes that cross his path. Such easy intercourse is possible because Alleyn, Bathgate, and Angela all belong to the same social class. It is to Alleyn's distinct advantage to be a member of the lower aristocracy—he can command respect and cooperation from suspects and witnesses in this still hierarchical society, and those who resent his social class would as likely have resented his position with the Yard in any case. The ease and charm of these young society people, as they take murder with a certain savoir faire, is the result of centuries of privilege and the self-assurance that it brings. Bathgate's friendship with Alleyn is a useful device for Marsh's purposes in that he helps describe and project certain of Alleyn's qualities. Nigel is a Watson-like narrator who provides appraisals of Alleyn's deductive powers, helps involve Alleyn in the resolution of the crime, and provides information and gossip picked up in unofficial circles. Finally, the Bathgate-Alleyn friendship helps emphasize certain truths about the nature of English society; for instance, even though these two Oxonians are working in professions not ordinarily associated with their class, they still receive the rank and status accorded the leisured classes. Like Wimsey and Campion, they have the indefinable air of "gents."

Had Marsh confined Alleyn to these circles and friends, he would have remained a rather rarefied "new breed" at the Yard, with his esoteric quotations and nervous sensibilities. His class background and his eccentricities might have overwhelmed him and seriously limited his appeal. Marsh refused to allow this; as she distracted Bathgate with the demands of matrimony, she began to expand the role of Alleyn's police subordinate, Edward Fox, "Alleyn's right-hand man: unambitious, contented, courageous, efficient and marvellously communicated from the very first."[5] It was unclear in the beginning, however, how companionable Marsh would allow Alleyn to become with Fox. In *A Man Lay Dead,* Detective-Constable Bailey appears to be the closest thing Alleyn had to a police confidant. Throughout the course of the novels Bailey will be kept in the stable of characters as a fingerprint expert whose clever work and deductions continue to assist Alleyn. By her last novels Marsh had promoted Bailey to the rank of detective-sergeant and, together with his cohort Thompson, the police photographer, they have grown "grey in the service."[6] When Fox appears in *Enter a Murderer,* he and Alleyn seem to have a somewhat uneasy relationship. Alleyn is still at his sardonic, affected best, and Fox appears stolid by comparison. In a rather fatuous exchange, Alleyn reports to Bathgate that he is playing detective, looking for clues, " 'little signs of footprints, little grains of sand. Fox, my valued old one . . . wing your way to Miss Vaughan's dressing room and get the foot of my grandmother's hare which you will find on the dressing table. Fetch me that foot and be thou here again 'ere the Leviathan can swim a league' " (*EM,* 63). Alleyn appears to be playing to Bathgate's literate foil in this conversation, and doing Fox an injustice in the process. When Alleyn demonstrates his prior knowledge of some facts that Fox has just unearthed, he does so in an airy, offhand fashion. ' "Very good, sir,' said Fox formally. 'And don't be cross with me, my Foxkin. You're doing well—excellent well, i' faith.' 'Is that Shakespeare?' 'What if it is? Away you go.' 'May I stay?' asked Nigel, as Fox went off. 'Do!' [said Alleyn]" (*EM,* 63). There is an air of condescension that would disappear from Alleyn's character before the next novel. Had it not, Alleyn would never have earned Fox's profound respect and affection, as he does, and would not have been likely to have asked Fox to be his son's godfather, which he does.

In *The Nursing-Home Murder* the Alleyn-Fox friendship appears far more easy and intimate.[7] Fox has interviewed the wife of the recently deceased home secretary. When she speaks of going to the prime minister with her request for an inquest, Fox urges her not to do so until he has spoken to Alleyn. She responds, " 'Alleyn? I think I've heard of him. Isn't he—' She paused. Cicely O'Callaghan had nearly dropped a brick. She had been about to say 'Isn't he a gentleman?' . . . Fox answered her very simply. 'Yes,' he said, 'he's rather well known. He's a very highly educated man. Quite a different type from me, you might say' " (*NHM,* 58). His complete lack of rancor and resentment deserves better than the crisp superiority with which Alleyn had treated him in the previous novel. In their first scene together in *The Nursing-Home Murder,* the tone is very different. " 'Hullo, Brer Fox,' said Alleyn, looking up from his desk. 'Where've you been in your new bowler? . . . Sit down and have a smoke. You look perturbed' " (*NHM,* 60). When Alleyn listens to Fox's story of Mrs. O'Callaghan's insistence on an inquest, he dismisses it as an exaggerated fear that she and others have of an anarchist plot. " 'I've no real faith in the British anarchist. Anarchist! The word is *vieux jeu.*' 'I suppose that's French?' 'Quite right, Fox. I always said you had a flair for languages.' 'I'm teaching myself with the gramophone. All the same, sir, these anarchists are no joke' " (*NHM,* 61). Fox is beginning to emerge as Alleyn's right hand, the voice of caution and working-class conservatism. Their mutual loyalty develops such depths that in the future Alleyn will encourage Fox to expand his education, while Fox will become Alleyn's professional anchor, as Troy is his personal anchor. Even though Alleyn sums up his cases for Nigel and Angela Bathgate, the emphasis has shifted to Fox in some significant ways.

By the time Alleyn travels to New Zealand for the first time and gets involved in *Vintage Murder,* he writes home to Fox affectionately with his same old flashes of wit but with far more warmth. In the forest scene with Carolyn Dacres, she comments about her husband's kind and understand-

ing nature and confesses that she loved him most because she never had to
"show off" for him. Alleyn responds that he has someone in his life who accepts him that way. Dacres thinks he is referring to a wife, which elicits a
laugh from the serious detective. No, he assures her, he is speaking of a colleague, Detective-Inspector Fox, who is deliberate and innocently candid.
He accepts Alleyn in all his moods and never expects to be entertained. In
this novel it is a letter to Fox that allows Alleyn to explain the method by
which he has deduced the killer's identity and what happened once he did.
Not only has Fox provided him with some vital information from London,
but also it is to Fox now, not the clever Bathgate, to whom Alleyn opens his
heart about his impressions of the new country and his excitement at the
discovery.

Alleyn even defers to Fox in *A Wreath for Rivera*. In this novel some of
Marsh's favorite elements were mixed together—upper-class eccentrics,
London's social scene with the "smart set" of Sloane Square, murder, and
the drug trade. Fox has been following a line on the drug traffic independent of his responsibilities to Alleyn. When the two investigations
intersect—Alleyn's murder inquiries and the drug trade case—Alleyn
steps aside for Fox's interests. In addressing Sir James Curtis, the surgeon
who does the postmortems for the Yard, Alleyn makes the division of
labor clear: "Sorry to drag you out, Curtis . . . but we may need you opinion on his fitness to make a statement. This is Fox's party. He's the drug
baron" (*WR*, 196). When the police confront their suspect, Fox issues the
warning. The suspect looks to Alleyn and whines, " 'What's the idea . . .
shooting this chap on to me? What's wrong with talking to me yourself?'
'Inspector Fox,' Alleyn said, 'is concerned with investigations about the illicit drug trade. He wants some information from you' " (*WR*, 197).
Alleyn has truly learned to appreciate his slow but steady colleague.

Appreciate Fox as he might, Alleyn appears never to have known very
much about him. Fox's background remains obscure. He is as he appears—
a hard-working and patient policeman. Where Alleyn is brilliant, Fox is
painstaking; where Alleyn shines, Fox is always unobtrusive. These qualities
and contrasts are underlined when Alleyn invites Fox into his and Troy's
home for a few hours' sleep, a bath, and a shave in the midst of the long
hours of questioning and chasing clues. Always the modest and somewhat
formal friend, Fox starts off to the bathroom with his compliments to Mrs.
Alleyn. It is a few moments later when Alleyn looks in on him: "He found
him lying on the visitor's room bed, without his jacket but incredibly neat;
his hair damp, his jaw gleaming, his shirt stretched tight over his thick pec-
toral muscles. His eyes were closed but he opened them as Alleyn looked in.

'I'll call you at half-past nine,' Alleyn said. 'Did you know you were going to be a godfather, Br'er Fox?' " (*WR*, 144). Alleyn has just paid his friend *his* highest compliment—the guardianship of his child. Marsh created a bond between these men that would only deepen with the passage of time, and Alleyn's marriage enhances the alliance because Troy is so obviously fond of Fox and recognizes his deep loyalty to her husband.

For the remaining seventeen novels Fox is a constant, and if he is not physically present, both Troy and Alleyn miss him. In his duties with Alleyn, Fox provides inestimable service. As Alleyn notes, Fox could disappear behind a mask of blandness while taking notes and observing every detail of a witness or a suspect's behavior. Very often when the two of them enter a room together, Fox almost literally does disappear into the background. Fox also provides a running commentary of wrong conclusions, enabling Alleyn to dispute them and thereby eliminate suspects and explanations. Each of these disputations is carried out in the kindliest manner possible since Alleyn's old facetiousness and sarcasm have long since disappeared from his personality. Fox carries the investigations into the servants' quarters where, as Alleyn chides him, he never fails to charm the ladies and earn a good meal or a special culinary treat for himself. Frequently the information that he digests there is crucial to solving the crime. Marsh and Alleyn have a bit of fun at Fox's expense as he struggles with his gramophone French lessons—frequently injecting a bon mot pronounced with as much difficulty as if he were trying to crochet lace with his massive hands. He may not be clever, erudite, or graceful, but he never loses his dignity. He is self-possessed and utterly professional.

Fox's personal life remains a blur even to his intimate friends, the Alleyns. The only information on his own history comes out as almost idle conversation during a prolonged stakeout. " 'Dull,' Fox said, 'doing your beat in the city of a Sunday afternoon. I had six months of it as a young chap. Catch yourself wondering why the blazes you were there and so on.' 'Hideous,' Alleyn said. 'I used to carry my *Police Code and Procedure* on me and try to memorize six pages a day. I was,' Fox said simply, 'an ambitious young chap in those days' " (*WR*, 200). Just what happened to modify his ambitions in the force is never made clear. Neither he nor Alleyn appear to have ever won any special commendation for their labor, no matter how spectacularly successful they might have been. Fox may not have ever made the higher ranks, but he is the quintessential professional, sticky about detail and proper procedure.

Ironically, though he tolerates a good bit of eccentric apostrophizing in his chief, he will not tolerate any deviation from form in his subordinates.

When a Detective Sergeant Sallis is reporting to Alleyn and Fox and begins to build an elaborate explanation in a "loud public school voice," Fox interrupted, " 'Get on with your report now. . . . Don't meander. . . . Use your notes and get on with it' " (*WR*, 151). His disgust at verbal excess carries over into his view of policemen who use elaborate disguises. In *Black as He's Painted*, Sergeant Jacks, wearing jeans, a dirty jacket, and "an excellent wig of the Little Lord Fauntleroy type" (*BHP*, 188), sits behind his easel and watches the homes of several suspects from his vantage point out in the open. When Fox is informed of his activities, "he remarked that the painter-chap seemed to be reasonably practical and active even if he did get himself up like a right Charlie. Mr. Fox had a prejudice against what he called 'fancy-dress coppers.' His own sole gesture in that line was to put on an ancient Donegal tweed ulster and an out-of-date felt hat. It was surprising how effectively these lendings disguised his personality" (*BHP*, 197).

Fox's sanity, his professionalism, and his very chameleonlike blandness provide the perfect anchor for Alleyn's more mercurial personality and fastidious temperament. Fox represents what most of the upper and upper-middle classes of the early twentieth century would have regarded as the best of working-class virtues. His loyalty and utter lack of offense-taking in situations where a more sensitive or less secure soul would have bridled at the social snobbery he encounters make Fox the ideal vision of a working-class conservative.

The only event that elicits passion from Fox is finding Ricky bound with wire and gagged on a bed, in a filthy apartment used by two dope dealers, one of them an addict. When Fox sees that his godson has been beaten and savaged in such a way, his outrage and his vengefulness can only be reined in by Alleyn's calm and Ricky's assured survival. When his two tormentors are led from the room, "as they were about to pass the bed, looking straight before them, Fox laid massive hands upon their shoulders and turned them to confront it. Ricky, from out of the mess they had made of his face, looked at them" (*LD*, 200). When Alleyn and Fox prepare to explore the apartment, the suspects have to be searched as well. " 'What about them?' Fox asked with a jerk of his head and an edge in his voice that Alleyn had never heard before. 'Should we wire them up?' " (*LD*, 201). Fox's quiet rage spends itself finally in the ordinary business of wrapping up the case. In the final scene of the novel, Troy and Fox are keeping vigil in Ricky's hospital room. Alleyn returns after the arrest to find them "quietly contented with each other's company" (*LD*, 244). Fox's home and family have become with his chief and his godson, who accept and embrace him as their own.

The hero's confidant and assistant is a traditional role in most forms of literature. In detective fiction the role was almost a necessity in order for the detective to ruminate aloud. Marsh created more than a mirror or cardboard-cutout assistant for her detective. She avoided the sociological as well as the literary stereotype, although the Fox-Alleyn connection explored some of the aspects of class tensions and assumptions that each group might have about the other. In Fox she had, with her usual flair for characterization, created a distinct man in his own right—made specific by her descriptions of his many little personal characteristics; made lovable by his warmth and loyalty; and made memorable by his patient spade work in the cause of justice and the solution of crime.

These are Alleyn's intimates, each of them contributing to his peace of mind and to his conviction that justice is both desirable and possible in a world so often shaded with gray uncertainties. Alleyn's full humanity as husband, father, comrade, and policeman is affirmed and reflected in the relationships that Marsh provided for him. According to the strictest rules of the detective genre, Marsh had overstepped her boundaries here, but in so doing she enhanced the texture of her novels.

Chapter Five
Characters: Supporting Roles

Over the course of thirty-two novels Marsh carefully developed Alleyn and his inner circle of family and friends. They are the constants, recurring in almost all the stories. Their relationships undergo change: for instance, Ricky ages, attends Oxford, and embarks on a creative career. Around the core group swirl a variety of glittering theatrical folk, society matrons, and ingenues, retired men with differing pretensions and selective memories, snobs of all ages, eccentrics, earnest village folk, a rural "natural," physicians—both rural and urban specialists—pairs of young lovers, middle-aged adulterers, the vain, the foolish, the churlish, murderers and victims, suspects and witnesses. Marsh's books never lack for interesting individuals, many of whom were described in such detail and with such a skillful use of dialogue that they engage the reader in their fate. Marsh used her characters to comment on social conditions—but never directly, and always with a humorist's eye. It was in her characters and her description and analysis of them that Marsh illuminated the manners and conventions of the England and New Zealand of her day. Even when her plot becomes a bit artificial or the murderer's motivation is weak, the lives of Marsh's people provide sufficient interest for us to overlook such flaws. Frequently, the murder does not even occur until halfway or more through the book, but the reader seldom misses it because, in the meantime, Marsh was busily plotting the tensions between personalities, and probing the tender psyches of all who become ensnared in the murder and the subsequent investigation.

As a group perhaps the most dominant characters of Marsh's novels after theater folk were the upper-class social set of London, whether enjoying "the season" or attending rural house parties. In several of her novels a murder occurs amid the debutantes, the "smart set," and these characters, who are unaccustomed to unpleasant reality, scurry for cover. In *A Man Lay Dead,* Marsh took Nigel Bathgate to Frantock, the home of "unique and delightfully original house parties" hosted by Sir Hubert Handesley. Among the guests are two very conventional figures of British society: the unmarried roué (here named Charles Rankin) and his married mistress (Marjorie Wilde). Rankin appears to Bathgate to be "getting on in years . . . forty-six or seven" (*MLD,* 11), but women adored him for his looks and his flirtatious charm. He is the complete bounder, disdaining the serious, intense woman who truly loves him and humiliating his mistress's husband in front of the other guests. He is foolhardy both in his affairs of the heart and in his disregard for the effects of his insulting actions on others. Not surprisingly, he is the murder victim, done in, as Alleyn ascertains, by his lover's husband. Marjorie Wilde, married to the scholarly Arthur in one of the great mismatches, reveals her shallowness and artificiality with her "rather high-pitched 'fashionable' voice" (*MLD,* 15), described elsewhere as an "italicized treble." She has little of substance to contribute beyond mundane observations and a rather exaggerated fear of knives and violence. She refuses to read her husband's archaeology books because, according to her, he "butchers [his] pages with native horrors" (*MLD,* 29). Marjorie, however, has "it"—sex appeal, which Rankin could not resist. In a tango they dance together, Nigel finally understands her raw sensuality:

There are some women who, when they dance, express a depth of feeling and of temperament that actually they do not possess. He saw that Mrs. Wilde was one of these women. Under the spell of that blatantly exotic measure she seemed to flower, to become significant and dangerous. Rankin, rapt and serious, was at once her foil and her master. He never took his eyes off hers, and she, unfriendly, provocative, stared back at him as though she were insulting him. (*MLD,* 50)

This is precisely the kind of defiant sexual invitation, unmistakable to those watching the dance, that often marks such torrid affairs.

Marsh examined similar society women and their relations with men in two other novels, *Death and the Dancing Footman* and *Tied up in Tinsel.* In the former, Marsh created the beauty expert Madame Lisse, a woman similar to Marjorie Wilde. All the men notice her, but the only one who objectively and most closely analyzes her qualities is Aubrey Mandrake, not as young or as naive as Nigel Bathgate but occupying the same position in this novel as Bathgate in *A Man Lay Dead.* When Mandrake first sees Lisse, he perceives a woman subtly groomed with sleek dark hair and a beautifully complected oval face: "Her mouth alone proclaimed her art, for it was sharply painted a dark red. Her dress was extremely simple, but in it her body seemed to be gloved rather than clothed. She was not young . . . but she had to the last degree the quality that Mandrake . . . spoke of and thought of as 'soignée' " (*DDF,* 47). Her greeting to Nicholas Compline, later revealed as her lover, is "coloured by that particular blend of composure and awareness with which Austrian women make Englishmen feel dangerous and delighted" (*DDF*, 47). Madame is the "sort of woman whose natural habitat was the center of a group of men and, with the utmost tranquility she dominated the conversation" (*DDF*, 48). Nicholas, unlike Rankin, ultimately murders his own brother, though he manipulates events so that a series of threats appear to have been made against Nicholas himself. He responds to ladies' charms, like Rankin, with a sort of "defiant showmanship." "He stood beside her in an attitude reminiscent of a Victorian military fashion-plate, one leg straight and one flexed. Occasionally he placed one hand on the back of her chair, while the other went to his blonde moustache" (*DDF*, 47–48). Nicholas, however, lacks Rankin's amatory sangfroid, and he turns into a blithering schoolboy when he tries to persuade Lisse to elope with him. His decision to murder his older brother evolves from his conviction that if he inherits the title and family wealth, Lisse will indeed have him. His obsession with her is his undoing, as Rankin's obsession with seduction is his. Seducers as a rule do not fare well in Marsh's novels—witness Sir Derek O'Callaghan in *The Nursing-Home Murder* and Luke Watchman in *Death at the Bar* (*1940*)—both murder victims.[1]

The other great seductress Marsh painted (and Troy Alleyn refuses to), is Cressida Tottenham in *Tied up in Tinsel*. She attempts no unnerving of other males, but she controls her fiancé Hillary Bill-Tasman through her explicit sensuality. She certainly has little else to recommend her. In a match as ill conceived as the Wildes', Bill-Tasman, who is both an aesthete and a sophisticate, is determined to play country squire and, therefore has become engaged to a lady who looks the part of chatelaine. Cressida is so elegant "that her beauty seemed to be a second consideration: a kind of bonus, a gloss. . . . When her outer garments were removed, she appeared to be gloved rather than clad in the very ultimate of expensive simplicity. . . . She was very composed and not loquacious, when she did talk she said 'you know' with every second breath" (*TT*, 45). Though her speech is so imbued with slang as to render her virtually inarticulate, and her manners border on the vulgar, she holds Bill-Tasman enrapt. She appears for dinner dressed in a "metallic trousered garment so adhesive that her body might itself have been gilded . . . in molten gold. She looked immensely valuable and of course tremendously lovely" (*TT*, 55–56). Troy senses the sexual bond between Hillary and Cressida, who finally kills her servant father to hide her lowly origins and protect her engagement. Such highly placed women were accepted in polite and well-to-do society, and each of them plays the role of femme fatale, sometimes quite literally. Marsh seemed to enjoy these characters: they are not automatically condemned to being loathsome, unlike their male counterparts. Each serves to move the plot along by contributing to the tension their actions produce.

If these women linger too long in the ranks of coquetry and do not develop substance of character or depth of wisdom along the way, they become sad and ridiculous. Marsh saw as pathetic the older woman who attempts to manipulate others by her physical appeal alone. In what would have been her own middle age, Marsh created one elderly and two middle-aged vamps, all of whom continue to seek their fulfillment through manipulating men. The two youngest, Kitty Cartarette in *Scales of Justice* and Mrs. Dillington-Blick of *Singing in the Shrouds (1958)* are in their last years of successful seduction.[2] Kitty, whose thoroughly decent husband Maurice treats her with a bewildered courtesy because he cannot understand why he married her, takes up a flirtation with their neighbor George Lacklander. He is rather obtuse and falls "into a muddled, excited dotage upon her" (*SJ*, 51). "She told him repeatedly how chivalrous he was and so cast a glow of knight-errantry over impulses that are not usually seen in that light. She allowed him only the most meager rewards, doling out the lesser stimulants of courtship in positively homeopathic doses" (*SJ*, 23). The flirtation is noticed with some anger by George's mother, who quite correctly sees Kitty Cartarette as a common sort of schemer but never imagines her as a murderer. Like Cressida Tottenham, however, Kitty Cartarette longs for more: prestige and a title that her reasonably well-off husband cannot provide. It is she who murders Maurice, with the intent of becoming Lady Lacklander. Marsh described her as "so fair without her make-up she would have seemed bleached. Her figure was well disciplined and her face had been skillfully drawn up into a beautiful cared-for mask. Her greatest asset was her acquired inscrutability. This of itself made a *femme fatale* of Kitty Cartarette. She had, as it were, been manipulated into a menace" (*SJ*, 23). A menace indeed, and a murderer. Without her charms, however, the tensions leading to such an extreme act would have been muted. Like the other ladies of this sort, Kitty Cartarette stokes the fires of middle-aged passion and, because at that age new love or excitement can seem to be "the last chance," her doing so has an air of desperation.

In *Singing in the Shrouds* Mrs. Dillington-Blick occupies the role of middle-aged siren. Far less lethal than Kitty or Cressida, she is also less interesting. This novel, in fact, strays from Marsh's traditions—it contains Alleyn and some of her favorite types, but the motivation for murder is far different. Marsh dipped into a psychological study—complete with oedipal complexes. At large is a serial murderer who, it turns out, murders women whose names are associated with jewels. Mrs. Dillington-Blick has, in one of

her fanciful moods, dressed as the Spanish dancer Esmeralda, or "emerald."
This is enough to trigger the killer's obsession. In fact, Alleyn sets the events
in motion by flattering Mrs. Dillington-Blick into cooperating. He knows
just the note to strike with this vain, aging woman. "He found her, still re-
clining on the verandah and fanning herself, enormous but delectable.
Alleyn caught himself wondering what Henry Moore would have made of
her. . . . 'You look as cool as a cucumber,' Alleyn said. . . . 'You dress quite
beautifully, don't you?' 'How sweet of you to think so,' she cried delight-
edly. 'Ah!' Alleyn said leaning towards her. 'You don't know how big a compliment you're being paid. I'm extremely critical of women's clothes . . .
and yours are clever enough to express the charm of their wearer.' 'Now I do
call that a *perfect* remark! In the future I shall dress 'specially for you. There
now!' promised Mrs. Dillington-Blick" (*SS*, 181). Alleyn has charmed the
charmer, for so many of these women, whether good or bad, measure themselves by their superficial attributes—clothes, makeup, masks and second
skins. These are their stock-in-trade. There is no depth or substance to
them, only the mirroring of the fantasy that they project—the sensual, always available, and sexually cooperative woman. That they do commit
crimes is always a shock, it is so contrary to the fantasy image. Playing men
like they would stroke a musical instrument, they scheme and manipulate
through their flattery. Using woman's oldest weapons to obtain "unwo-
manly" goals of power, influence, and money, they are fundamentally dishonest but such an ingrained part of the culture that their presence and their
ancient bag of tricks still enflame a Charles Rankin or a George Lacklander.
As they grow old these women become insubstantial, possessing only out-
moded charm and incapable of being attractively packaged. They cast no
shadow, they are nothing but illusion.

When in Rome provides a chilling portrait of an aged seductress. Lady
Braceley, who accompanies her nephew Kenneth Dorne to Rome, is one of
the most pathetic creatures in Marsh's gallery. Marsh referred to this aunt
and nephew as older and younger versions of the same wasted image. Lady
Braceley is very careful to "examine the precarious mask she still presented
to the world" (*WR*, 28). As attentive as she is to her looks, however, she cannot hide her age successfully. Alleyn notes, "The face was not too good. . . .
Even if we discounted the ruches under the eyes and the eyes themselves,
there was still that dreadfully slack mouth. It was painted the fashionable
livid color, but declared itself as unmistakably as if it had been scarlet: the
mouth of an elderly maenad" (*WR*, 40).

Despite her sagging looks and the ravages of her indulgent style of living,
Lady Braceley believes she maintains her seductive abilities. When she is in-

troduced to Alleyn, she shakes his hand and looks beseechingly into his eyes. Alleyn finds himself revolted by her suggestive behavior, recognizing the bathos but eager to be rid of her limpetlike attentions. But Lady Braceley must cling—it is all she knows how to do, since she is aware of no other reality beyond the reflection of herself that she sees in men's expressions. In two startlingly grim passages, Marsh let Lady Braceley's damaged and vacuous qualities show through the windows to her soul; she wrote, "Lady Braceley . . . let her ravaged eyes turn from one man's face to another" (*WR,* 44), and, "Lady Braceley turned her huge deadened lamps from one man to another, eager to respond to whatever mood she might fancy she detected" (*WR,* 50). Lady Braceley, the famous viper and victim, is not physically murdered but with the assistance of her drug-addicted nephew she takes another step toward complete degradation. She is the final result, the finished product, of one of high society's most vivid nightmares: the wasted woman who has pawned her very soul for the ephemeral rewards of male approval, and who later finds herself bereft of the means to reclaim it. Lady Braceley has been secretly dead for years—by her own hand.

Despite their certifiable status as femmes fatales, as women who quite literally bank on their physical appeal of proffered sexuality, none of them ever kills out of jealousy. Here Marsh gave the lie to the old cliché that women claw each other's eyes out in order to dominate masculine attention. With her usual irony and sense of humor, Marsh assigned that role to the two distinctly "non-fatale" women in *Overture to Death.* Eleanor Prentice and Idris Campanula are iron-willed, sexually repressed spinsters, yet theirs is the real crime of passion, perhaps because their natural sexual instincts are so denied. The two "old maids" are descended from the two oldest families in the area. Prentice is of direct Jernigham lineage, of the county squire Jernighams of Pen Cuckoo House. Idris Campanula lives at the Red House in Chipping, her wealth inherited from a father who was quite successful in business. They represent the best of county society, in both blood lines and money. They claim to be best friends but are in constant competition for the domination of county good works and for the affections of the naive rector, Walter Copeland.

The physical contrast between the two women, and between them and the other Marsh women, could not be more marked. Whereas the femmes fatales exude sexual fantasy and thereby stir conflicting passions around them, Eleanor and Idris repress all suggestion of sexuality and, like energy turned inward, such repression stirs deep conflict within them. Marsh described Eleanor Prentice as "a thin colorless woman of perhaps forty-

nine years. She disseminated the odor of sanctity. . . . Her perpetual half-
smile suggested that she was of a gentle and sweet disposition. This faint
smile caused many people to overlook the strength of her face, and that
was a mistake, for its strength was considerable. . . . [Her] prominent grey
eyes stared coldly upon the world through rimless pince-nez" (*OD*, 18).
Her rival and most deadly competitor, Idris, is her physical opposite, "a
large arrogant spinster with a firm bust, a high-colored complexion,
coarse grey hair, and enormous bony hands" (*OD*, 18). Her manner is also
far different; whereas Eleanor displays a mincing walk and a false modesty
of speech, Idris "was one of these women who pride themselves on their
outspokenness. The truth was that she reserved to herself the right of
broad speech, but would have been livid with rage if anybody had replied
in kind" (*OD*, 19).

Throughout the novel the tension between their artificial civility toward
each other and their jaw-snapping, claw-sharpening ill will fuels the plot.
Appearing at a fete before the entire village, Idris is the victim of a bizarre
and deadly booby trap: she is shot in full view of the audience while playing
the piano. When she depresses the soft pedal, a string that is attached at one
end to the batten and at the other end to the trigger, is pulled taut, causing
the pistol to discharge in her face. Alleyn's probing unearths the two wom-
en's carefully concealed hostility. Their jealousies and their grand passions,
their fantasies and their repressions, would have startled their beautiful
counterparts in other novels. These two women are driven by furies that
would have frightened Cressida Tottenham, who is at best a languid murderer. Accustomed as she is to various plots and counterplots, even Madame
Lisse would have found their middle-aged, ugly-duckling snarling ridiculous. As Alleyn discovers, Eleanor, driven to desperation by what she mis-
takenly regards as her rival's ultimate success with the rector, cleverly utilizes
for her nefarious purposes what had begun as a harmless joke set with a
child's water pistol. Her opportunism is reminiscent of Kitty Cartarette's
murder of her husband; but Eleanor's motive springs not from avarice but
from obsessive emotions finally exploding.

As Marsh so correctly reckoned, older women experience the tumults of
frustrated emotion much more deeply than the young. In most of her books
there are a pair of lovers who, following the classic tradition, fall in love, encounter a barrier to their match, and persevere to form a union. Shakespeare
used this device repeatedly in his comedies. It is the very stuff of romantic
entanglement, and Marsh made good use of it to spice up her detective
stories. The barrier, whatever it may be—family disapproval, most
commonly—never drives these resilient young people to murder. Marsh

suggested that even in the throes of intense youthful devotion there is a healthy optimistic detachment, but that in older women romantic/sexual fantasies become tainted with neurotic possessiveness. Even when the couple does not consummate their love—and this is rare—there is little rancor in their failure.

In thirteen of her novels Marsh threaded young love through her story. The most famous of these romances is, of course, between Roderick Alleyn and Agatha Troy. Alleyn meets Troy in *Artists in Crime* and wins her in *Death in a White Tie*. They are married by *Death and the Dancing Footman,* and parents by *Spinsters in Jeopardy.* Though Alleyn is scarcely young at the time he courts Troy, she is in her twenties and there are elements of awkwardness in their initial contacts, characteristic of the less experienced. Nigel Bathgate and Angela North manage a far more decorous and successful courtship from their first acquaintance in *A Man Lay Dead* to their marriage before *Vintage Murder.* Marsh occasionally employed the Shakespearean comedy convention of the clever and strong-willed young woman who waits impatiently while the obtuse young man matures or awakens to love. In *Death in a White Tie* Bridget O'Brien and Donald Potter offer a classic example of this kind of relationship, and with some modifications in form, the same purpose is filled by the romances of Carlisle Wayne and Ned Manx in *A Wreath for Rivera,* Camilla Campion and Ralph Stayne in *Death of a Fool,* Anelida Lee and Richard Dakers in *False Scent* (1959), Emily Dunne and Peregrine Jay in *Killer Dolphin,* and Sophy Jason and Barnaby Grant in *When in Rome.*

The romances in all these books offer more than a pleasant diversion from the murder investigation, for these characters and their love affairs entwine with the main puzzle in ways that offer clues, produce red herrings, and complement the action. The romances provide, as they adhere to the ancient rituals of courtship, the reminder that life does go on even in the presence of brutal death. Alleyn often remarks to himself that, though these young lovers may have been shocked and saddened by the murder, their real concern quickly returns to each other. They are insulated by youthful optimism and the natural high spirits of those as yet unburnished by love's disappointments. Such sentiments are echoed in *Death of a Fool* when Alleyn and the local doctor interview Camilla Campion. As the book opens, she has been reunited with her estranged grandfather, only to witness his murder a short time later. In the midst of the investigation, Camilla is distracted by her need to rehearse her vocal exercises for drama school and also by her elaborate flirtation/withdrawal with Ralph Stayne, the local solicitor. As Alleyn and the doctor watch the conflicting emotions entrap Camilla, the latter comments that "an infallible sign of old age is a growing inability to understand the toughness of the young" (*DF,* 153). To Ralph's protest that Camilla is really quite sensitive, the doctor agrees that she is "perfectly enchanting." It is simply that "her perfectly enchanting little inside mechanisms react youthfully to shock" (*DF,* 153). After the shock and horror wear off, Marsh left little doubt that these couples, whose bonds are forged in the fire of murder investigations, move into the future together.

In *Death of a Fool* Camilla and Ralph represent not only young lovers but also the tensions of class consciousness that still permeated English rural society. Camilla is the granddaughter of the South Mardian blacksmith, William Andersen. Her mother married "above herself," and worse still, married a Roman Catholic. For this she and her child have been shunned by her humble relations in a fever of reverse snobbery. Camilla is reluctant to make her engagement to Ralph a formal one because she is "village" and he is descended from the local aristocracy and related to Dame Mardian of "the manor." Ralph sees this as no obstacle to their betrothal, but Camilla does. Marsh explored some sensitive nerves in the English psyche, not quite evolved beyond the deep class divisions of previous centuries. Dame Mardian and William Andersen oppose the match for the same reason, which each instinctively and historically understood—marriage between the classes is an evil omen to this older generation steeped in deference to the values of the landed aristocracy.

In examining class distinctions in a twentieth-century Britain that had not yet shaken off the vestiges of past ideas, Marsh created several fastidious males who personify the ideals of gentry and high-born folk. Moving through their cloistered aristocratic world, these men, usually advanced in years, lament the transformation in their society that is slowly turning them into anachronisms. With great sensitivity, and avoiding the two extremes of parody or sentimentality, Marsh, a compassionate observer, portrayed their struggles to resist changes that they interpreted as signs of decay.

In *Death in a White Tie,* Lord Robert, known by the Dickensian last name Gospell, observes the rituals and manners of the Edwardian gentleman. Marsh even alluded to his looking like Mr. Pickwick. He wears an opera cloak as his evening dress, and a soft, wide-brimmed hat. In style he would have looked quite at home at an 1890s soirée, and the doors of high society are all open to him, not only because of his title but because of his kindly, avuncular interest in everyone. He is the perfect confidant for many great ladies, with none of the catty effeminacy that this role often implies. He is courtly to the less charming woman, whether debutante or household staff member. He uses *ain't* and drops the *g* on *ing* words, a popular speech pattern among the wealthy and titled (see also Peter Wimsey's conversations). His ideas about art are conventional and old-fashioned, as Agatha Troy discovers at her one-woman show when he pronounces that he likes "clean" pictures. He has distinct ideas about gentlemanly conduct; after paying several large debts for his wastrel nephew Donald Potter, he cuts off the young man's allowance. Young Potter has fallen in with a bad lot who gamble excessively, and Bunchy (as Gospell is known among his friends) wishes to break his nephew's habits and discourage his ill-advised social connections. Perhaps because of his own extensive friendships, he is respected as a sound judge of character—especially by Alleyn, for whom he performs some services that assist Scotland Yard in tracking down a blackmailer. It is in this service that Bunchy is murdered when his activities are discovered. Moments before his murder a weary Bunchy, dispirited by his nephew's behavior and his discoveries of blackmail, bastardy, and adultery among his high society friends, "suddenly felt as if an intruder had thrust open all the windows of the neat little world and let in a flood of uncompromising light. In this cruel light he saw the people he liked best and they were changed and belittled. . . . He saw . . . no honesty or ambition . . . unscrupulousness . . . pomposity . . . and . . . stupidity. How many of these women were what he still thought of as 'virtuous'?" (*DWT,* 68). Lord Robert wonders whether his own "proper" past era has been "no more than incidents in the history of society and if their proprieties had been as artificial as the paint on a modern woman's lips" (*DWT,* 69). In *Death in a White Tie* Marsh quietly opened the drawing room door onto the secrets, misery, and shallowness of those involved in the debutante season in London.

Another Marsh creation, Percival Pyke Period of *Hand in Glove* (1962), would have firmly defended the values of the Victorian-Edwardian era had he conversed with Lord Robert Gospell on the subject.[3] Mr. Period is indeed a "period piece," for by the time Marsh developed his character he is more out of sympathy with modern times than Bunchy would have appeared in 1938. Mr. Period is writing a book of manners, and the examples of his wisdom date him more effectively than his conventional sporting prints, silver-framed photographs, or well-thumbed copies of Debrett, Burke, Kelly's, and *Who's Who.* His chapter headings are "The Ball Dance," "Trifles That Matter," "The Small Dinner," "The Partie Carre," "Addressing Our Letters and Betters," "Awkwiddities," "The Debutante—Lunching and Launching," "Tips on Tipping," and "The Compleat Letter-Writer." His young typist, Nicola Maitland-Mayne, is amused by his rather childish humor and his little formalities. Mr. Period is also given to abbreviation and slang: "diffy" means difficult, and "begatteries" refer to genealogical descent. He loves to discuss family connections, especially his own high birth through the Pyke line, and to gossip about the indiscretions of the aristocracy. With her usual irony and twist of plot, Marsh arranged for Alleyn to discover that P. P. P., as he comes to be known, actually falsified the parish register of births and deaths to provide his pedigree. At first it appears as though this might have been a motive for murder, but the innocence of the blameless Mr. Period remains assured and his one guilty secret undisclosed.

Hand in Glove may have been Marsh's most pointed novel of social tension. With Mr. Period at one end, she ranged over the spectrum of social classes and the relations between them. There are the eminently respectable and conservative servants of Mr. Period, Alfred Belt and Mrs. Mitchell, who have long tolerated his snobberies because, like Bunchy, he is essentially a kind employer who treats them well. They plan to marry after leaving service and entering retirement, and they disapprove heartily of Harold Cartell, Mr. Period's housemate, who is murdered. Cartell had earned his income and possessed the manners of a middle-class professional man rather than the refinement they attribute to their master's high breeding. Most offensively, Mr. Cartell and his dog interrupted their accustomed routine when he came to share Mr. Period's house. Their irritation grows throughout the novel, but their motives for wishing him dead certainly lack the passion of others. When Alleyn, in a general review of the facts, includes them as suspects, several of his upper middle–class listeners sigh in relief that here at last are suitable suspects—people not from among their own class. Alleyn finds their reaction, the "veiled eagerness" with which they accept this solution, most unpleasant. He scotches their enthusiasm moments later when he tightens the noose of guilt on the victim's sister, Connie Cartell.

Though the servants might have despised Harold Cartell, he and his sister occupy quite secure positions in the upper-middle class because his profession of law is acceptable in the social scheme. Connie is one of the gruff women whom Marsh created so well. Like Eleanor Prentice and Idris Campanula, she is unmarried, awkward, and physically unattractive but cares passionately for her adopted child, Moppett. It is for Moppett's sake that she kills her brother, because he had uncovered the fact that Moppett and her disreputable male friend Leonard had stolen a valuable cigarette case from Mr. Period. She also attempts to kill Mr. Period to quiet the scandal. Like an outraged harpie, she strikes at anyone who threatens her precious child.

Moppett seems scarcely capable of eliciting such passionate commitment. She is a manipulator who instinctively recognizes her guardian's vulnerabilities and plays on them. Alleyn can barely restrain his contempt as he watches this game played by Moppett, who is "conceited, shifty and complacent . . . without scruple or compassion" (*HG*, 110). She has been indulged in her every wish by Connie Cartell and has become a brittle "modern girl" turned monster. She seems totally in the thrall of Leonard Leiss, whom everyone but Moppett recognizes as a bounder. He appears among county society wearing a "violently checked jacket" that "displayed an exotic amount of shirt cuff and link" (*HG*, 29). He has a sensual look about him, but also a telltale weak chin, greasy hair, and a speech pattern that fluctuates between ill-fitting formality and either "near Americanisms," or "unrepentent barrow-boy" (*HG*, 107). When Alleyn looks at Moppett, he knows the meaning of the Victorian phrase "lost girl," and Fox dolorously predicts that Leonard will be in prison before long. Moppett sees Leonard's visit to her guardian, Mr. Period, and others as a daring attempt to crash county society; that they are being indulged by those who penetrate their ruse never occurs to Moppett. She believes that she and Leonard are living dangerously. By book's end her shallow loyalties and maliciousness are amply documented, and her determined effort to shock is successful. Without Connie Cartell's support and protection, wrong-headed and obsessive as it might have been, Moppett and Leonard appear condemned to follow a dissolute lifestyle.

Another social type that Marsh examined in *Hand in Glove* was Desirée, Lady Bantling. An outrageous woman who prides herself on breaking the mold of proper society, Desirée has, however, acted within the matrimonial boundaries that Moppett abhors and defies. Her first marriage earned her a title, which, as a widow she retained during her brief second marriage to Harold Cartell. Her present marriage to Bimbo Dodds (who is described by one character as "a rather negative, fashionable, ambiguous sort of person" [*HG*, 145]) represents a distinct drop in status from that of her first two husbands. None of these social disasters, however, cost Lady Bantling her sense of humor. Looking on Moppett and Leonard with an amused and completely knowing air, she sits chain-smoking and listens to their flattery and stories created to win them an invitation to her evening party. Perhaps she recognizes social climbers so easily because she has married one in Dodds. She presents a mask of inscrutability to these two: "It would have been impossible for anyone to say what she thought of them. Her ravaged face, with its extravagant make-up, and her mop of orange hair made a flagrant statement against the green background of her chair" (*HG*, 44). Yet Desirée has no trace of meanness in her; she forgives slights quickly and has a good heart. Even P. P. P. dotes on her for, though socially improper and defiant, she is a loving gentlewoman beneath it all. This is the lesson that

Moppett misses—the key ingredient in those who are worthy of respect in the highest circles is a spirit of generosity and tolerance rather than title or connections. In this novel Marsh skillfully analyzed the false snobs, the lower bounders, the impeccable servants, and the eccentric aristocrat. Under the glare of a murder investigation their strengths and defects are ruthlessly exposed. In her own ironic way, she had examined the issues of personal quality and the nature of real respectability, revealing that there are no noble creatures here, all were flawed by secrets and fears of discovery. It was the detective story itself that enabled Alleyn to serve as a social surgeon, skillfully cutting into the body of pretensions and excising the fatal growth. Whether the patient, social conventions as Marsh knew them, would survive, was in serious doubt.

Besides Mr. Period, the other great snob Marsh created is Hillary Bill-Tasman in *Tied up in Tinsel*. The novel opens with his recitation of his parentage and fortunes to Troy Alleyn, who has been commissioned to paint his portrait. Although he makes no secret of the hard times his family has been through, or the fact that they bought their way back into social standing by hard work in trade, he also assures her that the trade prospered so well that as a paying student he attended the same private school as his father. By diligence and hard work, furthermore, he has become known as the European expert on Chinese ceramics. This is a fine English success story: the old landed class losing money in one of the economic slumps (perhaps the 1870s or the 1880s, Bill-Tasman is not specific), selling off the land, the manor house, and all the valuables, and then, through tenacity and skill, being restored to economic favor. Hillary Bill-Tasman carries on his father's successful antique business and by chance wins two national lotteries that enable him to buy back the family estate and house. The house, Halberds, suffered great damage in the decades of neglect but is being restored under its proud new master. Bill-Tasman insists on a restoration that is historically faithful and is determined to hold sway over county affairs in the manner of an eighteenth-century squire.

Bill-Tasman's ambitions pose a problem that would have daunted a less creative man: the familiar difficulty of the twentieth-century Englishman, who wishes to enjoy the amenities of a former age, finding suitable, affordable household staff. Halberds is located in a rural area of England, possibly Dorset. Even Bill-Tasman's considerable fortune cannot restore the house and pay the inflated salaries necessary to attract servants to this remote area. The solution lies just across the valley in the maximum security prison known as the Vale. Hillary Bill-Tasman simply offers to employ any paroled or released prisoner for decent wages, thereby hiring a household staff

made up entirely of murderers who, he insists, killed only once under extreme stress and are not average thugs but intelligent, if nervous, sorts.
When a murder occurs on the premises, however, it is easy for all the house
guests to conclude immediately that one of the staff has again gratified a
blood lust. Respectable upper-class English folk do not accept the idea that
one of their own could commit a heinous crime, especially if there are servants on whom to fix the blame—and Bill-Tasman's are completely vulnerable to such a charge.

The murder, it turns out, hinges not on Bill-Tasman's "social experiment" with murderers but on his social arrogance. Having become engaged
to Cressida Tottenham, his uncle's ward, Hilary takes great pride in pro-
nouncing that she is of a lineage suitable for his chatelaine. Cressida believes
it, too, and indulges herself and her fiancé in fantasies of her obscure but
aristocratic past. When she discovers that her father is Alfred Moult, servant
and former sergeant to her guardian, she is horrified. Although she has little
understanding of Bill-Tasman's county society, she is determined to learn
and to play the role of lady of the manor. Knowledge of her lowly birth
would ruin her chances, so she quickly kills Moult to avoid such an embarrassing disclosure. Marsh was clear in her indictment of the snobbery and
sex appeal underlying Hilary and Cressida's proposed union, which has
nothing of substance that might have helped it survive such a crisis. Cressida
instinctively knows this and kills as she has lived, flailing to survive in shallow water.

Bill-Tasman's drive for social propriety affects his relations with his
neighbors as well. Wishing to appear the generous, almost feudal overlord,
he arranges an elaborate Christmas ritual for the neighboring folk. The
adults are to enjoy cocktails and supper and the children are treated to a
druidical Father Christmas who distributes presents to each of them. It
would be tempting to regard this as an expansive gesture, but other parts of
his character suggest that he is playing the role of grand seigneur with a certain amount of egotistical condescension. Although innocent of the crime,
Bill-Tasman, like Percival Pyke Period, contributes to the possibilities for
wrongdoing by his single-minded, narrow standard for evaluating worth in
others, and ultimately in himself. Marsh implies that those characteristics,
extended to society at large, encourage envy, malice, and social hypocrisy.

As if to temper the more serious tones of social criticism that run
throughout her novels, Marsh introduced some of the most delightful eccentrics in modern fiction. From the mildly off-center to the madcap, she
peopled her books with lovingly sculpted, unadulterated, whimsical individuals. The presence of these folk reflected the English reputation for pro-

ducing the "compleat individual" with a totally singular view of the world. None of these characters is insane, none is out of touch with reality, each merely has his or her own particular angle on it. Sometimes they are from families such as the Lampreys in *Death of a Peer* or the Ancreds in *Final Curtain*. Most of them amuse Troy and Roderick Alleyn, but occasionally they outrage anyone who has more conventional views. More often in Marsh's books, it is the unusual individual who is tolerated by his bemused family and neighbors. Never are any of these characters murderers, which raises the question as to what behavior is normal: the flamboyant eccentric or the apparent conformist who erupts into homicidal rage?

One of Marsh's earliest descriptions of a humorous eccentric was in *Death at the Bar* in 1940. She wrote about the people of Ottercombe, a remote fishing community where the rare intimacy of the village pub persists. At the Plume of Feathers, George Nark, a regular and a prosperous local farmer, loves to expound his views of capitalism, scientific government, evolution, and self-education. In Mr. Nark's expostulations, all these rather complicated themes that he has absorbed from Winwood Reade, H. G. Wells, Charles Darwin, and Karl Marx become inextricably mixed and garbled. These serious ideas "had, with the passage of time, become transmuted into simplified forms which, though they would have astonished the authors, completely satisfied Mr. Nark" (*DB*, 52). He defends what he regards as his sophisticated understanding of these issues and philosophies by memorizing a dictionary. To Alleyn's astonishment, Mr. Nark announces that he has absorbed fifty-eight million words: "Nigh on it. Not reckoning twice-overs. I've soaked up four hundred words, some of 'em as much as five syllables, mind you, every night for the last forty years. Started at the age of fifteen. 'Sink or swim.' I said, 'I'll improve my brain to the tune of four hundred words per day till I passes out or goes blind!' And I done it" (*DB*, 197).

He reports that the *Evvylootion of the Spices (sic)* took him a year to master, but from there he went on to every branch of science. When asked to recall the fatal evening, he harangues Alleyn with his personal view of the solution to the murder. In the midst of his almost indecipherable and wandering comments, Alleyn does ferret out a clue, but it is a tiny gem amid a verbal rock slide. George Nark gives an early indication of Marsh's sense of humor, her ability to capture a wonderful rural raconteur, her sensitive ear for dialect, and her blending of the comic with the serious business engaging Alleyn.

In *A Wreath for Rivera* Lord Pastern represents yet another kind of eccentric—the self-indulgent peer whose rampages through popular causes and public idiosyncrasies drives his proper Edwardian-style wife to utter despair and distraction. She lives with him only periodically, for his moods and passions are often beyond her capacity for tolerance. In the opening pages of the novel she, in a tone that suggests wry humor and perhaps a sort of artificial despair, explains to her niece her difficulties in adjusting to her husband's interest:

I found myself confronted in turn by Salvation Army Citadels, by retreats for Indian yogis, by apartments devoted to the study of Voodoo; by a hundred and one ephemeral and ludicrous obsessions. Your uncle has turned with appalling virtuosity from the tenets of Christadelphians to the practice of nudism. He has perpetrated antics which, with his increasing years, have become the more intolerable. Had he been content to play the pantaloon by himself and leave me to deplore, I should have perhaps been reconciled. On the contrary he demanded my collaboration. (*WR*, 2)

Lady Pastern recites her woes and embarrassments at her husband's hands, yet she confesses that silence bores her; where he is, noise is, so she continues to live with him. By the end of the novel Lord Pastern has played in a popular jazz band and is revealed as a secret "advice to the lovelorn" columnist. When Alleyn confronts him with some of the facts of the murder, including some of his own activities that have thwarted the investigation, Lord Pastern shouts that someone must stir things up. Alleyn remains calm and tolerant as His Lordship rants and curses cautious police procedure. As the solution to the crime is laid out for him step by step from such procedure, Pastern reluctantly gives ground on his own theory. Finally convinced, he abruptly grins and asks Alleyn if there are age limits on becoming a detective. This shocks even the patient Alleyn, who makes a hasty exit.

Unlike Mr. Nark, Lord Pastern is not a relatively passive commentator, for he participates in the events leading to the murder. His peculiarities and demands help to pressure the murderer to act. Lord Pastern remains one of the most energetic and delightful of all Marsh's eccentrics, not content to sound off at his local pub like Nark but insisting on being in the midst of all the confusion and on trying to arrange all the outcomes.

In *Scales of Justice* Marsh painted a much quieter portrait of eccentric cat fancier Occy Phinn. Phinn lives in Swevenings, in the Cheyne valley, a peaceful rural setting of great beauty and outward tranquillity. All is not tranquil within Occy Phinn's breast, however; his son's suicide many years before had unsettled his wits, but not to the point of insanity. He is disturbed to the extent that he has forsaken most of the pleasantries required by human society and has withdrawn into his family of felines, whom he frets over in maternal fashion. He is especially attached to Mrs. Thomasina Twitchett, a mother to several kittens whom she alternately nurses and ignores. Phinn constantly exhorts Thomasina to behave in a more responsible manner, but she merely rolls on her back to have her belly rubbed. Phinn, in the manner of a Victorian aunt, fusses, saying, "Thomasina . . . hold your body more seemly" (*SJ*, 34). His appearance is quite peculiar; his tattered old smoking cap with a tassel is wont to fall into his face when he grows agitated. Over his cap he cocks his reading glasses, which he removes and uses as a baton to accompany his verbal sallies.

Phinn is indeed peculiar, but he is no fool. Obsessive as he may be about his cats, he nevertheless maintains a wry sense of humor, makes perfectly lucid observations, and has a secret shrewdness that Alleyn uncovers in the course of his investigation. Phinn has known for years that the local squire betrayed Phinn's son, bringing on his son's suicide, yet he remains quiet, withdrawn into his feline fantasies and unembittered. At the story's end he and the traitor's widow, neighbors for many years, have forgiven the past's dreadful shame and secrets and have reached rapprochement. For all his scattered thoughts, Occy Phinn is heroic in restraint and far more noble than his titled and conventional neighbors.

A similar contrast exists in Hillary Bill-Tasman's aunt and uncle. Known as Aunt Bed and Uncle Flea, they appear to be slightly dotty in their ideas and personal habits but are a stable and loving couple. Having had no children of their own, they took Bill-Tasman under their wing when he was a boy, and they accept the shallow Cressida Tottenham as a ward at the wish of her father, who yearns to see his daughter have the advantages of wealth and status they could give her. Their unselfishness elicits tenderness and loyalty from Bill-Tasman, who regards them as surrogate parents. With a tone of bemused affection, he describes their habit of using ancient green umbrellas to avoid the direct morning sunshine. They travel with all their jewelry, a good deal of which Aunt Bed sprinkles liberally over her bosom and wears all at once. They also carry most of their stocks, bonds, and important documents in a metal box that is placed under their bed at night. They talk incessantly, constantly sharing each day's events and impressions; they enjoy a truly intimate union and mutual interest in each other's well-being. Like Occy Phinn, they have a nobility that transcends the limited and self-indulgent Bill-Tasman and the vicious amorality of Cressida Tottenham.

Marsh created so many lively characters that it is difficult not to savor each of them in turn. It is possible to group certain kinds of people together from her various novels, but she gave each such specific qualities that none can be reduced to types or "the mixtures as before." She created, for example, physicians as varied as Dr. Te Pokiha, the Maori dignitary; Sir Daniel Davidson, the fashionable society doctor who is discovered to be a murderer; Dr. Otterly of Yowford, a general practitioner and fiddler for ritualistic folk dances; Dr. Ali Baradi, a surgeon with ties to the illicit drug trade; and Dr. James Mordant, a coroner who "saw human beings as mere playgrounds for brawling micrococci" (*DB*, 73). She also portrayed the occasional lawyer who oversees the probate of the deceased's will and is a valuable resource for Alleyn's investigation. One who recurs in several novels is Mr. Rattisbon, a member of an old and respected firm of solicitors. He has a precise personality, a humorously described speaking style, and occasionally shows a flash of dry, professional humor. Alleyn appreciates both his discretion and, very often, his help. Rattisbon's son, also a solicitor, makes an appearance in *Grave Mistake* (1978), a late novel. Although younger, he and his father both "behaved as if they were character-actors playing themselves in some dated comedy. Both had an extraordinary mannerism: when about to pronounce upon some choice point of law they exposed the tips of their tongues and vibrated them as if they had taken sips of scalding tea. They prefaced many of their remarks with a slight whinny" (*GM*, 72). Doctors, lawyers, ex-military men, a few businessmen, and one extraordinary priest in *Singing in the Shrouds* wend their way through Marsh's murder mysteries. Each was carefully drawn with individual mannerisms, often in the form of peculiarities of speech, noted in full.

It was through these characters, who became living individuals at Marsh's skillful touch, that she explored the manners and mores of twentieth-century British society. A fragment of social truth is exposed in their attitudes and actions toward one another. From the femme fatale and her machinations to the socially elitist males who make Burke's or Debrett's their missals, Marsh examined the social milieu that produced and nurtured their fantasies of blood and power. Her pairs of lovers—youthful, naive, and full of hope—are initiated into the ethically gray by the murder investigations. Although she did not disillusion them too severely—they are left with most of their youthful resiliency in place—she did darken their vision and temper their trust. Marsh was extremely sensitive to older women as well, understanding the eruptive passions of the middle-aged as compared to the more elastic emotions of younger people. Her eccentrics are typically noble, if highly individual, sorts. They are not social iconoclasts, merely people with a slightly different view of reality, and their truth is often more valid than that of those who rigidly conform to the expectations of others.

While no honest critic could ever argue definitively that an author cre-

ated characters directly from life, consciously designed to represent an attitude or class, Ngaio Marsh painted such a convincing social tableaux, with
characters of such profound depth and vibrant color, that the psychological
tension virtually crackled among them. This tension, arising out of their
personalities and their stations in life, reflects much on their creator's world,
a world that was being transformed from a more traditional and comfortable hierarchical society into one with a newer, less certain structure. Marsh
never analyzed or instructed, but she created completely credible and fascinating characters who, by playing their roles so skillfully, do "hold the mirror up to nature."

Chapter Six
Theater: Murder on the Marquee

Throughout her life, Ngaio Marsh modestly refrained from accepting the celebrity status to which the popularity of her detective fiction entitled her. Indeed, in the first edition of her autobiography she scarcely mentioned her achievements as a mystery writer. In the second edition, published in 1981, she finally yielded to the public's demand that she address those accomplishments. Throughout her life she maintained that her detective fiction embarrassed her intellectual friends, who preferred to see her as the Shakespearean producer/director of the Canterbury University Players. In 1966, when Queen Elizabeth II named her Dame Commander of the Order of the British Empire, she was being recognized for her theatrical rather than fictional contributions. Certainly love for the theater permeated Marsh's being, and it enriched her detective stories in clearly discernible ways. How theater functions in the novels and why she turned so frequently to theatrical people deserves close attention in any critical study.

The most obvious contribution that theater made to her fiction was by providing the setting for five of her novels: *Enter a Murderer, Vintage Murder, Night at the Vulcan, Killer Dolphin,* and *Light Thickens.* There are other novels that do not take place in theaters but are peppered with theater folk: the fledgling actress Diana Copeland in *Overture to Death* and *Death and the Dancing Footman,* Geoffrey Gaunt in *Colour Scheme,* the Ancreds in *Final Curtain,* and the Sommita in *Photo Finish.* These portraits range from warmly affectionate to satirical.

Beyond these obvious examples, however, there was subtle theatrical influence in many of Marsh's other works. In *A Man Lay Dead* the murder is committed during a blackout staged as part of a murder game. The homicide in *The Nursing-Home Murder* takes place in the operating theater. In *Artists in Crime* the victim is a model killed on her stage. *Death in Ecstasy* and *Spinsters in Jeopardy* present murder committed during rites of bogus religious sects steeped in dramatic rituals. In *Overture to Death* a booby trap fells the featured pianist performing before a village play. *Death of a Fool* features the murder of the leading dancer during a folk dance performance. In *Colour Scheme, Tied up in Tinsel,* and *Photo Finish* a murder is committed just after a performance. Finally, *A Wreath for Rivera* and *Black as He's Painted* concern killings that occur during public entertainments. Each of these novels, though set far away from Marsh's backstage world, has the same distinct flavor of crimes boldly committed by and upon famous, infamous, and very visible people, sometimes directly in front of an audience of witnesses.

In each of these three categories—theatrical locale, theatrical folk, and quasi-theatrical settings—Marsh, an intimate of the theater world, examined its boundaries, its temperaments, and its backstage tensions. Surely few events are more suited for dramatic exploration than a single unsolved murder. Massacres and genocide daunt Aristotle's unities, dwarfing attempts at artistic representation of events of such magnitude. Furthermore, as events of the twentieth century have demonstrated, the technical efficiency with which genocide can be exercised often reduces our sense of horror to numb incomprehension. For a woman like Marsh, for whom theater was not merely a place but also a state of mind, the connection between murder mysteries and dramatic structure was irresistible. The theater, like the murder mystery, requires its audience to redefine perceptions of illusion and reality. In a play every energy is bent toward maintaining illusions that resemble reality, whereas in a murder investigation false illusions of innocence have to be dispelled in the interest of justice. Both playwright and detective are holding the mirror up to nature, exploring facets of character, deception, and truth.

Given the range of possibilities, how did Marsh utilize the theater in her mysteries? There are three major functions of theater and its environs as Marsh presented them: to define space, to suspend or measure time, and to illuminate eccentricities of character. In the last, she created motive while honoring the unities of detective fiction that called for a limited group of suspects. In defining space, Marsh conformed to detective story conventions by creating a specifically bracketed environment, one limited in physical size and of limited access through a stage manager. Given the pretensions of the proscenium stage, a room with one wall removed, the space is both confined and at the same time limitless, expanding across the footlights. Yet those footlights also provide a barrier between actor and audience more sacred and unbreakable than any manor house's garden wall. Her skillful evocation of space and time and her sensitive portrayals of theatrical personalities give Marsh's detective novels a unique atmosphere and flavor unequaled by other detective fiction writers of her time.

Her second novel, *Enter a Murderer,* takes place almost entirely in the fictional Unicorn Theater in London's West End. The crime is committed when a climactic murder scene on stage becomes frighteningly real: Felix Gardener shoots Arthur Surbonadier at the end of the melodrama *The Rat and the Beaver.* Much to the horror of all concerned, the victim turns up literally dead, shot not with blanks as rehearsed but with real ammunition substituted by an unknown hand. As Alleyn uncovers the offstage hostility between the two men, their rivalry in love, and conflicts stemming from their college days, he unravels a web of jealousy, blackmail, and illicit drugs. During his investigation, one of the stagehands, Props, is hanged from the backstage gallery. This second murder and its "ineffable effrontery," according to Alleyn, reveal the double murderer's identity. The crimes, the vital clues, and the solution lie almost completely on stage, where the action begins and ends with Gardener exposed as the murderer in both cases.

By the final revelations, the theater itself has become a character in the drama—more intense and real, in fact, than the ephemeral humans who tread its boards. Alleyn and Nigel both sense its personality as they arrive that fateful evening: the silence of the theater is pregnant with shadows of dead plays. Nigel realizes that his mind has slipped from its moorings in reality into his imagination and back again in a confused rapture. He expects "the ghosts of old mummers to step out from behind the waiting doorways and mouth their way intently through forgotten scenes" (*EM*, 80). Yet just as it could be brooding, mysterious, and haunted, the theater could be bright and comforting. When the footlights spring to life, the stage becomes a warm and welcoming place. The very theater itself pulses with life.

Marsh creates a special atmosphere from the first visit that Nigel Bathgate and Roderick Alleyn make to the Unicorn's backstage. They at once sense the indescribable flavor of the "working" half of a theater when the nightly show is coming on. The stage door leads them to a separate place—a separate state of mind. That place is both familiar and strange to outsiders, whose air of excitement and expectancy is tantalized by the theater's peculiar odor: a combination of paint, greasepaint, and dust. This ancient incense wafts through the semidarkness welcoming them to the rites and the shrine of Thespis.

Foreign as the stage world might appear to the observers who sit at a discreet distance from it, the play draws them unwillingly toward it, across the footlights into the intense confrontation of the last scene. They feel rudely propelled across this no-man's-land, the blank space between stage and house, and ensnared in the fury of the fatal scene between Gardener and Surbonadier. As though it senses that real mayhem is afoot, the audience fidgets and then freezes, riveted by the breakdown of its role as observer into that of participant in the action. Nigel feels himself sucked into a vortex of emotions, with the space between fantasy and reality growing smaller and smaller for him until he dreams that he is mingling with the players. Alleyn experiences this, too, but because his sensibilities are more protected, his rational faculties continue to function. He knows that this confusion obscures the ultimate clue. In order to solve the crime, he calls the players back and resets the scene, springing a trap on the guilty man. Only by returning the actors to the stage can they be made to enact the real final scene.

Alert, all sleep banished, the stage is now ready to trap the killer. Just as he murdered Arthur Surbonadier and Props on the Unicorn stage, Felix Gardener trips on his own arrogance and is arrested in the same place. Marsh added her observation that if Roderick Alleyn is interested in dramatic symmetry he should note that the last act of this drama is played out on the stage where it began—appropriately enough, she suggested, for the place that had been the consummate scene of all the action.

She treated the stage of *Light Thickens,* a late novel, in a similar fashion. Here, in a reprise of her theater and characters of *Killer Dolphin,* Marsh created a mystery interwoven with the rehearsals of *Macbeth.* The stage and the play's blocking are again the central focus. Again, one actor kills another in a mock murder scene that becomes chillingly real. The death, by decapitation, does not actually occur *on* stage but just offstage in the wings. Sir Dougal Macdougal, playing Macbeth, is found dead, his body in a dark corner, his head actually gibbeted and brought back on stage for the final triumphant scene. Alleyn is again in the audience. The murderer, as Alleyn ascertains, is fellow actor Gaston Sears, swordmaster-choreographer of the final, brutal duel between Macbeth and Macduff. Sears, in what had to be one of Marsh's weaker motives, is a fanatical believer in the power of the claidheamh-mor, his revered ancient sword of Scotland. When Macdougal fails to show the proper respect for his treasure, Sears, convinced that the sword demands blood for revenge, does the dreadful deed.

In *Light Thickens* Marsh leads the reader through successive rehearsals of *Macbeth.* Director Peregrine Jay exhorts his charges to high passion and horror, while he attempts to mitigate the superstitious beliefs of actors who perform *Macbeth.* As the cast gathers for a read-through, "the stage was lit by working lights, and the shrouded house waited, empty, expectant, for whatever was to be poured into it" (*LT,* 32). What is poured into it are sets designed to accentuate the cold, grim reality of multiple murder —stone staircases, gallows, and a courtyard, all painted in grays and browns tinged with dull red. The final fight between the two rivals is elaborately staged on platforms of alternating heights. Gaston Sears had broken the stage plan down into a complex grid on which the actors had been instructed as to the precise height and degree to which their swords should be raised. Such detailed stagecraft enables Alleyn to check on the cast's movements up to the moment of the murder. Given this precision, it appears more and more impossible that any cast member would have had the time to complete the decapitation and make his reentry for the finale. It remains for the director's sons, attending the play for the first time, to point out that the same actor portraying Macbeth throughout is not the man dueling Macduff at the end. By altering the timing of the murder, the guilty man's identity becomes clear.

Light Thickens is littered with theatrical lore, superstition, and stagecraft, as Shakespeare's darkest play, according to some scholars, is described and played out on each page of the novel. Marsh brought the experience of a lifetime of acting and directing Shakespeare to this imaginary, "perfect" *Macbeth*. She wrote the book in, and revealed the story's layers almost completely through, dialogue. As though to honor the playwright, she presented her novel in a way that most resembled a play, thereby paying tribute to both the theater and its leading dramatist.

Although in *Enter a Murderer* and *Light Thickens* the primary murders are committed in the course of a play on the stage, in *Vintage Murder* Marsh created a subtle variation. Here the murder is committed on the stage but during a post-performance birthday celebration for the company's leading lady, Carolyn Dacres. In one of her famous booby-trap murders, Marsh has Alfred Meyer, manager of the acting company and husband of its star, killed by a falling jeroboam of champagne. As in *Enter a Murderer,* the rigging of and the traffic across a dusty iron walkway in the upper reaches of the backstage area yield crucial information for solving the crime. Alleyn is in the theater both to view the play beforehand and to attend the fatal supper party as a guest. As he begins his investigation, he muses on the depressing regularity with which crime haunts his theatrical visits and wonders if his very presence is a cue for murder. Certainly Marsh did display a predilection for bringing Alleyn in on theatrical crime more often than might normally occur. By setting *Vintage Murder* not only in a theater but also in New Zealand (Theatre Royal in Middleton, North Island), Marsh weaves together her favorite interior space, theater, with her favorite exterior place, New Zealand. The book provides a fascinating counterpoint between the two.

Marsh, who was familiar with the peculiarities of most provincial playhouses in New Zealand, created specific characteristics and atmosphere for her fictional Theatre Royal. She described it as a large playhouse with an audience capacity of one thousand, containing an adequate light system and the standard galleries, ropes, and grids. The stage manager, who is not accustomed to improvising in older, less well equipped theaters, turns up his nose a little at the old-fashioned lighting. Marsh's concrete descriptions of the technical crew's backstage activity bring to life the bustling business side of a touring company's evening performance as they haul in the familiar flats that appear more artificial under the working lights. The crew swarms about the stage and galleries, moving with a sure-footed grace across this different but familiar setting. For the actors and technical staff the playhouse is always the focus-point of the company, but it is a shifting focus-point.

The company in *Vintage Murder* is on tour and, therefore, is likely to "carry their *lares et penates* in a bandbox."[1] Theaters, large and small, well equipped or not, become simply "theater" to actors on tour because once the greasepaint and costumes are unpacked and arranged, the actor feels at home. Carolyn Dacres and her husband attempt to create something of the family atmosphere of the old-fashioned actor-manager's touring company: a sense of common purpose, with shared comforts and discomforts. One of the means by which they hope to foster this espirit de corps is to fashion a space for the community in a common room, an improvised version of the traditional greenroom.

Despite these well-intentioned efforts to maintain intimacy, Alleyn knows that the "family" and the theater atmosphere create protective masks and illusions. He has to pry his chief witness away from them in order to strip off the falsehoods. He concocts a trip out into the country and lures Carolyn Dacres to accompany him on the pretense of providing a respite from the interrogation's intensity. She is not deceived, however, for she sees through *his* illusion and realizes, correctly, that she is leaving one stage only to step onto another. Bantering in theatrical jargon, she comments to Alleyn that the New Zealand landscape is lovely and that it is kind of him to arrange such a splendid set in the vistas of the purple mountains upstage. Ultimately, however, neither can resist the beauty, neither can ignore the "clean" smells and the clear voice of the bell-bird that sweeps away the cacophony of their human dilemma. As Alleyn watches her, she removes her fashionable hat and, by that action, removes her "brave widow" veneer. The Carolyn Dacres who he had seen, vague and delightfully artificial, becomes the exhausted and grieving human being left alone with him. At last he earns her trust and learns the truth about her actions during a critical period after the murder. Both investigator and suspect have been touched and cleansed by this excursion—not into wild and boundless nature (for Marsh is too sophisticated to indulge in a variation on the "noble savage" theme) but by a natural space and place, a stage even, although far different from the structured one they have left behind in Middleton. Alleyn admits to himself that he has deliberately produced a set and created a mood, hoping that away from her protective coloring in the theater Dacres will relax and speak the truth. He has not, however, calculated New Zealand's effect on him: a walk into the forest sets his imagination reeling, filling the silent woods with mysteries, dark-skinned people soundlessly slipping through the trees—reminiscent of Bathgate's fantasies about deserted theaters in *Enter a Murderer*. Alleyn wonders at his lapse—his flight from the harsh reality of his murder investigation—but his creator repeatedly insists that special environments produce heightened emotional responses even from literal-minded detectives. *Vintage Murder* provides the most interesting juxtaposition between theatrical interiors and natural exterior spaces, from one kind of beauty and fantasy to another.

Marsh returns to the theater in two later novels, *Night at the Vulcan* and *Killer Dolphin*.[2] In neither case is the murder committed on stage as it had been previously. In the former, an unpopular actor is slain in his dressing room, and in the latter, a night watchman is murdered on one of the landings in the house. In both cases, however, the setting is critical in establishing atmosphere and motivation for the crime. In *Killer Dolphin*, Marsh again contrasts the structured space of the playhouse, this time to the larger, structured cityscape of London rather than, as in *Vintage Murder*, to a natural wilderness. She illuminates the Dolphin's presence in the squat and monotonous warehouse district on the banks of the Thames by illustrating its exterior grace and embellishments with florid prose.

Her use of theatrical space in *Night at the Vulcan* was almost entirely confined to the playhouse itself. Her heroine, the young New Zealander Martyn Tarne, in London seeking an acting job, has developed "a sensitivity to theatres. She was aware of them at a distance" (*NV*, 12). Once inside the Vulcan she moves with the assurance of one to whom the theater is home: "She waited for a little while longer, to accustom herself to the dark. The shadows melted and the shape of the auditorium filtered through them like an image on a film in the darkroom. She thought it beautiful: the curve of the circle, the fan-like shell that enclosed it, the elegance of the proscenium and modesty of the ornament—all these seemed good to Martyn, and her growing sight of them refreshed her. . . . She was on her own ground" (*NV*, 20).

As the tension in the novel builds toward the performance and its eruption into murder, the theater, too, is expectant. Backstage, Martyn revels in the excitement. "There is perhaps nothing that gives one so strong a sense of theatre from the inside as the sound of invisible players in action. The disembodied and remote voices, projected at an unseen mark, the uncanny quiet offstage, the smells and the feeling that the walls and the dust listen, the sense of simmering expectancy; all these together make a corporate life so that the theatre itself seems to breathe and pulse and give out a warmth" (*NV,* 96).

For all its warmth and comfort, the theater also reflects life as it has become in the modern age, a "shifting world" (*NV,* 129), a kaleidoscope, a world of impermanence, a world where the most imposing edifice is merely a backdrop for the players who move through its space, a world of landscapes painted on a wrinkled canvas. In this world loyalties and commitments are only negotiable until the season ends. Like the theater, Marsh suggested, life is filled with the hope of stability but, on closer examination, that hope proves to be a dream—all the characters of the piece are merely mouthing lines. Most of all, the world, like the backstage of the theater, is in constant motion, hurrying through the clutter of yesterday's values, toward tomorrow. Not even the murder of Clark Bennington, another leading lady's husband, can stop this rush of activity. Alleyn steps onto the revolving stage and flushes out the actors "like rabbits from their burrows" (*NV,* 238), thinks Martyn. Then Alleyn suspends the characters in time and space in order to entrap the murderer. In an ending worthy of Agatha Christie's *The Murder of Roger Ackroyd* (1926), the killer, also a physician and a playwright, is allowed to commit suicide—on the stage, of course. Dr. Rutherford's motive is Bennington's threat to expose his latest play as plagiarized, and his opportunity comes in the moments between the final exit and the curtain calls. The stage and its environs permeate the action, the motive, and especially the tone of the novel. It is the play itself, its rhythm and climax, that eliminates suspects and ultimately traps its very creator.

Marsh employed a wider perspective in *Killer Dolphin*. Peregrine Jay, a young playwright and director, first views the bomb-damaged playhouse from Wharfingers Lane in the warehouse district along the Thames. There the playhouse is, Jay observes, a stolid building set among other uninspiring buildings. From his vantage point, he only sees the wrought-iron ornament of the tower, but he lusts after this awkward and ugly edifice. Marsh envisioned a theater almost under siege, crowded and beleaguered by its surroundings. Once Peregrine, through a series of astonishing circumstances, restores the theater, it quite naturally assumes a dominance over its neighbors. The freshly painted theater with its shining dome and gilded flagpole shines among the drab warehouses that surround it. As Jay watches, like a lover filled with longing, the gold-and-black flag with a dolphin logo is unfurled atop the flagpole. As if to mark this moment, "Big Ben and all the clocks in the city struck eight and Peregrine's heart's blood rose and pounded in his ears. The glory of London was upon him" (*KD,* 87).

The transformation of the interior is equally noticeable. It had been a derelict, tattered house marked by a deep scar in the stage made during the blitz; now it is renovated, alive with color and restored to its former glory and splendor. From the rococo exterior of gilded caryatids to the cherubims in the foyer, the plush carpeting, and the wrought-iron embellishments on the bannisters and seats, Peregrine Jay's fantasy has become reality. His patron, the mysterious and wealthy Vassily Conducis, has sponsored the restoration. More miraculous than that, he has revealed his ownership of an ancient glove and a handwritten note that the Victoria and Albert Museum staff confirm is in Shakespeare's handwriting. The glove belonged to the playwright's son, Hamnet, who died very young. It and the note are displayed at the Dolphin in a secure glass case for the audience to view while enjoying the intermission of Jay's original play, "The Glove," which opens the Dolphin's season.

Tragedy associated with the story of the dead child continues to stalk this famous memorabilia when a night watchman is murdered in the midst of a theft and a boy actor is seriously hurt at the same time. Alleyn's ultimate solution of the crime revolves around a past encounter between Mr. Conducis and one of Jay's actors. Blackmail and the greed of unscrupulous art collectors who lust after the glove and letter inspire the crime and its perpetrator, with the actual murder taking place on the landing by the glove display. Uncovering the killer depends on the timing of various actors' entrances and exits after the performance. In this *Killer Dolphin* bears a certain similarity to *Night at the Vulcan.* The exact structure of the house itself also plays a critical role in resolving the questions of who could have been hiding where, but seen by whom at what time. In this respect and in its contrast of interior and exterior space the book also resembles *Vintage Murder. Killer Dolphin* allowed Marsh the exquisite pleasure of a restoration project denied to her in life. As Earl Bargainnier suggests in his article "Ngaio Marsh's Theatrical Murders," the work on the Dolphin reflects Marsh and Dan O'Conner's ideas of repairing a bomb-damaged theater in Woolwich.[3] Since this plan did not materialize, Marsh created a Mr. Conducis to finance her fantasy of the Dolphin's rebirth.

Not only did Marsh provide fascinating settings for her murders, she also peopled her books with as colorful and as eccentric a group of theatrical characters as one might find crowding a novel by Dickens. Theaters as

places, and the actors who inhabit their stages, were at one level inseparable
for Marsh. In her first theatrical novel she observed assembled actors standing quietly onstage awaiting instruction. She described them in their native
habitat, the stage, where their ephemeral selves disappear and they gain
substance. "They no longer seemed preposterous or even artificial. They
were in their right element and had become real" (*EM*, 176). Though their
"reality" is one of greasepaint, costumes, and rehearsed lines and gestures,
they are not necessarily false, though outsiders, especially the police, tend to
interpret them as such.

To integrate the theatrical world and the detective novel, Marsh added an
adroit touch: she made Alleyn the balance wheel between the land of theatrical invention, where people create their personas with care, and the more
pragmatic world of the other police officers. His is the consciousness that
translates one world into the other. And he is indeed altogether accustomed
to the theatrical scene and to theatrical people, having been involved in four
police investigations in which actors had played—and *played* had been the
operative word—leading roles. As a result of these cases he is sardonically
regarded at the Yard as something of an expert on the species. Classifying
the plumage and habits of this species, in and out of its natural habitat, is
Alleyn's chore. He knows, along with the author, that for actors there is a
fine line between insecurity and habitual posing, exaggeration and outright
lying, jealous malevolence and murderous rage. Marsh mentioned this twice
in her second theatrical novel, *Vintage Murder*. She remarked that in everyday life actors appear to dramatize and heighten their actions and emotions.
This begins as an affectation in young apprentices and, by maturity, has become a habit, unconsciously motivating their attitudes and actions. If their
critics charge them with always acting, it is true, but that does not mean
they are insincere. Later on Marsh also observed that actors have a separate
mask for occasions when they mix with the nontheatrical world. It is a mask
of normalcy worn to show the world how ordinary they are. This persona
enables the actor to pass unnoticed among his fellow beings.

In *Killer Dolphin* Marsh put these sentiments into Alleyn's mouth, as
though he has truly absorbed these truths about actors. He explains to Fox,
"When you and I and all the rest of the non-actors do our damndest to un-
derstate and be ironical about our emotional reflexes, the actor, even when
he underplays them, does so with such expertise that he convinces us laymen
that he's *in extremis*. He isn't" (*KD*, 179). Of course, the audience who
truly counts in these novels is Roderick Alleyn, as he sorts through a welter
of contradictory emotions and personalities. Marsh provided him with col-

orful suspects whose portraits are tinged with sympathy or satire, and whose masks are knocked askew in the murder probe.

On the whole Marsh was generous in her portrayal of leading ladies. In her two earliest theatrical novels, *Enter a Murderer* and *Vintage Murder,* she created women of such charm that Alleyn, despite himself, is attracted to them. In *Enter a Murderer,* Stephanie Vaughan is initially seen exhibiting both personal and professional grace in handling a difficult encounter with the victim-to-be, an angry Arthur Surbonadier. In talking with him, she takes "her time lighting a cigarette and quite unconsciously adapt[s] the best of her six by-the-mantlepiece poses" (*EM,* 14–15). Surbonadier knows from her routine how she will manipulate him with her repertoire of poses and her deep throaty purr. When Alleyn sees her after Surbonadier's murder, she turns toward him as he watches her curiously, and then, with touching dignity, she lets herself be led off by Susan Max. As she exits the stage, she glances back at the corpse, shudders, and sweeps into the wings. "Lovely exit, wasn't it?" (*EM,* 35), said the inspector. Yet this same woman of artifice turns in a courageous performance when she attempts to steal evidence from the dead man's apartment. Alleyn, who has expected such an attempt, confronts her and, as she is about to faint, he chastizes her, reminding her that she is too strong to faint, she is a woman with iron nerve who keeps her wits about her in a crisis. Alleyn knows that her delicacy is an act to earn his pity. Though Stephanie Vaughan continues to exhibit bits of stage tricks, from that moment she ceases to pose and emote so self-consciously. Vaughan's gain in stature contrasts with the responses of a secondary actress, Janet Emerald, who "achieved the feat known to leading ladies as 'running through the gamut of emotions.' . . . She wept unfeignedly and said that her heart was broken" (*EM,* 135). Though the coroner reacts coldly to this display, Alleyn, knowing the lady's predisposition to histrionics, has expected it.

In *Vintage Murder* Marsh created a similar contrast. The leading lady, Carolyn Dacres, is introduced when the first attempt is made on her husband's life. She adopts a sprightly, unconcerned air that causes Alleyn to wonder what kind of part she is playing—vague and foolish woman or plucky heroine? He decides that Dacres is merely making a little cameo part for herself in the midst of the melodrama. Later, at her birthday party, she makes the grand and belated entrance for which she is famous, smiling benevolently and saucily on all the assembled party goers. Alleyn is charmed by her warmth and her famous personality, but after her husband's murder, he has to break through that same charming facade to discover the truth. Like Stephanie Vaughan, Carolyn Dacres attempts no more levity or self-promotion. By contrast, the ingenue Valerie Gaynes is in good theatrical form during Alleyn's questioning, thoroughly enjoying the attention of his official audience. She declares that her delicate temperament is upset by this investigation and uses every stock phrase and every bit of theatrical jargon she can interject to demonstrate how professional she is. Sensing her attempts to distract them, Alleyn waits patiently through the tedium with "polite interest," and then swoops on her with critical questions. She continues to prevaricate and, affecting wounded dignity, makes an exit, but not before Alleyn has gotten the information he needs. He dismisses her as a "silly young woman."

Night at the Vulcan offers the portrait of a darker personality. Though often gracious to her dresser, Martyn Tarne, Helena Hamilton, the star of the company, retains an air of emotional distance throughout the novel. Unlike Stephanie Vaughan or Carolyn Dacres, after her husband is murdered Hamilton does not act decisively to protect others, nor does she grieve for him. Her presence does not dominate the novel, and Alleyn, now that he has married Agatha Troy, does not respond to her beauty and grace as he did with the previous leading ladies. The contrast in this story is between sensible Martyn and the hysterical actress Gay Gainsford, the ingenue whom Martyn ultimately replaces. Gainsford's acting offstage, both before and after the murder, surpasses any skill that she is capable of demonstrating onstage. Martyn's impression of her acting voice is that it is "slight" and "uncoloured," and playwright John James Rutherford cannot discuss Gainsford's performance without breaking into wild, Falstaffian epithets.

Gainsford, herself, facing Alleyn's initial questions about the murder, chokes on her cigarette smoke and seeks protective cover from her one admirer in the cast, who sees her as a "frail little thing." In a manner reminiscent of Janet Emerald and Valerie Gaynes, Gay enters Alleyn's presence speaking "in a high grand voice that seemed to come out of a drawing-room comedy of the twenties" and moving "with a Mayfairish gallantry that was singularly dated" (*NV,* 196). Alleyn "wondered if she had decided that her first reading of her new role was mistaken. 'She's abandoned the brave little woman for the suffering *mondaine* who goes down with an epigram,' he thought" (*NV,* 196). Despite Alleyn's alternating patience and forcefulness, Gainsford never really breaks, she never becomes vulnerable. Perhaps, as Marsh suggested, the distinction between a legitimate leading lady and a minor actress is that not far beneath the surface of the former is a layer of humanity that gives her performance an element of verisimilitude, while the minor poseurs always remain imposters.

Marsh's two most unsympathetic leading ladies, not surprisingly, are murder victims themselves. Mary Bellamy in *False Scent* and Isabella Sommita in *Photo Finish* are interesting, contentious women, so passionately bound up in their own dominating personalities that they are largely unaware of the complications arising from their conduct and the exasperation of others.[4] These women earn a certain amount of sympathy when their insecurities so blatantly dictate their insufferable arrogance. Mary Bellamy's murder is the result of her outrageous possessiveness, her determination to control everyone about her. Her bad moods are legendary and becoming worse as she celebrates her fiftieth birthday. The day of her party she unleashes her fury on two close friends. "Mary Bellamy's temperaments were of rare occurrence but formidable in the extreme and frightening to behold. They were not those regulation theatre tantrums that seem to afford pleasure both to observer and performer; on the contrary they devoured her like some kind of migraine and left her exhausted. Their onset was sudden, their duration prolonged and their sequel incalculable" (*FS,* 25). In this instance, however, the sequel proves fatal when her long-suffering husband finally rebels against her contempt and puts poison in her perfume atomizer.

Mary Bellamy's murder is better plotted and more persuasively motivated than is that of Isabella Sommita, who is stabbed as a part of an ancient Sicilian family vendetta. Though her tantrums are equally feared by the men in her life, her passions, her greed, and her hysterical outbursts are all red herrings. The Sommita dominates and bullies her men, but the beauty of her voice overwhelms all who hear it. She is the "celestial fire engine" to her former vocal coach and "bella" to other admirers. It is her lover who murders her, having plotted for years to wreak his generation's vengeance in the centuries-old feud.

Marsh passed rather quickly over other husbands and lovers of her leading ladies. In *Enter a Murderer* the most complicated menage is untangled: Stephanie Vaughan had been Arthur Surbonadier's lover for a brief time and had broken with him for Felix Gardener. Jealousy and a shameful past haunt Gardener, who finally kills his rival in front of an audience. Had his only murder been that of Surbonadier, and love his primary motive, Gardener might have captured some sympathy, but his callous second murder and a barely repressed violence toward Vaughan robs him of that. An adulterous love tryst seems to be at the core of *Vintage Murder,* but when Alfred Meyer's murderer is discovered, far more prosaic reasons for his death are uncovered. His partner in theatrical management murdered him for business reasons, and Meyer's wife, Carolyn Dacres, it develops, never betrayed her husband. Clark Bennington, husband to Helena Hamilton in *Night at the Vulcan,* has long accepted her coldness toward him and her affairs with others; though he rapes her in the course of the book, this does not lead to his murder. Rather, he is killed by the man he blackmailed, Dr. John James Rutherford. Mary Bellamy's husband in *False Scent* is a despised and long-suffering businessman who feels that he has "spent the greater part of [his] life among aliens" (*FS*, 87). He is her foil and her murderer. These men, whether in major or minor supporting roles, never draw Marsh's full attention, nor the best of her prose.

There are other males in her cast of theatrical characters who are more fully developed egos and talents. *Colour Scheme* concerns itself far more with the atmosphere in wartime New Zealand and the delightfully anachronistic Claire family, but the famous actor Geoffrey Gaunt is critical to the plot. It is Gaunt's visit to the Wai-ata-tapu Springs Hotel and Spa that brings some of the elements of the intrigue to a head. He has been in New Zealand performing and has remained to seek treatment for fibrositis in his leg. The excitement on his arrival at the Claires' hotel, and Barbara Claire's obvious hero worship once he has settled in, provide his opportunity to strut and preen himself on this romantic stage, even while bewailing its inconveniences. Of the Claires he remarks, "Marvellous character parts. Overstated of course. Not quite West End. A number-one production on tour shall we say?" (*CS*, 68). His quiet, unassuming secretary Dikon Bell looks on his behavior with responses ranging from bemused indulgence to outrage. Long ago he had decided that Gaunt is a creature of extremes: at times dissembling and at other times sincere and charming, but all to the same end—promoting his need for praise and attention. Nevertheless, Dikon Bell has to admit, he likes his employer. When Gaunt agrees to perform for a gathering of Maori and Paheka at the Maori village, he is treated like royalty. Marsh described this evening at length—the crowded Maori meetinghouse bedecked with native arts, ironically reverberating with the best of Shakespearean soliloquies. This in fact is what redeems Gaunt; for all his vanity and duplicity, he is able to capture the meaning and the music of Shakespeare's lines even if he himself is an unworthy vessel. Indeed, Gaunt believes that he can win an audience's love both for himself and for Shakespeare. Bell's ultimate disillusionment with Gaunt marks a stage of new maturity and independence in his life, as Gaunt's utter foolishness and insensitivity propel the young man forward into his own loves and challenges.

Like Geoffrey Gaunt, Sir Henry Ancred is never seen in a formal performance in *Final Curtain*. His reputation as Macbeth has achieved the proportions of legend, so when Troy Alleyn is summoned to paint his portrait she is too intrigued to refuse. Nigel Bathgate describes the "Grand Old Man" to Troy: "Because he is an actor, his friends accept his behavior as part of his stock-in-trade" (*FC*, 18). Though he has had to surrender the demanding roles of Shakespeare, he still appears in drawing room comedies, giving exquisite performances of charming or irascible buffers. "Sometimes he forgot his lines, but by the use of a number of famous mannerisms, diddled his audience into believing it was a lesser actor who had slipped" (*FC*, 21). However, to his family his most marked characteristic is his mercurial temperament, which results in a frequent altering of his will. Not surprisingly, this plays a major role in the unfolding of the mystery. To Troy he is courtly, with only a hint of an improper advance. Her first impression of him is that "he looked as though he had been specially designed for exhibition. . . . You could hardly believe that he was true" (*FC*, 55). He is vain and stubborn, yet rather pathetically vulnerable and easily manipulated by family factions. It is his vanity and possessiveness that lead him to his death at the hands of a daughter-in-law determined to protect the inheritance of her son, his nephew.

Since he has dominated all the other males in *Final Curtain* except for Alleyn, Sir Henry's death deprives the Ancreds of any real focus or leadership. His brooding masculinity is underlined by contrasting him with his bland son Thomas and his mincing nephew Cedric. In *Colour Scheme* Marsh had achieved somewhat the same effect by balancing Geoffrey Gaunt against Dikon Bell. Bell emerges, however, as more the hero of the two, more sensitive and more truly courageous. Cedric, on the other hand, is despicable, not because he is effeminate—in fact, he lusts for his grandfather's mistress—but because he is cruel and utterly self-serving. Alleyn describes him as smart, "but what a cold-blooded little worm it is, Fox. . . . I could kick that young man . . . in fourteen completely different positions and still feel half-starved" (*FC*, 233). Offensive as he might appear to his family, his mother poisons two people to ensure his inheritance.

The two leading men Marsh presented at the height of their careers are Marcus Knight of *Killer Dolphin* and Sir Dougal Macdougal of *Light Thickens*. Each man is chosen for his role in the productions by playwright and director Peregrine Jay, who is guided not only by his instincts as to acting ability and reputation but also by looks. He selects Knight to play Shakespeare and Macdougal to play Macbeth. Jay repeatedly emphasizes how much Knight's features resemble the bard's. He also realizes that nurturing such talent to give a first-rate performance requires patience. Even as the actor argues, "Peregrine listened to the celebrated voice and as he listened he looked at the beautiful face with its noble brow and delicate bone structure. He watched the mouth and thought how markedly an exaggerated dip in the bow in the upper lip resembled that of the Droushout engraving and the so-called Grafton portrait" (*KD*, 57). Because Knight's looks and voice so perfectly match Jay's view of Shakespeare, Jay decides to endure his temperaments. Macdougal, like Sir Henry Ancred, has a magnificent head and voice for the tragically ambitious Scotsman. Both actors display petty vanities of such limited proportions that they threaten only to disturb, not disrupt, the fragile harmony of their respective casts, and they never threaten the integrity of the play. Marsh treated them both with respect for their professional assiduity.

In these two "leading man" dramas Marsh also provided detailed descriptions of rehearsal techniques and the painstaking precision required of the conscientious actor. When both men apply themselves to their craft, gone are the self-indulgent sulks. As Peregrine Jay watches Knight approach his part, he feels excited. "Marcus was an actor of whom it was impossible to say where hard thinking and technique left off and the pulsing glow that actors call star-quality began. At earlier rehearsals he would do extraordinary things: shout, lay violent emphasis on oddly selected words, make strange, almost occult gestures and embarrass his fellow players by speaking with his eyes shut and his hands clasped in front of his mouth as if he prayed" (*KD*, 57). Growing out of these peculiarities is a transfiguration occurring before the director's eyes. Marcus Knight is a superb actor who by opening night performance, would *be* Shakespeare.

Although one could scarcely define Macbeth as "joyful," Peregrine expresses a similar admiration for Sir Dougal's efforts. Macdougal is required to learn a complicated choreography for his last fight with Macduff, and is being trained by a minor actor and weapons expert, Gaston Sears. At 7:30 each morning, Sears, Simon Morton, who plays Macduff, and Macdougal meet to rehearse the physically demanding duel, which is planned right down to the individual blows and parries. Both actors suffer and sweat, but both remain committed and professional. To get the correct rhythm, Gaston has found a record of the Anvil Chorus, which he plays at a slower speed. Very occasionally Macdougal protests Sears's insistence on absolute fidelity to the ancient swords and the sword fight. When Sears calls him a "weakling," Macdougal responds grandly that he refuses to be treated with such niggardly respect and whines that the sword fight would be easier if it were faked. Gaston's fanaticism, however, intimidates him, and he agrees with grumpy geniality to keep working on it. These encounters are designed to build the tension between Sears and Macdougal that erupts in the offstage murder of the latter. Marsh created such an essentially mild leading man, however, that the conflict between the two does not quite work. Peregrine compliments Dougal Macdougal for "playing like the devil possessed"

(*KD,* 63); the actor accepts the compliment on his performance with a smile and a half-hearted protest against Sears's manner with him. Jay brushes off this bit of temperament with ease. Sir Dougal, like Marcus Knight, is really a likable sort, not given to the serious tantrums that can disrupt performances. These qualities make his murder by Sears all the more peculiar. Macdougal's death is a result of Sears's obsessions and hallucinations that the sword itself demands Sir Dougal's blood, but the motive remains weak and unconvincing. Nevertheless, as chronicles of a director's passions, both *Killer Dolphin* and *Light Thickens* reveal a great deal about theatrical intensity. Both sustain interest primarily by their evocation of an alien world and culture, not for the suspense usually attendant on a murder mystery.

There are dozens of other dramatic roles in Marsh's novels, in which she could scarcely resist including references to theatrical qualities and characters. *Final Curtain* alone provides the reader with an entire generation of a theatrical family. Lesser actors fill out the lists of suspects for Alleyn in all these theatrical settings. Marsh also included a few voices of reason and balance among all these flamboyant folk, such as the older character actress, Susan Max, who appears in *Enter a Murderer* and *Vintage Murder.* In each she provides a vital piece of evidence for Alleyn, who realizes that he can count on her to keep her head and report to him in a calm and orderly manner while all the others are being histrionic. A few innocent young women who get their men also appear from time to time. Martyn Tarne in *Night at the Vulcan* and Emily Dunne of *Killer Dolphin* respond to the sad circumstances of murder with appropriate but controlled emotions, and each earns the admiration of her selected male in the process. Tarne wins the love of Adam Poole, a relatively sensible actor-manager, and Dunne sweeps the young playwright/director Peregrine Jay into her comforting arms when together they discover a grisly murder in his proudly restored Dolphin. Diana Copeland, the fledgling actress-director, wins the love of Henry Jernigham in *Overture to Death,* but she reappears in *Death and the Dancing Footman,* four years later, single, with no references to Jernigham. Aspiring young actresses like Anelida Lee in *False Scent* and Camilla Campion of *Death of a Fool* are included among these gentle women whom Alleyn recognizes as essentially sane despite their theatrical ambitions.

Critics disagree on how well these theatrical settings and characters served Marsh's purposes as a writer of detective fiction. Jacques Barzun and Wendell Hertig Taylor in their *Catalogue of Crime* excoriate *Night at the Vulcan* as undeserving of serious consideration. "The crime is committed at the dressing table. Almost the whole cast deserves to perish in the same way." A theatrical setting, they opine, "brings out the worst in Ngaio."[5]

With the exception of *Overture to Death,* which has a theatrical murder, and *Enter a Murderer,* Barzun and Taylor find Marsh's loyalty to her theatrical world unfortunate and its effects on her fiction deleterious. Julian Symons does not focus on the effects of theater per se in his criticism of Marsh; instead he commends her skill as a novelist of social satire. Had Marsh written purely theatrical novels, he suggests, with her ear for dialogue and her eye for eccentricities of character, she might have been a first-rate writer. Symons is more offended by the addition of police procedure to an otherwise compelling read.[6]

Two more critics, Howard Haycraft in *Murder for Pleasure* and Anthony Boucher in his review of *Killer Dolphin,* see the positive contributions of theatrical settings and characters to Marsh's detective fiction. Boucher says that Marsh wrote about the theater "delightfully, vividly and inimitably"; *Killer Dolphin* is, therefore "a novel of theatre with a good mystery attached."[7] Haycraft, unlike Barzun and Taylor, sees the connections between her skill at writing detective fiction and her theatrical bent. He maintains that "it is doubtful if any other practitioner of the form [detective fiction] to-day writes with so vivid a talent for picturization, so accurate a grasp of 'timing,' or so infallible a sense of dramatic situation."[8]

Had Marsh remained an actress, her perspective on the theater would have been quite different from what it became as she moved into producing and directing. As producer/director one must see the larger scene—the movements and motivations of all the characters and how props and sets complement or inhibit action. Marsh blended these skills of blocking, inspiring, and clothing her characters with her skill as a writer of detective fiction.

Ngaio Marsh knew and respected the Aristotelian unities of time, place, and action in drama, or, as they were translated to detective fiction by S. S. Van Dine, the rigid rules of the puzzle story. It was her skill as a novelist, trained in the theater, that enabled her to work within their confines. The theater provides some of the same advantages to plot as does the classic country house or the small village. It is a specific place, easily described and understood. It offers a sense of confinement; that is, it is not accessible to large numbers of suspects, at least backstage. It is ordered by conventions and routines that, if disturbed or broken, are immediately verifiable. These characteristics are all well within the strictures of the craft. As a creative producer/director Marsh paid homage to the rules even as she departed from them. Though theater is a familiar symbol to many, Marsh noted that its backstage grids, galleries, small, dark hallways, dressing rooms, and tiny, grimy windows and doors suggest a setting almost Gothic in tone. The theater is a confined, but not inaccessible, area whose boundaries are guarded by often distracted stage managers and their minions. These are boundaries, furthermore, that bear the illusion of openness: the stage with the curtain up invites an audience to watch and respond to actions writ larger than life. If those actions include murder, then the apparent open space between players and audience becomes a shattered glass wall—reality breaks through the illusions of the play. In three of Marsh's theatrical mysteries, *Enter a Murderer, Night at the Vulcan,* and *Light Thickens,* the murder occurs during the performance, when access to the stage would have been most limited. In *Vintage Murder* and *Killer Dolphin* homicide occurs at a moment when outsiders could have been on the scene. Although Marsh used her theatrical settings to set place and define space, she integrated her murders into the routine of the setting and the actions so skillfully that Alleyn is still required to resolve the conundrum. *Vintage Murder* and *Killer Dolphin* also suggest that although the theater is home for both victim and murderer, as well as the scene of the crime, the motives for it lie outside the theatrical world; one is a murder waiting to happen, and the other is an impulsive, self-protective act. In these two novels the theater could have been as easily a country house or a village, for it intrudes far less than in the first three books.

Marsh's characterizations of theatrical folk revealed similar respect for the conventions of detective fiction, with some individual digressions. Her characters obey a hierarchy, a pecking order as rigid as any in proper society. From the stars and their management to bit players, from the stage managers to the maintenance men, each knows his place. There are, of course, abrasions, jealousies, and backbiting—all of which add colorful insights into character. As detective conventions dictate, it is a closed society, but Marsh played with this illusion as she did with the illusion of openness in the edifice itself. She commented throughout on the theatrical personality—read by some as emotionally open, by others as simply emotionally excessive—within the confines or norms of theatrical society as compared to other social divisions. Often she defended the excesses as simply conventions that are appropriate to theater itself but have been taken out of context. These characters are extraordinarily intense, and it is difficult to remain neutral about their personalities. It heightens the effect of the murder if the victim has inspired affection, and it intensifies the sense of betrayal and disappointment if the murderer also comes from these ranks. Although Marsh was usually careful to shield her victim and her murderer from too much sympathy, lest she slipped into maudlin melodrama, she created such memorable eccentrics, with their temperaments and their childlike vulnerabilities, that they become full character studies, not the single-dimension characters of other golden-age detective fiction.

How did the theater affect Marsh's detective fiction? It is quite obviously more than just a place for murder to happen, and its denizens are more than just groups of prospective victims or murderers. It is an area, a region in Marsh's mind, almost as vivid as New Zealand, where actions and characters acquire intense coloring. The passionate act of murder seems oddly at home among these theater folk, whose emotions are charged to fever pitch, yet such an act is peculiarly out of place—a rude intrusion of reality into a world of illusion. Marsh utilized theatrical settings and people to accent her palette of violence and suspense. If she did not always conform to the detective story conventions, or color within the lines, she can be forgiven her embellishments by readers who enjoy her familiar yet exotic settings and her characters who personify every aphorism of theatrical lore, from the self-indulgent "darlings" to the nobility of "the show must go on."

Chapter Seven
Marsh and the Golden Age of Detective Fiction: Her Legacy

All major critics of the mystery story place Ngaio Marsh among the grand dames of the golden age of detective fiction. Like her sister crime writers, Agatha Christie, Dorothy Sayers, and Margery Allingham, she produced a solid body of work that is honored for its skillful construction and its popularity. Some critics would argue for including Josephine Tey in this august company, and others would drop Margery Allingham, but Ngaio Marsh's rightful place is never questioned. Indeed, she is often said to have combined the better qualities of Christie and Sayers to create an improved detective story. Marsh herself felt that she had much in common with Allingham, whose novels she read with pleasure.[1]

That each of these eminently reputable English ladies excelled in a genre created by men and presumed to be most attractive to masculine tastes for violence and analytical reasoning is a puzzle that no critic has yet solved. Most agree, however, that they established a tone for detective fiction that has lasted to the present day among women writers. When critics of the genre expand their vision from the mere solving of the murders to a mature assessment of the social order presented, it becomes evident that these women had more in common with the subtle touch of a Jane Austen and her drawing rooms than with the mean streets and tough guys of Raymond Chandler. Ngaio Marsh stands very comfortably alongside the rest of the "Big Four," enjoying a reputation for quality next to Sayers's and for popularity second only to Christie's. Within the body of Marsh's work a discerning critic finds a unique synthesis of three major traditions: the detective story, the novel of manners, and a strain of social analysis. Furthermore, Marsh's skillful characterization, her theatrical experience, and her New Zealand heritage, give her works a flavor that distinguishes them from those of her contemporaries.

Besides placing Marsh in the context of her fellow authors, it is important to place her in the context of the historical era in which she lived. Although she wrote mysteries until 1982—in fact, over half of her writing was done after World War II—she was most influenced by and most closely associated with the so-called golden age of detective fiction during England's interwar years. These years were intensely unsettling for the ruling classes of Britain, a theme that is sounded most forcefully by other fiction writers but that amounts to nothing more than a nervous giggle in mystery writers' works.

Woodrow Wilson best expressed the hopes of Americans and Britons entering the post–World War I period: "I believe that . . . men are beginning to see, not perhaps the golden age, but an age which at any rate is brightening from decade to decade, and will lead us some time to an elevation from which we can see the things for which the heart of mankind is longing."[2] Unfortunately, the developments of the two decades between the world wars met neither Wilson's nor his contemporaries' expectations. By 1920 the English governing classes had survived war carnage of unprecedented proportions, the crumbling of the German and the Ottoman empires, and the aggressive socialism of the emerging Labour party. Ahead lay the decade of boom-bust economic cycles, anger and despair among the coal miners, and finally, the flare-up of a general strike that, although it was extinguished, left smoldering embers. The thirties appeared even more unstable, with economic breakdown at the beginning and the disintegration of peace in Europe at the end. At home all appeared unsettled; manners and morals undermined by the vicissitudes of war had never quite recovered their Victorian decorum. Class distinctions blurred beneath the intense scrutiny of ambitious working people, newly outspoken women, and former domestic servants seeking other employment. The insecure middle class looked on this threat from below and trembled. Its members assuaged their fears by reassuring themselves that politics remained their secure bailiwick. Indeed, even with the intrusion of the Labour party, England escaped the clutches of the visionary and the radical, her interwar political policies remaining rooted in the past as inappropriate old solutions continued to be applied to new problems.

Politics may have remained conservative, but literature, ideas, and art did not. This was a great age of experimentation by writers such as James Joyce and Virginia Woolf. In the thirties art reached out to enhance the proletariat with a social consciousness and to promote an expansive worldview that was in direct contrast to the insularity of national leaders. The study of psychology and its rapid development in the interwar years challenged the comfortable view of human reason that had been dominant in Western culture since the Enlightenment. Science and the new physics contributed another unsettling note to the cacophony of change; technology jarred the senses with motion pictures, wireless broadcasting, and motor coaches. New styles and new techniques of contraception freed bodies from past constraints, and morals were presumed to have loosened commensurately. Since Wilson's "golden age" was insecure in so many areas, it is not surprising that some forms of popular culture reflected resistance to change rather than acceptance of it.

The most prominent of those forms, detective fiction, especially that written by the grand dames, presented a conservative view of the world. In all of their books the English class system continues to function with minimal challenge: the murderer is always caught, and the world is purged of its taint of disorder. Detective story readers could depend on this satisfactory resolution. They could also expect a highly structured plot involving reasonably predictable characters in situations bound by rules and conventions. The writers were themselves well-bred women of the upper-middle class who shared this worldview with their readers. With no intent to distort, they wrote about the world they knew and hoped would prevail, but they did not ignore its volatility—they simply chose to relegate disturbing elements of change to the periphery, leaving their central characters undisturbed. Except for the occasional Bolshevik or leftist sympathizer, their detective novels do not address the Russian Revolution or the Third International's call for world revolution. Likewise, rather than plotting strikes and canvassing for Labour candidates, most of the working-class characters in detective fiction are well behaved and deferential toward their betters. It is a world where middle-class readers could find reassurance that, despite a few disturbing signs, all is in order. The values of their class are preserved in innumerable social rituals. Those guilty of crimes are tracked down and punished, the innocent are protected, and there would, indeed, always be an England. Christie, Sayers, Allingham, and Marsh offered differing slants on these themes, but all provided a similar worldview.

Of the four, Agatha Christie certainly claims the greatest fame and most prodigious publishing record. She remains the standard by which other writers of detective fiction are judged. But many critics insist that Marsh was superior to Christie in every area: plot, characterization, and prose style. Considered the ultimate flattery, these sentiments appear on thousands of paperback copies of Ngaio Marsh's books. A question remains, however: how good a writer was Agatha Christie? How well does she set the standards for others of the genre? What are her strengths and her weaknesses?

From her first novel, *The Mysterious Affair at Styles,* published in 1920, to her posthumous *Sleeping Car Murder* (1977), Christie received attention and adulation for her narrative style and her ability to deceive readers and offer surprise solutions. Unlike Sayers, and even Marsh on occasion, Christie did not offer clues based on bits of obscure knowledge or Shakespearean quotations; she led up to the solution through ordinary objects and information. She confused readers by the convoluted shifting of suspicion and by similiarities among the suspects. In her most famous mystery of the golden age, *The Murder of Roger Ackroyd,* she broke with convention and revealed the narrator as the murderer. This book, with its twisting of conventional plot techniques, created such a stir that critic Edmund Wilson used the altered title "Who Cares Who Killed Roger Ackroyd" to excoriate all detective fiction as shallow and unreadable. His curmudgeonly protest hardly checked the flow from Christie's pen and the fortune accruing from it. She continued to emphasize plot over atmosphere and character and to resolve the puzzle in clean, well-reasoned, if wooden prose.

Dorothy L. Sayers, beloved by the more academic critics of the genre, wrote a series of mysteries beginning with *Whose Body?* in 1923. Each work in the series revolves around her detective hero, the aristocratic, eccentric Lord Peter Wimsey, who stumbles into and solves murders with astonishing alacrity. Lord Peter and his man Bunter display sophistication and courage in their various entanglements, each possessing an amazing range of skills. Bunter can develop photographs and run complicated forensic tests as well as lay on an elegant tea. Lord Peter knows rare manuscripts and code deciphering, and he accomplishes athletic feats of skill and daring. Wimsey may intrigue readers, but his eccentricities and his very perfection begin to cloy after a few novels. His exploits reveal his creator's ingenuity and intellectual bent, but they eventually become dull. Many critics consider *The Five Red Herrings* (1931) downright unreadable, and Sayers herself wryly referred to her later books as conversation pieces with "detective interruptions."[3] Sayers's production of detective novels remained small, although for *Omnibus of Crime* (1929) she wrote an extensive examination of the genre that introduced a collection of short stories, and she was active in the Detection Club when Ngaio Marsh was inducted into it. Even so, her critical reputation remains high among those who maintain that she injected a more respectable, intellectual tone into her novels than her contemporaries did.

Margery Allingham, the third member of this exclusive group, produced twelve mysteries. Her detective, Albert Campion, has distinct ties to the Peter Wimsey model. He is a peculiar fellow who appears deceptively dull to most who meet him, and quite foolish even to those who know him well. He has a secret identity hinted at by his creator—he may, in fact, be royalty, and at times he is reminiscent of Christie's Harley Quin, a magical sort of detective/hero whose identity and even substance is never quite ascertained. Campion can perform astonishing feats of derring-do while appearing rather silly and disoriented. His personality reveals Allingham's quirky imagination and her talent for bringing strange and grotesque characters to life. For this very reason Marsh declared that she had more in common with Allingham than with Sayers—both women created memorable villains and supporting characters in the tradition of Charles Dickens. Allingham's books are a mixed lot, from the early formula thrillers to her later, more satisfying novels, *The Tiger in the Smoke* (1952) and *The China Governess* (1962). Her style began to change with the 1931 publication of *Police at the Funeral;* her detective stories became more traditional, with more emphasis on the doctrines of fair play enumerated by S. S. Van Dine in 1928. She added the character of policeman Stanislas Oates and filled her books with details of the detective's analytical chores. She also developed character more fully than before, endowing Campion with more normal qualities, including falling in love, first with an unavailable woman and later with Amanda Fitton, an independent woman who enables Campion to integrate his two sides: silly eccentric and serious man of compassion and action.

Marsh conforms well enough to the strictures of Van Dine and others to earn the praise of those conscientious critics who zealously guard the gates of the genre. She is often compared favorably to Christie, whose characters, except for Poirot, were sketchy at best and whose descriptions of place were no more substantial than pastel watercolors. With Christie, plot was the thing; the puzzle and its solution dominate her novels. Marsh created devilishly clever plots that hold up well compared with Christie's. Toward the end of Marsh's work, most notably in *Photo Finish* and *Light Thickens,* her motives become a bit thin, but the puzzle is still meticulously drawn, if not as "inspired" as the puzzles in Christie's best work. Alleyn also provides more interest than Poirot, being less mannered and young enough for Marsh to develop other sides of his nature besides his detecting skill. Marsh stressed character, and her finely drawn portraits of Britons and New Zealanders, underscored by her brilliant dialogue, far outshine any of Christie's types.

Marsh shared Christie's love of travel and set her mysteries in more exotic locales than did Sayers or Allingham. Christie's *Man in a Brown Suit* (1924) and Marsh's *Singing in the Shrouds* offer an interesting comparison of views of South Africa. Although separated in time by twenty-four years, they both project essentially the same tensions. Christie's place description in *Man in a Brown Suit,* written shortly after she had returned from South Africa, was unusually complete—ordinarily she provided no more than a thumbnail sketch of a locale. By comparison, Marsh's descriptions of South Africa were, for her, abbreviated; she reserved her deepest tones and most evocative prose for her New Zealand stories, which are her best for giving readers a sense of place.

Of all of these writers, Dorothy Sayers has the greatest critical reputation. Marsh probably ranks just behind her, and Marsh's novels are often considered even more readable than those of Sayers. Roderick Alleyn, many critics maintain, wears better than Peter Wimsey, who is almost a caricature, part Bertie Wooster and part Sherlock Holmes. Alleyn became less affected and facetious as Marsh developed his character, allowing him to mature beyond the light, bantering sarcasm of the early stories. On closer reading one discovers that his humor is frequently that of the gallows variety, as well as self-deprecating, as if to parody the gushing tone in which the daily press describes him. Beneath Alleyn's preciosity Marsh revealed an edge of social commentary all the more effective for its subtlety. Wimsey and his ilk truly belong to the years of Victorian and Edwardian England. Though Alleyn is a "gent," he suggests a major shift in England's social and professional structure. Both men marry independent women they meet in the course of murder investigations. Both quote Shakespeare and share in the homogeneous class tradition of university educations and aristocratic families. Each regards his older brother who inherited the title as a "bit of an ass." Nevertheless, Wimsey remains the quintessential amateur sleuth and Alleyn the refined but professional policeman.

These two men emphasize a deeply ingrained ambivalence in attitudes toward class and toward professionals in British culture after World War I. With their accents, their touches of refined sensibilities, and the way others treat them, both are quite clearly of aristocratic backgrounds. Ironically, the aristocracy was at low ebb in these years of the twentieth century. Its source of political power, the House of Lords, had been "reformed" in 1911 and, by the twenties and thirties, was virtually toothless in everyday politics. The House of Lords could still serve as a court in certain instances, as we see in Sayers's *Clouds of Witness* (1927), but these dramatic occasions were rare. Aristocrats fought and died in World War I; often the first to volunteer for military service out of noblesse oblige and patriotism, they perished alongside their working-class mates in the trenches of Flanders. Some historians maintain that neither the aristocracy nor Britain ever recovered from the shocks and losses of World War I. Yet, while political power might have ebbed, and the labor unrest of the twenties might have indicated cracks in the old class system, the social power of the upper class was not impaired. Society in these novels really reflects a prewar world of house parties and debutante seasons. Of course, Wimsey and Alleyn are both younger sons; Wimsey's brother is the Duke of Denver, and Alleyn's holds the lesser title of baronet. Alleyn's brother, unlike Wimsey's, actually served the state in the Foreign Office, but both brothers are portrayed as pompous. Nevertheless, they inhabit the higher social stratum that was the stuff of Britishers' fantasy—the sleek sophisticated women and the handsome if slightly ineffectual males. If the peerage was still producing such clever men as Wimsey and Alleyn, then the fabric of English life would surely remain stable. After the disruptions of life and the great loss of men from World War I had devastated the old Victorian and Edwardian certainties, many English people must have turned to Sayers and Marsh for escape and reassurance.

While a social revolution was taking place in the interwar years, the status of policemen was in some ways enhanced. Although English people still liked to believe that their government, their empire, and their police were run by dedicated amateurs, the truth was that the twentieth century was becoming the century of the competent professional. The university system had changed its curriculum in the late nineteenth century to accommodate the training of civil servants, but English society as a whole accepted the necessity for bureaucrats with reluctance. Marsh's books reveal Alleyn's ambivalence about his job: he believes that it is right and just to solve crimes, but he cannot escape the uneasy shame of his professional status. Others of his social class appear to be less offended by the necessity of investigations, but Alleyn carries his own stigmata, apologizing for the details of his work to all who will listen.

Ngaio Marsh ultimately parted company with her contemporaries Christie, Sayers, and Allingham in her sensuous evocation of place and atmosphere and in the extent to which she analyzed character. Her challenge to the formulaic boundaries lifts her books from the limiting definition of predictable puzzle whodunits to the more complicated realm of novels of manners. No other detective fiction writer of this period painted external nature and internal space with such carefully crafted images. Whether the mystery occurs in the mud flats of New Zealand or in the country houses of the English gentry, Ngaio Marsh's lush prose painted them with broad and colorful strokes. Even when she set a winter scene with snow, ice, and bitter wind, she filled it with smells and sounds that illuminate her themes of desperation and the chill of murder. In her three coldest novels, *Death and the Dancing Footman, Death of a Fool,* and *Tied up in Tinsel,* the crimes are the most chilling: fratricide and patricide. Marsh wrote detective stories with careful attention to the elements and the physical surroundings, both of which reflect qualities of character and provide many twists to the already Byzantine plots. Marsh's theatrical experiences greatly enhance her ability to

integrate sets, props, lighting, and character, thus providing her books with
intricate texture and vivid color.

All of Marsh's novels are about more than the solution of crime. They are
bursting with ideas and enthusiasm about a wide range of topics, from the
future of the British Commonwealth to the passing of Victorian-Edwardian
manners and morals. She explored a rather extensive sampling of Britons
and New Zealanders to delineate not merely personal traits but national
characteristics as well. As a social critic she deftly fileted England's class system, removing the skeleton still intact and exposing its shape and form to
the last tiny bone. She accomplished this, not by digressive essays, but by
the interaction of her characters in the throes of a murder investigation.

Perhaps nothing is so sacred to any society as the rites of passage of its
youth into the adult world. In several of her novels, including *Enter a
Murderer, Night at the Vulcan,* and *Death of a Peer,* Marsh examined these
traditions in England; a young woman or man becomes disillusioned and
is allowed to see beyond the superficial, beyond what he or she had supposed to be virtues in another, to a more accurate assessment of character
and, by extension, of the world. Their crucibles occur in the murder investigations. In this loss of innocence, Marsh suggested, is the beginning of
the wisdom that tempers their youthful hubris and bleaches the rosy tint
from their worldview. Alleyn is the priest at these rites of passage. Though
he often tries, with his wit, to relieve the funereal atmosphere as illusion
and innocence are laid to rest, he does not trivialize his role. By all of these
characteristics—sensitivity to atmosphere, a strong sense of place, and
character studies that prick illusions and probe into personal and national
values—Marsh distinguished herself as a writer skillful enough to utilize
the conventions of her genre when they suited her story, and confident
enough to discard them when they did not. She set a precedent for the
next generation of women writers, who may choose a similar blend of literary traditions or depart from them in good conscience.

All four of these golden-age novelists bequeathed their legacies to contemporary writers. To untangle the skeins of influence and determine where
Christie, Sayers, Allingham, or Marsh influenced recent novelists would be
an impossible and ultimately fruitless task. In publicity releases modern
mystery writers are usually compared to Agatha Christie, since their publishers hope that some of her extraordinary sales appeal will rub off on their
current authors. Of the recent crop, the writers who suggest comparison are
P. D. James, Patricia Moyes, and two Americans—Martha Grimes and
Carolyn Heilbrun writing as Amanda Cross.

Carolyn Heilbrun maintains that P. D. James is the most skilled contemporary writer of the classic detective tale; other critics agree that James's detective fiction deserves the same attention as "serious" novels. In her early writings, such as *Cover Her Face* (1962), James followed more closely the conventions of the detective story of the golden age. Set in a country house, the murder of a parlor maid introduces the reader to Adam Dalgliesh, James's solemn detective, who solves the mystery in traditional fashion. The book is noteworthy primarily for its descriptive language, which boded well for works to come. James broke with custom in *An Unsuitable Job for a Woman* (1972), in which she gives Dalgliesh only a minor role, building her plot instead around Cordelia Gray, a female private detective. James's other novels, especially *Innocent Blood* (1980), reveal a talent maturing beyond the golden-age standard; she probes more deeply into the psyche and reveals her sensitivity to moral issues and societal concerns.

James has written about detective fiction in her capacity as reviewer for the *Times Literary Supplement* and has repeatedly insisted that Dorothy Sayers and Margery Allingham were the most direct influences on her writing. Although James has been compared to Agatha Christie in book jacket statements (much as Marsh is), she insists that there is no valid similarity. James has referred to Marsh as a disciple of Sayers, although Marsh has often mentioned Allingham's work as most influencing her own. It is perhaps most accurate to say that each of these writers influenced the others to some degree. James is the most prominent heir to the traditions of the golden-age detective story, which she has developed into deeper explorations of modern social tensions.[4]

By 1987 Patricia Moyes had produced at least twenty detective novels, earning encomiums from the reviewers who protest that P. D. James and Ruth Rendell stray too far into psychological thrillers. Books by Moyes bear a striking resemblance to Marsh's in two ways: they focus on a professional policeman and his wife, and their dialogue and character analyses demonstrate a similar sense of humor. In the 1965 novel *Johnny Under Ground,* Emily Tibbett's Royal Air Force reunion brings together a squadron of pilots and support staff who had all been stationed at Dymfield Air Base during World War II. From this mixture, old wounds and jealousies are stirred and an old mystery revived. Chief Inspector Henry Tibbett is drawn into the story in much the same way that Alleyn involves himself in Troy's adventures. Henry and Emily Tibbett are not clever and urbane like the Alleyns; Roderick would never address Troy as "my dear girl," nor would she refer to him, even in jest, as "mild and mousy."[5] Nevertheless, the Tibbetts are a devoted, childless couple who encourage each other in their separate activities; their intimacy is an easy one, similar to the Alleyns, and

Henry is frequently concerned that his long and irregular hours are an unfair burden on his wife.

In the same novel Moyes revealed an ease with dialogue and a sardonic sense of humor reminiscent of Marsh's. Describing the father of the murdered man, Moyes wrote, "The Reverend Sidney Guest was a robust, white-haired man who wore his seventy-five years not so much lightly as with impatience. In the course of life, ostensibly devoted to the service of others, he had, in fact, never given a thought to anybody but himself. Being therefore quite unaware of the strain which consideration for others puts upon the human constitution, he was a picture of whole heartiness and was continually irritated by the spinelessness of his nearest and dearest."[6] Such a wry observation as this could sit comfortably among Marsh's ironic turns of phrase. Moyes's style, wit, and plot-through-dialogue reveal a writer who has absorbed the lessons of the expanded detective story formula as developed in Ngaio Marsh's canon.

Marsh's influence is not limited to British writers. Howard Haycraft believes her work combines the "best features" of both the British and American schools of popular fiction.[7] Not surprisingly, a number of her characteristics have found their way into the books of American writers, such as Martha Grimes and Amanda Cross. To Grimes, Marsh has bequeathed her outsider's view of the insiders of British society. Grimes writes the traditional detective novel; her Inspector Richard Jury is an introspective, lonely man who is responsive to feminine charm like the early Roderick Alleyn. Jury carries his still unrequited passion for Vivian Rivington through many murder investigations in ten mysteries. All of these novels are named for the pubs where parts of the mystery unfold. Pubs are to Grimes what the theater was to Ngaio Marsh; both writers employed their respective locales as specific, "carpentered" spaces, natural gathering places for victims, suspects, and witnesses. Marsh's *Death at the Bar* centers on a pub in much the same way. Marsh was also making a play on the word *bar,* since her victim is a barrister who is killed with a poisoned dart in the saloon bar of Ottercombe. Marsh and Grimes both develop subplots of police personalities and procedures. Unlike Alleyn, Jury is constantly harassed by his superior, Superintendent Racer; like Alleyn, he gradually develops a companionable relationship with Sergeant Wiggins, who assists him in his cases. Wiggins complements Jury in many of the ways that Fox complements Alleyn. A walking apothecary of medicines designed to ward off ailments from allergies to digestive disorders, Wiggins regales suspects and witnesses with sympathetic prescriptive suggestions and empathetic cluckings over aches and pains. Grimes has created a number of other important characters who appear and reappear in the course of the novels and give a sense of continuity similar to that provided by Alleyn's family, friends, and associates.

Grimes also reveals a skillful use of dialogue and class dialect. In *The Five Bells and Bladebone* (1987) she captured in description and accent the Limehouse area of London. In fact, Grimes probes into poor and working-class lives more profoundly than Marsh ever did. Her descriptions of the upper classes, however, are similar to Marsh's in that they resonate with snappy repartee and ironic humor. Elderly busybody Lady Agatha Ardry constantly annoys Jury's friend, her nephew Melrose Plant, with her domineering nosiness. Agatha and the rector of Long Piddleton "were dependent on one another in the mindless way of two gibbons dedicated to picking fleas off one another's fur."[8] Like Christie and Marsh, Grimes injects frequent commentary on detective fiction through Agatha (a name that suggests that Grimes was having a bit of fun here), whose ambition is to write long, rambling mysteries, and through Polly Praed of the same village, who actually publishes detective novels.

At first glance, Amanda Cross's novels appear to be quite different from Marsh's. She writes about a female amateur sleuth who is a professional academic in the English department of a New York university. Kate Fansler is drawn to murder investigations in a variety of ways, all of which appear outlandish to her less imaginative colleagues, whose only mysteries revolve around tenure decisions and annual raises. There are, however, some similarities in tone and character between Marsh's work and Cross's. Certainly Kate Fansler can be seen as a female Roderick Alleyn. Born into privileged circumstances and in possession of an independent income, she has the self-confidence that frequently accompanies such well-being. Both Kate and Roderick have eschewed the easy and comfortable lives to which their economic and social status qualify them, both have chosen to become professionals, and both have uneasy relationships with older brothers who enjoy their privileges to the fullest. The marriage of Kate Fansler and Reed Amherst is the closest parallel to Roderick and Troy Alleyn among detective novels. Kate and Reed truly regard each other as equals, and like Alleyn, Amherst is enormously solicitous of his wife's independent career. There is an easy bantering and exchange of intimate confidences in both marriages. There are also frequent separations brought about by career obligations. That Amanda Cross would create such a marriage in the 1970s and 1980s is not surprising; that Ngaio Marsh would do so in the 1930s and 1940s is more unusual.

Both Cross and Marsh write about people who exchange frequent liter-

ary allusions as a matter of course in their conversations. Neither Reed nor
Troy has specialized in academic studies, yet they both recognize their
mates' references and are perfectly capable of appreciating the aptness of
certain quotations and of returning allusions in kind. Troy frequently caps
Alleyn's quotations from Shakespeare by reciting lines from the same play.
Reed never has difficulty following Kate's conversations peppered with
phrases from Auden, James Joyce, and Shakespeare, among others. Both
couples are enormously articulate, playfully enjoying the magic of poetry
and the sensuality of language. Although their plots and their circumstances
may be vastly different, both Marsh and Cross draw on the educated and
professional aristocrats of their respective societies. Despite all that separates
them, Cross and Marsh share a number of assumptions about whom the
natural leaders and problem solvers of a society are or should be. Martha
Grimes occasionally indulges herself in a Shakespearean clue, as in *The Man
with a Load of Mischief* (1981) and in references to Melrose Plant's academic interests, but she writes a grittier novel with less rarefied, less sophisticated characters. Both Grimes and Cross, however, draw on the framework
of the detective novel that was established in large part by Ngaio Marsh.

In 1980, *Booklist* referred to Marsh as "one of detective fiction's two
reigning monarchs."[9] From her earlier inclusion in the "Big Four" of the
golden age to the end of her creative life, she enjoyed an international reputation for fine writing. Her better novels contain a great deal more than
clever plotting. Expanding beyond the classic puzzle story conventions, she
brought new life to the strict formula as she incorporated traditions of the
novel of manners, character study, and social commentary into the detective
story. Critics who pick nits with her work because she breached the conventions and challenged the rules are less charitable in their evaluation of her
works, which they damn by their narrow definition of the detective genre.
Discerning critics recognize that hers was a highly individual voice and an
imaginative vision.

Marsh did not defy the conventions as much as she appeared to rise ef-
fortlessly above them. Her achievements have been rewarded by her univer-
sal recognition as New Zealand's most famous author and as one of the
most significant women writers of the classic British murder mystery. Even
those critics who would limit her accomplishment to the detective story, as
well as those who would strictly segregate the detective story from the "legitimate" novel, acknowledge the skill of Marsh's characterization and style.

Later writers have clearly benefited by her example of a very professional
if slightly eccentric detective whose relatively conventional life and intriguing work were examined with wit and stylistic elegance against a back-

ground of complex social mores. P. D. James and Martha Grimes are most readily indebted to Roderick Alleyn as a model for Adam Dalgliesh and Richard Jury. June Thomson's Inspector Rudd and her treatment of the Essex countryside suggest the temperament, albeit less colorful, of Alleyn and Marsh's finely detailed descriptions of New Zealand. Sheila Radley's Chief Inspector Quantrill, like Rudd, is a countryman and, like Alleyn, a family man. Quantrill does not quote Shakespeare but he is an intelligent, humane policeman, a type introduced most effectively by Marsh. It is this very expansion, this coloring outside the lines of convention, that makes Marsh's mysteries so memorable and ensures the survival of the genre. Had detective fiction been confined to the pure puzzle writers, it might have died from its own effete traditions. Indeed, for decades scholars have predicted the imminent demise of the mystery story, but thanks to less conventional authors like Marsh, the rumors of its death have been greatly exaggerated.

In addition to her novels, which speak to a wider, more complex range of human experience than simply the extraordinary event of a murder, Marsh wrote plays, descriptive travel books about New Zealand, and an autobiography, *Black Beech and Honeydew*. In her autobiography, she chronicled the most satisfying moments in her primary career as a director of Shakespearean plays in New Zealand. Her work in theater was well received, not only for the quality of the productions but also for her missionary spirit in nurturing an appreciation of Shakespeare in the antipodes. Marsh's commitment to excellence, be it in popular fiction or classical theater, argues persuasively for recognizing her for what she was, a woman of letters.

Notes and References

Preface

1. S. S. Van Dine, "Twenty Rules for Writing Detective Stories," in *The Art of the Mystery Story: A Collection of Critical Essays,* ed. Howard Haycraft (New York: Simon and Schuster, 1946), 189–93; Dorothy L. Sayers, ed., *The Omnibus of Crime* (New York: Payson and Clarke, 1929), 9–47.

2. "The Oath for the Detection Club in Britain (1928)," quoted in Julian Symons, *Mortal Consequences: A History—From the Detective Story to the Crime Novel* (New York: Harper and Row, 1972), 2.

3. Elaine Budd, *13 Mistresses of Murder* (New York: Ungar, 1986), xi.

4. *Enter a Murderer* (Glasgow: Fontana Books, 1984), 56; hereafter cited in the text as *EM.*

5. Leroy Lad Panek, *Watteau's Shepards: The Detective Novel in Britain 1914–1940* (Bowling Green, Ohio: Bowling Green State University Popular Press, 1979), 185.

6. Earl F. Bargainnier, "Ngaio Marsh," in Earl F. Bargainner, ed., *10 Women of Mystery* (Bowling Green, Ohio: Bowling Green State University Popular Press, 1981), 103.

Chapter One

1. As quoted in John Elsom, "At the End of the World," *Contemporary Review* 237 (August 1980): 78.

2. Marsh uses this phrase, written in shop-girl's dialect, in several of her novels.

3. *Black Beech and Honeydew: An Autobiography* (Boston: Little, Brown, 1965), 7–8. Subsequent page references to this first edition are hereafter cited in the text as *BBH.* References to the second edition, which contains an added chapter on her detective fiction (London: Collins, 1981) are cited in the text as *BBH* rev. ed.

4. Howard Haycraft, *Murder for Pleasure: The Life and Times of the Detective Story* (New York: Biblo and Tanner, 1968), 194.

5. Claire Tomalin, *Katherine Mansfield: A Secret Life* (New York: Knopf, 1988), 7.

6. As quoted in Robert Paul Jordan, "New Zealand: the Last Utopia?" *National Geographic* 171 (May 1987): 662.

7. Bruce Mason, "In Memoriam: Dame Ngaio Marsh, 1899–1982," *Landfall* 36 (June 1982): 240.

8. Ibid., 244.
9. William Shakespeare, *Cymbeline,* act 4, scene 2.

Chapter Two

1. *Colour Scheme* (New York: Jove Books, 1982); hereafter cited in the text as *CS.*
2. Winston S. Churchill, *The End of the Beginning: War Speeches by the Right Hon. Winston S. Churchill* (Boston: Little, Brown, 1943), 268.
3. As quoted in John Ball, ed., *The Mystery Story* (San Diego: University of California at San Diego, 1976), 1.
4. *Vintage Murder* (New York: Jove Books, 1978); hereafter cited in the text as *VM.*
5. Carole Acheson, "Cultural Ambivalence: Ngaio Marsh's New Zealand Detective Fiction," *Journal of Popular Culture* (Fall 1985): 165.
6. Ibid.
7. *Died in the Wool* (New York: Jove Books, 1981); hereafter cited in the text as *DW.*
8. Leon Edel, "Writing Biography: The Nature of Psychological Evidence," the Cecil B. Williams Lecture delivered at Texas Christian University, Ft. Worth, Texas, 3 March 1981.
9. *Death of a Peer* (New York: Book League of America, 1940); hereafter cited in the text as *DP.*
10. *Photo Finish* (New York: Jove Books, 1981); hereafter cited in the text as *PF.*
11. *Light Thickens* (Boston: Little, Brown, 1982); hereafter cited in the text as *LT.*
12. *Black as He's Painted* (New York: Jove Books, 1978); hereafter cited in the text as *BHP.*

Chapter Three

1. *When in Rome* (New York: Jove Books, 1980); hereafter cited in the text as *WR.*
2. *Death in Ecstasy* (New York: Berkeley, 1977); hereafter cited in the text as *DE.*
3. *Artists in Crime* (New York: Jove Books, 1980); hereafter cited in the text as *AC.*
4. *Death in a White Tie* (Matlock, N. Y.: Aeonian Press, 1981); hereafter cited in the text as *DWT; A Wreath for Rivera* (Boston: Little, Brown, 1949); hereafter cited in the text as *WR.*
5. *Killer Dolphin* (New York: Jove Books, 1980); hereafter cited in the text as *KD.*

6. *A Man Lay Dead* (New York: Jove Books, 1978); hereafter cited in the text as *MLD.*

7. *Overture to Death* (New York: Furman, 1939); hereafter cited in the text as *OD.*

8. *Death and the Dancing Footman* (Boston: Little, Brown, 1941); hereafter cited in the text as *DDF.*

9. *Tied up in Tinsel* (Boston: Little, Brown, 1972); hereafter cited in the text as *TT.*

10. *Scales of Justice* (New York: Jove Books, 1980); hereafter cited in the text as *SJ; A Clutch of Constables* (London: Crime Club, 1968); hereafter cited in the text as *CC.*

11. *Death of a Fool* (New York: Jove Books, 1978); hereafter cited in the text as *DF.*

Chapter Four

1. Haycraft, *Murder for Pleasure,* 194.

2. Jessica Mann, *Deadlier Than the Male: Why Are Respectable English-women So Good at Murder?* (New York: Macmillan, 1981), 88–89.

3. *Final Curtain* (Boston: Little, Brown, 1947); hereafter cited in the text as *FC; Spinsters in Jeopardy* (New York: Jove Books, 1986; hereafter cited in the text as *SJ.*

4. *Last Ditch* (Boston: Little, Brown, 1977); hereafter cited in the text as *LD.*

5. Erik Routley, *The Puritan Pleasures of the Detective Story: A Personal Monograph* (London: Gollancz, 1972), 147.

6. Ibid., 148.

7. *The Nursing-Home Murder* (New York: Jove Books, 1982); hereafter cited in the text as *NHM.*

Chapter Five

1. *Death at the Bar* (New York: Jove Books, 1980); hereafter cited in the text as *DB.*

2. *Singing in the Shrouds* (Boston: Little, Brown, 1958); hereafter cited in the text as *SS.*

3. *Hand in Glove* (New York: Berkley, 1963); hereafter cited in the text as *HG.*

Chapter Six

1. O. Henry, "The Furnished Room," in *The Four Million* (New York: Doubleday, 1906), 239.

2. *Night at the Vulcan* (New York: Pyramid, 1974); hereafter cited in the text as *NV.*

3. Earl F. Bargainnier, "Ngaio Marsh's 'Theatrical' Murders," *Armchair Detective* 10, no. 2 (April 1977):181.

4. *False Scent* (New York: Jove Books, 1981); hereafter cited in the text as *FS*.

5. Jacques Barzun and Wendell Hertig Taylor, *A Catalogue of Crime* (New York: Harper and Row, 1971), 131.

6. Symons, *Mortal Consequences,* 7.

7. Anthony Boucher, review of *Killer Dolphin,* as quoted in Ann Evory, ed., *Contemporary Authors,* New Revision Series, vol. 6 (Detroit: Gale Research, 1982), 323.

8. Haycraft, *Murder for Pleasure,* 192–94.

Chapter Seven

1. As quoted in James Vinson and D. L. Kirkpatrick, eds., *Contemporary Novelists* (New York: St. Martin's Press, 1982), 435.

2. As quoted in Charles Loch Mowat, *Britain between the Wars 1918–1940* (Boston: Beacon Press, 1971), 1.

3. As quoted in Robert Barnard, "The English Detective Story," in H. R. F. Keating, *Whodunit? A Guide to Crime, Suspense, and Spy Fiction* (Van Nostrand Reinhold, 1982), 34.

4. There are many interesting and useful essays on P. D. James and her reflections on detective fiction. These remarks are a synthesis of comments from Budd, *13 Mistresses of Murder,* 65–75, Mann, *Deadlier Than the Male,* and Bruce Harkness, "P. D. James," in Bernard Benstock, ed., *Art in Crime Writing: Essays in Detective Fiction* (New York: St. Martin's Press, 1983).

5. Patricia Moyes, *Johnny Under Ground* (New York: Henry Holt, 1965), 44.

6. Ibid., 84.

7. Haycraft, *Murder for Pleasure,* 194.

8. Martha Grimes, *The Man with a Load of Mischief* (New York: Dell, 1985), 23.

9. Review of *Photo Finish, Booklist,* 15 June 1980, 1464.

Selected Bibliography

PRIMARY WORKS

Detective Novels

A Man Lay Dead. London: G. Bles, 1934; New York: Sheridan, 1942. Reprint; New York: Pyramid, 1973 (paperback); New York: Jove Books, 1978 (paperback).

Enter a Murderer. London: G. Bles, 1935. Reprint; New York: Berkley, 1963 (paperback); Glasgow: Fontana Books, 1984 (paperback); New York: Jove Books, 1988 (paperback).

The Nursing-Home Murder (with Henry Jellett). London: G. Bles, 1935; New York: Pocket Books, 1941. Reprint; New York: Pyramid, 1973 (paperback); New York: Jove Books, 1982 and 1988 (paperbacks).

Death in Ecstasy. London: G. Bles, 1936. Reprint; New York: Berkley, 1974 and 1977 (paperbacks); New York: Jove Books, 1989 (paperback).

Vintage Murder. London: G. Bles, 1937. Reprint; New York: Pyramid 1973 (paperback); New York: Jove Books, 1978 and 1987 (paperbacks).

Artists in Crime. London: G. Bles, 1938. Reprint; New York: Grosset and Dunlap, 1938; New York: Berkley, 1963 (paperback); New York: Jove Books, 1980 and 1985 (paperbacks).

Death in a White Tie. London: G. Bles, 1938. Reprint; New York: Pyramid, 1974 (paperback); Matlock, N.Y.: Aeonian Press, 1976 and 1981; New York: Jove Books, 1989 (paperback).

Overture to Death. London: Collins, 1939. Reprint; New York: Furman, 1939; New York: Pyramid, 1974 (paperback); New York: Jove Books, 1988 (paperback).

Death at the Bar. London: Collins, 1940; Boston: Little, Brown, 1940. Reprint; New York: Berkley, 1963 (paperback); New York: Jove Books, 1980 and 1985 (paperbacks).

Death of a Peer. London: Collins, 1940 (title *Surfeit of Lampreys*); Boston: Little, Brown, 1940. Reprint; New York: Book League of America, 1940; New York: Berkley, 1961 (paperback); New York: Jove Books, 1986 (paperback).

Death and the Dancing Footman. Boston: Little, Brown, 1941; London: Collins, 1942. Reprint; New York: Berkley, 1961 (paperback); New York: Jove Books, 1986 (paperback).

Colour Scheme. London: Collins, 1943; Boston: Little, Brown, 1943. Reprint;

New York: Berkley, 1961 (paperback); New York: Jove Books, 1982 (paperback).

Died in the Wool. London: Collins, 1945; Boston: Little, Brown, 1945. Reprint; New York: Berkley, 1978 (paperback); New York: Jove Books, 1981 and 1983 (paperbacks).

Final Curtain. London: Collins, 1947; Boston: Little, Brown, 1947. Reprint; New York: Berkley, 1961 (paperback); New York: Jove Books, 1986 (paperback).

A Wreath for Rivera. London: Collins, 1949 (titled *Swing, Brother, Swing*); Boston: Little, Brown, 1949. Reprint; New York: Berkley, 1962 (paperback); New York: Jove Books, 1984 (paperback).

Night at the Vulcan. London: Collins, 1951 (titled *Opening Night*); Boston: Little, Brown, 1951. Reprint; New York: Pyramid, 1974 (paperback); New York: Jove Books, 1983 (paperback).

Spinsters in Jeopardy. Boston: Little, Brown, 1953; London: Collins, 1954. Reprint (titled *The Bride of Death*); New York: Spivak, 1955; New York: Berkley, 1961 (paperback); New York: Jove Books, 1986 (paperback).

Scales of Justice. London: Collins, 1955; Boston: Little, Brown, 1955. Reprint; New York: Berkley, 1960 (paperback); New York: Jove Books, 1980 and 1984 (paperbacks).

Death of a Fool. Boston: Little, Brown, 1956; London: Collins, 1957 (titled *Off with His Head*). Reprint; London: Companion Book Club, 1956; New York: Pyramid 1973 (paperback); New York: Jove Books, 1978 and 1987 (paperbacks).

Singing in the Shrouds. Boston: Little, Brown, 1958; London: Collins, 1959. Reprint; New York: Pyramid, 1974 (paperback); New York: Jove Books, 1984 (paperback).

False Scent. Boston: Little, Brown, 1959; London: Collins, 1960. Reprint; New York: Berkley, 1967 (paperback); New York: Jove Books, 1981 and 1984 (paperbacks).

Hand in Glove. London: Collins, 1962; Boston: Little, Brown, 1962. New York: Berkley, 1963 (paperback). Reprint; New York: Pyramid, 1973 (paperback); New York: Jove Books, 1987 (paperback).

Dead Water. Boston: Little, Brown, 1963; London: Collins, 1964. Reprint; New York: Berkley, 1970 (paperback); New York: Jove Books, 1982 (paperback); New York: Jove Books, 1987 (paperback).

Killer Dolphin. Boston: Little, Brown, 1966; London: Collins, 1967 (titled *Death at the Dolphin*). Reprint; New York: Berkley, 1967 (paperback); New York: Jove Books, 1980 and 1989 (paperbacks).

A Clutch of Constables. London: Collins, 1968; Boston: Little, Brown, 1969. Reprint; New York: Berkley, 1978 (paperback); New York: Jove Books, 1987 (paperback).

When in Rome. London: Collins, 1970; Boston: Little, Brown, 1971. Reprint;

New York: Berkley, 1972 (paperback); New York: Jove Books, 1980 and 1987 (paperbacks).

Tied up in Tinsel. London: Collins, 1972; Boston: Little, Brown, 1972. Reprint; New York: Pyramid, 1973 (paperback); New York: Jove Books, 1978 and 1987 (paperbacks).

Black as He's Painted. London: Collins, 1974; Boston: Little, Brown, 1975. Reprint; New York: Pyramid, 1975 (paperback); New York: Jove Books, 1978 and 1988 (paperbacks).

Last Ditch. London: Collins, 1977; Boston: Little, Brown, 1977; New York: Jove Books, 1986 (paperback).

Grave Mistake. London: Collins, 1978; Boston: Little, Brown, 1978. Reprint; New York: Jove Books, 1980 and 1987 (paperbacks).

Photo Finish. London: Collins, 1980; Boston: Little, Brown, 1980. Reprint; New York: Jove Books, 1981 and 1987 (paperbacks).

Light Thickens. London: Collins, 1982; Boston: Little, Brown, 1982. Reprint; New York: Jove Books, 1983 and 1987 (paperbacks).

Uncollected Short Stories

"I Can Find My Own Way Out." *Queen's Awards 1946,* ed. Ellery Queen. Boston: Little, Brown, and London: Gollancz, 1946.

"Death on the Air." *Anthology 1969,* ed. Ellery Queen. New York: Davis, 1968.

"Chapter and Verse." *Ellery Queen Murdercade.* New York: Random House, 1975.

"A Fool about Money." *Ellery Queen's Crime Wave.* New York: Putnam, 1976.

Plays

The Nursing-Home Murder (with Henry Jellett), an adaptation of the novel produced in Christchurch, New Zealand, 1936.

False Scent, an adaptation of the novel; produced in Worthing Sussex, England, 1961.

A Christmas Tree (juvenile). London: S. P. C. K., 1962.

A Unicorn for Christmas, music by David Farquhar; produced in Sydney, Australia, 1965.

Murder Sails at Midnight; produced in Bournemouth, Hampshire, England, 1972.

Miscellany

New Zealand (with Randal Matthew Burdon). London: Collins, 1942. Reprint; Matlock, N.Y.: Aeonian Press, 1976.

A Play Toward: A Note on Play Production. London: Collins, 1942.

Perspectives: The New Zealander and the Visual Arts. Auckland: Auckland Gallery Associates, 1960.

New Zealand. New York: Macmillan, 1964; London: Collier Macmillan, 1965.

Black Beech and Honeydew: An Autobiography. Boston: Little, Brown, 1965; London: Collins, 1966. Revised edition; London: Collins, 1981.
"Entertainments." *Pacific Moana Quarterly* 3 no. 1 (January 1978): 28–32.

SECONDARY WORKS

Books, Parts of Books, and Articles

Acheson, Carol. "Cultural Ambivalence: Ngaio Marsh's New Zealand Detective Fiction." *Journal of Popular Culture* (Fall 1985): 159–74. Acheson is the only scholar to have made this topic her concentration. She maintains that Marsh had deep insight into the problems of her native land and, in hopes of ameliorating them, presented them in her detective novels in a deliberate but respectful fashion.
Bargainnier, Earl F. "Ngaio Marsh's 'Theatrical' Murders." *Armchair Detective* 10, no. 2 (April 1977): 175–81. A review of the effectiveness of the theatrical influences on Marsh's fiction. Bargainnier provides a skilled summation of the themes and concludes that *Enter a Murderer* and *Killer Dolphin* are the best of the theatrical novels.
_____."Roderick Alleyn: Ngaio Marsh's Oxonian Superintendent." *Armchair Detective* 11 (January 1978): 63–71. Bargainnier argues that Inspector Alleyn not only develops in the course of the novels but points the way toward the hard-nosed cop of the police procedural novels.
_____. "Ngaio Marsh." In *10 Women of Mystery,* ed. Earl F. Bargainnier, 78–108. Bowling Green, Ohio: Bowling Green State University Popular Press, 1981. Bargainnier emphasizes the variety of structure and the diversity of Marsh's canon. He insists that her work incorporates manners, romance, and satire with skillful character studies. His quantitative studies help sum up the grand themes of Marsh's fiction by dividing the works into categories—novels of setting, novels of theater, and novels taking place in country houses.
Bertram, Manfred A. "Ngaio Marsh." In *Twentieth-Century Crime and Mystery Writers,* ed. John M. Reilly, 1010–13. New York: St. Martin's Press, 1980. Bertram sees Marsh's work as serious literature and comments on her skill as a dramatist, which affected every aspect of her books.
Dooley, Allan J., and Linda J. Dooley. "Rereading Ngaio Marsh." In *Art in Crime Writing: Essays in Detective Fiction,* ed. Bernard Benstock, 33–49. New York: St. Martin's Press, 1983. The Dooleys admire Marsh for her skill in creating a strong sense of place and character, for looking beyond the cliché and pointing up the side effects of the murder investigation on characters and readers alike, such as a reconsideration in values. They maintain that Marsh's vision darkened after World War II.

Elsom, John. "At the End of the World." *Contemporary Review* 237 (August 1980): 78–83. Elsom builds on a personal visit with Marsh to reflect on her fiction. He identifies "Marshmarks" as storytelling in the grand manner of logical cause and effect portrayed by attractive characters, and he comments further on the effect of worldwide mass communication on New Zealand, the Maori, and the difficulties that the shrinking world has placed on the integration of the cultures. Dame Ngaio (of whom he does not appear to approve wholeheartedly) assisted her country in defining itself and its arts.

Joyner, Nancy C. "Ngaio Marsh." In *Novelists and Prose Writers,* Great Writers of the English Language Series, eds. James Vinson and D. L. Kirkpatrick, 813–15. New York: St. Martin's Press, 1979. A brief but laudatory overview of the themes and influences in her works down to *Grave Mistake.*

Klein, H. M. "Ngaio Marsh." In *Contemporary Novelists,* 3d ed., eds. James Vinson and D. L. Kirkpatrick, 434–35. New York: St. Martin's Press, 1982. Klein's article, though brief, touches on the major themes and influences and concludes that it was Marsh's genius to place the melodrama of murder in the ordinary lives of believable characters. He also praises Alleyn for his lack of peculiarities and eccentricities.

Knox, Valerie. "Ngaio Marsh: Crime Writer Who Admits She's Squeamish." *London Times,* 6 November 1968. Based on an interview with Marsh, Knox praises *A Clutch of Constables* and briefly reviews Marsh's life and the English influences.

Mann, Jessica. *Deadlier Than the Male: Why Are Respectable Englishwomen So Good at Murder?* New York: Macmillan, 1981. Mann's introduction and chapter on Ngaio Marsh suggest that Marsh's personal reticence inhibits an appreciation of the various influences on her novels. Mann sees Marsh as merely another clever writer well within the mold of detective fiction's formulas.

Nichols, Lewis. "In and out of Books." *New York Times,* 5 June 1960. Nichols writes about Marsh's first visit to America. He quotes Marsh as saying that her time in the theater distracted her from her detective novels, so that it took her seven or eight months to write them, rather than five.

Panek, LeRoy Lad. *Watteau's Shepherds: The Detective Novel in Britain 1914–1940.* Bowling Green, Ohio: Bowling Green State University Popular Press, 1979. A group of essays about the early years and the golden age. Panek believes Marsh was successful in transcending the limitations of the puzzle story because she hit her stride around 1940 when the rules were not as rigidly insisted on. The intervention of the war gave Marsh a breathing period to adjust her ideas about what form her stories would take next.

Penzler, Otto. "Roderick Alleyn." In *The Great Detective.* ed. Otto Penzler, 3–8. Boston: Little, Brown, 1978. A good summary of Alleyn's career and his development throughout the novels to that date.

Walbridge, Earle F. "Ngaio Marsh." *Wilson Library Bulletin* 15, no. 1 (Septem-

ber 1940). Walbridge sees Marsh as a savior for the detective story, which was
floundering between Sayers's abjuration of the genre and Christie's cardboard
characters. Marsh provided first-class writing and characterization to earn herself the title of leading lady of the proper mystery story. Walbridge also comments on her success as a London hostess in the most exclusive circles.

White, Jean M. "Murder Most Tidy." *New Republic,* 30 July 1977, 36–38.
White writes an appreciative overview of the Marsh canon down to *Last
Ditch.* She praises Marsh's "gently ironic eye to spot human and social foi-
bles." Even before Christie had died, she defends Marsh as the better writer.

Winn, Dilys. "Portrait of Troy." In *Murderess Ink.* ed. Dilys Winn, 142–43. New
York: Workman, 1979. An approving glance at the significance of Troy
Alleyn in the detective stories she appears in, by a longtime Ngaio Marsh fan.

Books on Detective Fiction

Ball, John. *The Mystery Story.* San Diego: University of California at San Diego,
1976. Ball, himself a distinguished detective novelist, has chosen a select
group of other novelists and academics to write about various aspects of the
genre. Most of these essays are graceful summations of developments to date.

Barzun, Jacques, and **Wendell Hertig Taylor.** *A Catalogue of Crime.* New
York: Harper and Row, 1971; 2d ed., corrected, 1974. An invaluable collec-
tion of their critical opinion about detective fiction based on 7,500 works.
Their biases are notable, especially toward Marsh's theater novels.

Freeman, Lucy, ed. *The Murder Mystique.* New York: Frederick Ungar, 1982.
Freeman's novels and her critical writing emphasize the "whydunit," a psychological analysis of the appeal of crime writing.

Hagen, Ordean. *Who Done It? A Guide to Detective, Mystery, and Suspense Fiction.* New York: R. R. Bowker, 1969. A useful reference work.

Haycraft, Howard, ed. *The Art of the Mystery Story: A Collection of Critical Essays.* New York: Simon and Schuster, 1946. An invaluable, but not always
accurate, collection of essays written by critics, fans, and practitioners, from
Sayers's introduction to *The Omnibus of Crime* in which she reveals many of
her own injunctions about the genre to Van Dine's rules, concluding with
Haycraft's survey of the detective novel since World War II.

―――――. *Murder for Pleasure: The Life and Times of the Detective Story.* New
York: D. Appleton, 1941. Reprint; New York: Biblo and Tannen, 1968. A
trustworthy survey of the genre as it has developed on both sides of the Atlan-
tic, with some provocative observations on the origins of the mystery story.

Keating, H. R. F. *Murder Must Appetize.* London: Lemon Tree Press, 1975. A
brief reminiscence of the great detective writers of the 1930s and 1940s.

―――――, ed. *Whodunit? A Guide to Crime, Suspense, and Spy Fiction.* New York:
Van Nostrand Reinhold, 1982. An illustrated dictionary/guide to the authors, developmental stages, and detectives of many different kinds of mystery stories, from the classic to the Gothic and espionage. A nice touch is the

addition of "How I Write My Books," confessions of ten highly successful authors like P. D. James and Len Deighton.

Mann, Jessica. *Deadlier Than the Male: Why Are Respectable Englishwomen So Good at Murder?* New York: Macmillan, 1981. In addition to her chapter on Marsh she surveys Christie, Sayers, and others. Though her conclusions about Marsh are less than laudatory, she does have some interesting comments about the heroes and heroines of these writers. Mann's book is a first and rather impressive attempt to address women's role in the development of this genre. She concludes that it was their instinctive conservatism and successful conforming to the rules of the genre that made these women so successful and popular. They challenged none of the comfortable notions of their day about a woman's place.

Maugham, Somerset. *The Vagrant Mood.* London: Heinemann, 1952. A personal essay about the age in which the professional in all areas of English life was coming to be recognized as necessary.

Murch, A. E. *The Development of the Detective Novel.* London: Peter Owen, 1958. Not terribly good for research on Marsh. He tends to focus on the pre–World War I novel.

Nevins, Francis M., Jr., ed. *The Mystery Writer's Art.* Bowling Green, Ohio: Bowling Green State University Popular Press, 1971. Takes up where Haycraft's *The Art of the Mystery Story* leaves off. Nevins includes essays on the conjunction of the mystery story and science fiction and on the crime story on film. He includes an especially provocative essay on the detective story as useful to historians.

Panek, LeRoy Lad. *An Introduction to the Detective Story.* Bowling Green, Ohio: Bowling Green State University Popular Press, 1987. A more general look at the development of detective stories, from Genesis to the present. In an act of historical generosity, he rescues Edward Bulwer Lytton from the utter ignominy to which he has been subject and sees his work as a necessary precedent against which Edgar Allan Poe would react.

Routley, Erik. *The Puritan Pleasures of the Detective Story: A Personal Monograph.* London: Gollancz, 1972. Some interesting observations about the field of British detective story writers. His rather idiosyncratic views of these authors, with his emphasis on the values of the society that produced such novels, are at times curious but always engaging.

Symons, Julian. *The Detective Story in Britain,* published for the British Council and the National Book League, Writers and Their Work, no. 145. London: Longmans, Green, 1962; rev. ed., 1969. Out of this brief pamphlet came the seminal ideas that were developed further in *Bloody Murder.*

———. *Bloody Murder: A History—From the Detective Story to the Crime Novel.* London: Faber and Faber, 1972; New York: Harper and Row, 1972 (titled *Mortal Consequences*). Symons argues that the classic detective story has been adapted to meet the needs of greater characterization and to move from the dead weight of the puzzle rules. By so doing it evolves from the detective story to what Symons calls the crime novel, which employs a wider range of literary devices. Probably the best overall survey of the genre.

Watson, Colin. *Snobbery with Violence: Crime Stories and Their Audience.* London: Eyre and Spottiswoode, 1971. An informal and highly personal look at popular literature, from the eighteenth century to James Bond. Watson examines the literature as it reflects and rebels against the social standards of the day.

Winks, Robin., ed. *The Historian as Detective: Essays on Evidence.* New York: Harper and Row, 1968. A collection of essays from noted historians and literary critics pointing out how the historian builds his case for asserting the truth of certain assumptions in much the same way that the detective goes about his investigations. A book most especially for professionals and graduate students, but the idea is clever enough to produce enjoyment for anyone interested in the structure of intellectual inquiry.

_____. *Modus Operandi: An Excursion into Detective Fiction.* Boston: David R. Godine, 1982. Once again this imaginative historian has produced an essay that connects the training of a professional academic with the enthusiasm of a true devotee of detective fiction. In the style of those informal graduate seminars in which ideas are pleasantly exchanged, Winks traces his own attraction to this genre and mentions his favorite writers and books. The student fear typical in such a setting is, for once, in inverse proportion to the pipe smoke.

_____, ed. *Detective Fiction: A Collection of Critical Essays.* Englewood Cliffs, N. J.: Prentice-Hall, 1980; rev. ed., expanded, Woodstock, Vt.: Countryman Press, 1988. Winks brings together a rather unusual collection of essays, eschewing many of the better known works for the more provocative and interesting. There are still the solid contributions of scholars like Jacques Barzun and John Cawelti, with the addition of others like W. H. Auden. Winks pleads for more attention to this form of cultural information on the part of American and British academics.

Index

Africa, 17, 22, 41, 43–44. *See also* South
  Africa
Alleyn, Roderick, ix, x, 1, 12, 14, 16, 22,
  24–26, 28–31, 37–38, 40, 42–43,
  47–53, 57–59, 62, 64–65, 68, 72,
  74–93, 95, 98–111, 115–16, 122–24,
  126, 129, 138–45; aristocrat, x, 64,
  75, 77, 85–87, 138
Alleyn, Troy, 7, 16, 40, 42–43, 52–53,
  58, 62–63, 67–68, 77, 79–80, 82–86,
  92, 96, 98, 101, 103, 124, 126–27,
  141, 143–44
Allingham, Margery, x, 1, 74, 133,
  135–37, 139
Almayer's Folly (Conrad), 5
Apartheid, 9
Aristotle, 114, 130
Asia, 22
Auden, W. H., 144
Austen, Jane, 133
Australia, 3, 9, 13–14, 17, 20–21, 24
Austria, 11, 96

Barham, R. H., 5
Bible, The, ix
Big Four, ix, 3, 75, 82, 85, 133, 144. *See
  also* Allingham, Margery; Christie,
  Agatha; Marsh, Ngaio; Sayers,
  Dorothy
Buchan, John, 44
Burma, 21
Burmese Days (Orwell), 31
Burtons, The, 6

Campion, Albert, x, 74–75, 88, 136–37
Canada, 20–21
Cary, Joyce, 44
Chandler, Raymond, 133
China Governess, The (Allingham), 137
Christie, Agatha, ix, x, 1, 4–5, 11, 44,
  62, 74, 78, 120, 133, 135–37, 139–41
Churchill, Winston, 21, 27, 36

Clouds of Witness (Sayers), 136
Collins, Wilkie, ix, 74
Collins, William, 13
Conrad, Joseph, 5
Cover Her Face (James), 141
Cross, Amanda, 140, 143–44
Cymbeline (Shakespeare), 19

Darwin, Charles, 108
David Copperfield (Dickens), 5
Dickens, Charles, ix, 5, 73–74, 102, 121,
  137
Dostoyevski, 58
Doyle, Conan, 74
*Dual Mandate in British Tropical Africa,
  The* (Lugard), 43

Eccentrics, 11, 19, 38, 61, 74–75, 88,
  90–91, 94, 107–110, 114, 122, 130,
  132–33, 136–37
Edel, Leon, 36
Elizabeth, Queen, 113
England, xi, x, 1, 3, 8, 10–11, 13–14,
  17–19, 21–22, 24–28, 30, 36, 40–42,
  46–62, 65–67, 72–74, 78, 102, 106,
  114–15, 119, 121, 126, 137, 140;
  London, x, 10–11, 13, 27, 30, 32,
  40–43, 46, 53, 56–57, 59–63, 74, 78,
  94, 119, 121, 126, 135, 137–40

Fielding, Henry, 5
Fiji Islands, 58, 62
Five Bells and Bladebone, The (Grimes),
  142
Five Red Herrings (Sayers), 136
Forster, E. M., 3
Fox, Inspector, 29, 62, 70, 72, 75, 77–80,
  85, 89–93, 105, 122, 142
France, 14, 82
Far East, The, 14

Galsworthy, John, 5

Gandhi, 31
Germany, 11–12, 134
Golden age, ix, x, xi, 1, 46, 62, 77–78,
    85, 132–36, 140–41, 144
Grimes, Martha, 140–42, 145

Haggard, Rider, 44
Hakluyt, Richard, 50
Hamlet (Shakespeare), 6–7, 12, 22
Hardy, Thomas, 5
Heilbron, Carolyn. *See* Cross, Amanda
Henry V (Shakespeare), 13, 16
Holmes, Sherlock, 74, 138
Hunter-Watts, Frediswyde, 22

India, 17–18, 21, 29, 44
Ingoldsby Legends, The (Barham), 5
Innocent Blood (James), 141
Ireland, 21
Italy, 11, 53–56, 98

James, P. D., 140–41, 145
Japan, 12
Jellett, Henry, 11
Johnny Under Ground (Moyes), 141
Joyce, James, 134, 144

Kipling, Rudyard, 44

Lamprey, Charlot, 10. *See also* Lampreys,
    The
Lampreys, The, 8, 10, 14
Lugard, Sir Frederick, 43

Macaulay, Rose, 5
MacBeth (Shakespeare), 40, 116–17, 126,
    128
Man in a Brown Suit, The (Christie), 137
Man with a Load of Mischief, The
    (Grimes), 144
Mansfield, Katherine, 17
Maori, 9, 18, 21, 23, 25–26, 28–34, 38,
    40, 48–49, 51–52, 71, 126
Marsh, Henry Edmund (father), 3–5,
    10–12, 19
MARSH, NGAIO, attitude toward her
    work, 1–2, 8, 11, 113; on class, xi,
1–3, 10, 15–17, 21–22, 26, 29, 33,
    37, 57, 60–61, 64, 74–76, 87–89,
    92–93, 96, 102, 104, 107, 134–35,
    138–39, 143; conservatism, 10, 135;
    early life, 3–4, 5–10, 85; education,
    5–6, 12–13, 83, 113; fears, 4, 7, 85;
    influences, 8, 74, 100–101, 133, 141;
    murder methods, 1, 4, 16, 34, 40–41,
    115–17, 120; Officer of the Order of
    the British Empire (O.B.E.), 1, 15;
    painting career, 3, 6–7, 51, 56, 82–83;
    reputation, 1, 113–14, 129–30, 133,
    135–38; theatrical career, 1–2, 7–8,
    12–14, 113, 130

WORKS:
Artists in Crime, 58, 62, 77, 79, 83,
    101, 113
Black as He's Painted, 58–61, 92, 114
Black Beech and Honeydew, 4–5, 6, 8,
    15, 21, 25, 42, 53, 113, 145
A Clutch of Constables, 67–69, 73, 84
Colour Scheme, 12, 20, 25–28, 31,
    33–35, 46, 48–49, 113, 126–27
Dead Water, 12, 20, 27, 35–38, 46,
    49–52, 69
Death and the Dancing Footman, 5, 46,
    63–65, 95, 101, 113, 129, 139
Death at the Bar, 96, 108
Death in a White Tie, 59, 79–81,
    101–103
Death in Ecstacy, 57, 61, 77, 86, 113
Died in the Wool, 20, 26–38, 69
Death of a Fool, 61, 70, 73, 77,
    101–102, 113, 129, 139
Death of a Peer, 38–39, 46, 59, 61,
    108, 140
Enter a Murderer, 11, 23, 77–78,
    86–88, 113–14, 117, 119, 123,
    125, 129, 131, 140
False Scent, 101, 125–26, 129
Final Curtain, 81, 108, 113, 127, 129
Grave Mistake, 111
Hand in Glove, 103–105
Killer Dolphin, 40, 60, 101, 113,
    115–16, 119–22, 127, 129–31
Last Ditch, 83, 85–87

Light Thickens, 40–41, 113, 116–17, 127, 129, 131, 137
A Man Lay Dead, 11, 61, 75–76, 78, 86, 88, 94–95, 101, 113
Night at the Vulcan, 40, 113, 119, 121, 124–26, 128–29, 131, 140
The Nursing-Home Murder, 11, 89, 96, 113
Overture to Death, 62–64, 99, 113, 129–30
Photo Finish, 40, 46, 51–53, 59, 113, 125, 137
Scales of Justice, 61, 67, 69–70, 73, 81–82, 97, 109
Singing in the Shrouds, 97, 137
Spinsters in Jeopardy, 46, 84, 101, 113
Tied Up in Tinsel, 46, 65, 95–96, 106, 113, 125, 139
Vintage Murder, 10, 22–23, 25–28, 31–34, 39, 46–50, 78–79, 81, 101, 113–14, 118–19, 121–23, 131
When in Rome, 46, 53, 90
A Wreath for Rivera, 59, 90, 101, 108–109, 114

Marsh, Rose Seager (mother), 2, 4–11
Marx, Karl, 108
Mason, Bruce, 17
Maugham, Somerset, 14, 22, 32
Moore, Henry, 98
Moyes, Patricia, 140–42
Murder of Roger Ackroyd, The (Christie), 120, 136
Mysterious Affair at Styles, The (Christie), 135

Nazis, 11–12, 36, 48
New Zealand, x, xi, 1, 3, 7–8, 10–14, 17–59, 69, 71, 81, 89–90, 94, 117–19, 126, 132, 137–38, 140, 144–45; Canterbury, 4, 12; Christchurch, 3–8, 12–13, 18–19; North Island, 13, 46

O'Connor, Dan, 13
Oliver, Ariade, Mrs., ix
Omnibus of Crime (Sayers), 136

Orwell, George, 31, 33, 34
Othello (Shakespeare), 13

Passage to India, A (Forster), 31
Pickwick Papers (Dickens), 5
Pirandello, Luigi, 10, 13
Poe, Edgar Allen, ix, 15
Poiret, Hercule, x, 74–75, 78, 137
Police at the Funeral (Allingham), 137
Priestly, J. B., 10
Professional police, xi, 51, 59, 75–76, 86, 138–39, 141, 143, 145

Radley, Sheila, 145
Reade, Winwood, 108
Rendall, Ruth, 141
Royal, Jonathan, 5
Russian Revolution, 135

Sayer, Dorothy, ix, x, 1, 11, 74, 77, 82, 133, 135–39, 141
Seager (grandfather), 4–5, 7
Shakespeare, 10, 12–13, 16–17, 20–22, 26, 33, 40, 68, 76, 84, 100–101, 113, 116–17, 121, 126–28, 136, 138, 144–45
Sleeping Car Murder, The (Christie), 135
South Africa, 9–10, 14, 20–21, 137
Soviet Union, 14, 135

Tey, Josephine, 133
Thomson, June, 145
Tiger in the Smoke, The (Allingham), 137
Tom Jones (Fielding), 5
Troy, Agatha. *See* Alleyn, Troy
Twelfth Night (Shakespeare), 13

Unsuitable Job for a Woman, An (James), 141
United States, ix, 14–15, 24–25, 27

Van Dine, S. S., ix, 62, 78–79, 81–82, 130, 137
Verdi, 52
Victorian era, 2–3, 5, 17–18, 26, 96, 102–103, 134, 138–39
Voyages (Hakluyt), 50

Waves, The (Woolf), 17
Wells, H. G., 108
West Indies, 14
Whose Body? (Sayers), 136
Wilkie, Allan, 7–8, 22
Wilkie, Allan, Shakespeare Company, 7–8, 12
Wilson, Edmund, 136

Wilson, Woodrow, 134–35
Wimsey, Lord Peter, x, 74–75, 77, 82, 88, 136, 138, 139
Woolf, Virginia, 17, 134
Wooster, Bertie, 138
World War I, 43, 49, 134, 138–39
World War II, 12, 18, 20, 25, 27, 48–49, 81, 134, 141

The Author

Kathryne Slate McDorman was born in Birmingham, Alabama, and attended Birmingham–Southern College. She received her B.A. from the University of Kentucky, her M.A. from the University of North Carolina at Chapel Hill, and her Ph.D. in history from Vanderbilt University in Nashville. She has published articles on fiction and history, especially on the popular English novels of the early twentieth century as they reflect the decline of the British Empire. She has taught at Western Kentucky University and East Texas State University and at present is an associate professor of history at Texas Christian University.